PORTRAITS OF THE SIXTIES

THE TREATY OF PARIS, 1860

Bazley Baines Kershaw Palmerston Pilkington Cowley Wilson
Persigny Crossley Cobden Gibson Pereire
Fould Kergorlay Bright Chevalier Dollfus Villiers Rouher Gladstone
Baroche Dufour

PORTRAITS OF THE SIXTIES

BY

JUSTIN McCARTHY

ILLUSTRATED

Essay Index Reprint Series

BOOKS FOR LIBRARIES PRESS
FREEPORT, NEW YORK

First Published 1903
Reprinted 1971

INTERNATIONAL STANDARD BOOK NUMBER:
0-8369-2061-9

LIBRARY OF CONGRESS CATALOG CARD NUMBER:
79-142661

PRINTED IN THE UNITED STATES OF AMERICA

CONTENTS

ILLUSTRATIONS

ILLUSTRATIONS

PORTRAITS OF THE SIXTIES

PORTRAITS OF THE SIXTIES

CHAPTER I

THE EARLY SIXTIES

The early sixties have left a clear and deep impression on my memory. It was in the earliest of the sixties that I settled in London for a life of journalism and literature, to be much interrupted afterwards by politics. The London of the early sixties had no Thames Embankment and no underground railways and no tram-cars; the Law Courts on the Strand had not yet been dreamed of, and some of the judges still held their tribunals within enclosures opening from what I may call the off-side of Westminster Hall. But the outer aspect of London street life was not very different from that which we can contemplate at the present day. The hansom-cabs and the "growlers," familiar to all eyes now, were familiar to all eyes then. The great, palatial restaurants where fashion now entertains its friends at luncheons, dinners, and suppers were not in existence then, and the smart Londoner of the early sixties would not have thought of inviting his friends to a banquet in the taverns of the time. I may observe that the word "smart" used as I have just used it in the conventional language of the present reign would have conveyed no such meaning to the mind of a Londoner in the sixties.

The Thames tunnel was still the wonder and delight of provincial visitors, there were still some toll-bridges spanning the Thames between Westminster and London Bridge, and Westminster Bridge and London Bridge and Blackfriars Bridge were erections of very different shape and structure from those which maintain the names in our present time. The river traffic in the early sixties was carried on by an immense number of incessant steamers, which, indeed, relieved the streets of a large proportion of passengers, and did in their much smaller way something like the work now accomplished by underground lines and "tubes." But I think I am warranted in saying that, even when we take the latest schemes of metropolitan improvement into view, the general appearance of the streets of London has not undergone, since the early sixties, anything like the changes which have been made in New York and in Paris during the same time. Many of the great theatres which were fashionable or popular, or fashionable and popular, in the sixties still hold their position and their repute, but, of course, many new theatres have been added, and in the early sixties the suburban theatres can hardly be said to have had any existence. When we consider the changes which have taken place in other European countries since the time when this book opens, it might almost seem as if the people of England had been living just the same life during the lapse of all these forty years and more.

Let us take the condition of France, for instance. The Emperor Napoleon the Third was then at the zenith of his power and his fame. He had but lately defeated the Austrians in the campaign of which Solferino was the greatest triumph, and he was universally regarded as the most powerful sovereign on the Continent of Europe. Even those in England who most strongly condemned his usurpation of power and his despotic rule felt reluctantly compelled to regard him as the founder of a new dynasty and as the force which had finally extinguished in France the republican system brought in by the great Revolution. On the other hand, almost all Englishmen were agreed in regarding the position of Prussia as one of mere insignificance, and out of all consideration so far as political influence was concerned. Not one of our statesmen or our leading political writers seems to have given any indication, in the early sixties, that Prussia impressed him as a rising power or a power capable of rising in the political affairs of Europe. I do not know of any phenomenon in modern history more curious than the apparent incapacity of English statesmen and political writers, at that time, to make any forecast as to Prussia's political possibilities. The American republic was just then engaged in its great domestic struggle, and the war between North and South created naturally an intense excitement throughout England. It may, indeed, be said to have divided the people of England into two hostile camps—the advocates of the Northern States and the advocates of the Southern Secessionists. It may be said, not unfairly, that the whole of what we describe as "society" in England was in favor of the South, and fully believed that the South was certain to make itself an independent republic, while the advanced Radicals of whatever order in England and all the English working population were on the side of the Northern States, and were confident that the Northern cause must ultimately triumph. Egypt was still under the rule of its Pachas, and the Ottoman power in Turkey was still regarded by many Englishmen as a needful bulwark of British interests against the possible encroachments of Russia. The wildest dreamer had not yet thought of a system of railways extending from Egypt to the Cape of Good Hope, or of Russia opening up the resources of Siberia by the pathway of the iron rail.

Palmerston and Lord John Russell were still rivals or colleagues; Brougham and Lyndhurst were still waking up the House of Lords by their curiously contrasted styles of eloquence; Gladstone had already achieved some of his most splendid financial triumphs; Cobden had accomplished a great commercial treaty with France; Bright was the foremost democratic orator in the House of Commons. Disraeli still held his place without a rival as the brilliant leader of the conservative party in the representative chamber, and Sir Edward Lytton Bulwer was able to convince the audiences in that same chamber that a writer of showy and fascinating novels might, notwithstanding the most serious defects of articulation, prove himself in his later years a successful parliamentary orator. In literature our acknowledged leaders were Tennyson, Dickens, and Thackeray, but Thackeray's life came to a close at a very early period of the sixties. Carlyle was creating a school of thought and of letters all to himself, and John Stuart Mill was teaching us the principles of political economy and of expanded political liberalism. Robert Browning had not yet become the fashion, and only by men and women of intellect was recognized as a great and genuine poet. Macaulay's career as essayist, historian, verse-writer, and parliamentary debater had just come to an end. George Grote had still some years of noble work before him, and although he never could be called a popular historian in the ordinary sense, his influence on the study of history was inestimable. Maclise and Landseer were probably the most universally admired among painters at that time. The great singers of the opera-houses—Covent Garden and Her Majesty's—were Grisi, Alboni—Jenny Lind had ceased to sing on the operatic stage—Mario, Tamberlik, and Lablache. In the homes of the regular drama Charles Mathews, Charles Kean, the Keeleys, and Buxton were most popular, and Helen Faucit was recognized as the most successful actress in the Shakespearean drama. Macready had taken his final farewell of the English stage before the time with which our narrative opens, and Frederick Robson had just begun to make himself famous in his short career as the creator of a style which combined in original, fantastic, and unsurpassed fashion the elements of the broadly burlesque and the deeply tragic.

There is one peculiarity belonging to the early sixties which I cannot leave out of notice, although assuredly it has little claim to association with art or science, with literature or politics. The early sixties saw in this and most other civilized countries the reign of crinoline. It is well for the early sixties that they had so many splendid claims to historical recollection, but it may be said of them that if they had bequeathed no other memory to a curious and contemplative posterity, the reign of crinoline would still have secured for them an abiding-place in the records of human eccentricities. I may say, without fear of contradiction, that no one who was not living at the time can form any adequate idea of the grotesque effect produced on the outer aspects of social life by this article of feminine costume. The younger generation may turn over as much as it will the pages of *Punch,* which illustrate the ways and manners of civilization at that time, but with all the undeniable cleverness and humor of *Punch's* best caricaturists, the younger generation can never really understand, can never fully realize, what extraordinary exhibitions their polite ancestresses made of themselves during that terrible reign of crinoline.

"Hang up philosophy," says Romeo, "unless philosophy can make a Juliet." I should not like to say hang up caricature unless caricature can make a crinoline, because such a sentence, if it could by possibility be carried out, would only speak the doom of the caricaturist's amusing and delightful art. The fashion of crinoline defied caricature, for the actual reality was more full of unpicturesque and burlesque effects than any satirical pencil could realize on a flat, outspread sheet of paper. The fashion of crinoline, too, defied all contemporary ridicule. A whole new school of satirical humor was devoted in vain to the ridicule of crinoline. The boys in the streets sang comic songs to make fun of it, but no street bellowings of contempt could incite the wearers of this most inconvenient and hideous article of dress to condemn themselves to clinging draperies.

Crinoline, too, created a new sort of calamity all its own. Every day's papers gave us fresh accounts of what were called crinoline accidents—cases, that is to say, in which a woman was severely burned or burned to death because of some flame of fire or candle catching her distended drapery at some unexpected moment. There were sacrifices made to the prevailing fashion which would have done the sufferers immortal honor if they had been made for the sake of bearing some religious or political emblem condemned by ruling and despotic authorities. Its inconvenience was felt by the male population as well as by the ladies who sported the obnoxious construction. A woman getting into or out of a carriage, an omnibus, or a train, making her way through a crowded room, or entering into the stalls of a theatre was a positive nuisance to all with whom she had to struggle for her passage. The hoop-petticoats of an earlier generation were moderate in their dimensions and slight in the inconvenience they caused when compared with the rigid and enormous structure in which our ladies endeavored to conform to the fashion set up by the Empress of the French.

I remember well seeing a great tragic queen of opera going through a thrilling part at one of the lyric theatres. Her crinoline was of ultra-expansion, was rigid and unyielding in its structure as the mail corselet of the Maid of Orleans. The skirt of silk or satin spread over it was so symmetrically and rigidly conformed to the outlines of the crinoline that it seemed as if it were pasted to the vast arrangement beneath. The thrill and tragedy of the part were wholly lost on me. I could only see the unpicturesque absurdity of the exhibition. I could feel no sympathy with the dramatic sufferings of the melodious heroine thus enclosed. Every movement and rush of passion, of prayer, of wild despair, or distracted love was lost on me, for each change of posture only brought into more striking display the fact that I was looking at a slight and graceful woman boxed up in some sort of solid barrel of preposterous size over which her skirt was artificially spread. To this day I can only think of that glorious singer as of a woman for some reason compelled to exhibit herself on the stage with a barrel fastened round her waist. A lyrical heroine jumping in a sack would have been graceful and reasonable by comparison. Do what we will, we who lived in those days cannot dissociate our memories of the crinoline from our memories of the woman of the period.

We had not in the early sixties the vast, splendid, and artistically arranged music-halls of a later generation. We had music-halls indeed, but they were comparatively small and darksome enclosures, where comic songs were sung and grotesque buffoonery was enacted, but which women were not expected to visit—at least as part of the audience. We have made distinct improvement in the style of our music-halls since those days, and the ordinary man of the world who belongs to our time would find himself much amazed and not a little abashed if he could by some magical power be carried back to listen to some of the songs at the Caves of Harmony or the Cyder Cellars, or to be present at the Judge-and-Jury performances which we attended unabashed during the passing of the early sixties.

I devote my opening chapter to these few rapid and disconnected illustrations of London life in the early sixties as a general introduction, which I propose to set off by written descriptions. These portraits bring back the likenesses of men and women who were famous, or conspicuous, or peculiar and odd and eccentric in the years which, at the suggestion of Mr. Fisher Unwin, I am endeavoring to illustrate and to bring back to life for the public of the present century. Many of the portraits bring their own fame with them, and must ever be studied with interest. Others are the likenesses of men and women who made themselves, or were made, conspicuous in their own time, and in every instance the likeness is that of one on whom, for some reason, the attention of the world was for a while directed, and each portrait tells a story characteristic of the events and the movements occupying attention just then. After this short and prefatory chapter I shall go on to pass my portraits in review. I may add that I am not relying on contemporary records for any of my descriptions, and that I am telling of men and women whom I have seen and most of whom I have known. I have to make a further explanation.

There are grave authorities upon literature and its

rules who maintain that nothing should be explained in advance, and that the narrative, whatever it is, should tell its own story as it unfolds itself, on the principle that if it does not thus tell its own story it is the fault of the narrator, and only shows that he is not equal to his work. Despite those edicts, however, I venture to tell my readers that this book does not by any means profess or pretend to be anything like a description or history of the early sixties, or of the figures which have given it a place of mark among the ages. I find ready to my hand a collection of portraits belonging to the period, and I shall merely discourse of these and of the men and women whom they represent without the slightest effort or intention to make of them a complete illustration of their time. Some of the most important events and figures of those days are entirely outside the range of my purpose. I take the figures as they pass before me just as one might describe to a stranger the persons who moved along in some public procession, and have no pretension to do anything more than to tell him something about each of those who come under our momentary observation. Such a description cannot be given without helping the younger generation of readers to become more familiar than before with many of the characteristic figures which distinguished the period, and in this way to bring the early sixties more clearly to their minds. I speak of those whom I have seen and known. I give my own recollections and impressions only and act merely as showman to my friend Fisher Unwin's gallery of portraits. For the convenience of the reader I shall endeavor to arrange these pictures in separate groups, and to describe the representatives of arts and science, of letters and politics, of commerce and of social life as if they were passing in separate processions before our eyes. As my recollections are aided by the portraits, I shall endeavor to make the portraits more lifelike to the minds of my readers by the help of my own recollections. "The best in this kind are but shadows; and the worst are no worse if imagination amend them." This is the kindly saying of Theseus in *A Midsummer Night's Dream,* and I cannot offer any better apology for my shadowy recollections.

CHAPTER II

CHARLES DICKENS

THE portrait of Charles Dickens is the most appropriate illustration with which to open these sketches from memory of men and women who were living in the early sixties. This likeness of Dickens represents him in one of those moods of rather melancholy thoughtfulness with which those who knew him then were familiar. There was a certain depth of melancholy underneath all the joyous activity of Dickens's ordinary moods, and it is profoundly characteristic of even his most humorous and exhilarating stories if only we pause to look a little beneath the surface. It is not thus that he presents himself to our memory if we trust to our recollections of him as he appeared when delivering one of his lectures or making, on some joyous occasion, one of his after-dinner speeches, or talking with cheerful animation in the company of his friends.

Readers of the present generation will find it hard to understand how supreme and universal was the influence of Dickens at the time which this volume endeavors to recall. So far as mere popularity was concerned, he had then absolutely no rival. We have at present no such reigning monarch of fiction. Dickens was read by every one, high and low, the cultured and uncultured, who cared to read a novel. Walter Scott was the only writer who in modern days could claim a popularity surpassing or even equal to that of Charles

Dickens. Thackeray was admitted by most readers, even then, to stand on a literary level with Dickens and to dispute his absolute supremacy, but Thackeray's readers never approached in numbers to those over whom the novels of Dickens exercised a complete sway. Thackeray himself once said that the readers of his books did not number one in seven of those who devoted themselves to the green-covered monthly numbers which gave forth in serial form such books as *Pickwick, Nicholas Nickleby*, and *David Copperfield.* Dickens was a year younger than Thackeray, and he outlived him for seven years. Thackeray has described in some striking sentences how the young man Charles Dickens suddenly moved up from the ranks of the beginners, and took his place as if by right at the very head of the literary class, and kept his leadership as a matter of course. I am not now entering into any comparison between the two great men who represented two such different schools of fiction, and I regard all such comparisons as futile, needless, and thankless. I am merely recording the absolute fact that in popularity Dickens stood without a rival.

When I first came to London, Dickens was at the very zenith of his fame and his influence. To meet him in the Strand or in Piccadilly was an event to be remembered in the life of a young man then passing through the streets of London. Dickens began his literary career as a reporter in the gallery of the House of Commons, and in my early days of journalism I heard from elder men engaged in the same occupation many an interesting and delightful anecdote of his remarkable skill in his work and of his genial and companionable qualities. It was his gift to be able to make himself a master of any craft to which he applied his mind and his energies, and I have often been assured that he was the quickest

CHARLES DICKENS

and most accurate reporter of his time in the House of Commons gallery. We may judge what a capacity he had for success in any path which inspired him with interest, from the opinion which I have often heard given by some of the leading actors of that time, that if the novelist had thought fit to turn his artistic talents to the business of the stage he would have won for himself a place among the highest of the theatrical profession. At one period Dickens felt strongly drawn towards such a career, but his peculiar genius was too commanding to allow of any deflection, and the world has the best reason to be glad that he kept himself steadily to his calling as a writer of novels. Amateur acting was, however, always one of his favorite recreations, and he was universally regarded as the most capable amateur actor in England.

Dickens did not forget his old friends and associates when he had attained his supreme height in the literature of fiction, and it was to that fact that I owed the honor of his personal acquaintance. I was for one session a reporter in the gallery of the House of Commons, and through some elder brothers of the craft I had the honor of being introduced to the great novelist. I may say at once that my acquaintance with Dickens was of the slightest, and I never had the good fortune to be ranked among his friends. But it was a source of unspeakable delight and pride to me to have an opportunity of meeting him now and then in private intercourse, and to have acquired the right of going up to him and inviting his recognition. I need hardly say that I felt as if I had achieved a triumph whenever I happened to meet Dickens and he remembered who I was and addressed me by my name. When a small boy living in an Irish southern city I had written once to Dickens and asked him for his autograph, and to my inexpressible delight I received within a very few days a kindly line from the great novelist with his peculiar and characteristic signature.

I had heard all of Dickens's readings when I was working as a journalist in Liverpool before I ventured to attempt the business of journalism in London, and I certainly believed that I had attained the very pinnacle of self-satisfaction when I found myself, as I have described, within the circle of his personal acquaintances. Our casual meetings in London only brought me to the interchange of a few words each time with Dickens, for I was young and rather shy and totally obscure, and I hardly ever ventured in his presence to offer any observation on my own account. This certainly did not arise from any discouragement in Dickens's manner, for he was always genial and friendly, seemed naturally inclined to welcome and encourage young men, and I had heard many stories from companions in journalism about the generous interest which Dickens took in those who were beginning their work as newspaper reporters or writers. The great novelist seemed to make it a part of his work to discover literary talent in rising young men and to give practical help to its development. When he started *Household Words* he gathered around him quite a school of men who were then very young, and most of whom became under his fostering care successful and distinguished writers. Most of them have passed away since that time, but the names of such men as George Augustus Sala, Andrew Halliday, Edmund Yates, Wilkie Collins, and many others are still remembered. John Hollingshead, who was one of the cleverest and best writers of that school, and who afterwards turned his attention almost altogether to theatrical management, is still living.

Dickens discovered and brought out the lyrical genius

of Adelaide Anne Procter, daughter of Bryan Waller Procter, the poet who disguised his identity for a long time under the assumed name of Barry Cornwall. Adelaide Procter sent some verses to *Household Words* without giving her real name. Dickens read them and saw at once that they had high poetic promise in them, and he welcomed the young writer to the ranks of his contributors, and gave her ample opportunity of proving her capacity before he came to know of her relationship with his old friend. Of course the prose contributors to *Household Words* got into the habit, unconsciously it may be, of forming their style upon that of their master, and thus a whole school of writers came into existence who reproduced the Dickens mannerisms in unnumbered magazines and newspapers. I can well remember hearing the editor of a great London daily paper making humorous complaint that he could not keep the imitations of Dickens out of the columns of his journal when his staff of writers had to do the work of description. If, for instance—so he went on to declare—he wanted a preliminary account of the preparations being made for some great London procession or other public ceremonial, he was sure, no matter whom he trusted with the work, to get a long account beginning with "Seats everywhere. Seats outside the Abbey; seats inside the Abbey; seats in Palace Yard; seats in Piccadilly; seats in High Holborn"; and so on through at least the first half-column before the writer condescended to come down to anything like a plain and practical account of the operations which he was called upon to depict in prose. The same editor occasionally spoke in the same mood of the increasing proportion of persons with whom literature meant Dickens. It was, indeed, almost impossible for a young writer at that time to keep himself from falling into an imitation of the Dickens strain, even though he were profoundly conscious of the fact that his best efforts in that direction could be nothing better than a grotesque and pitiful imitation of the great and unique original. There was a sort of Dickens language which people unconsciously spoke and wrote under the spell of the master. The fact itself was but another tribute to the genius of Dickens, and may help us, even, still to understand how wide and deep was the influence then exercised by the spell of the enchanter.

The contributors to *Household Words* and to *All the Year Round,* the periodical which Dickens afterwards started in consequence of his quarrel with his publishers, were not all by any means mere imitators and nothing else. Men like Wilkie Collins, Shirley Brooks, John Hollingshead, George Sala, and many others, brought out books entirely their own, and made a mark for themselves, although, of course, no one among them could ever have won for himself anything like such a place in literature as that to which Dickens mounted almost by one step. I should say it was always the desire of Dickens himself to find out the real and individual gifts of his regular contributors, and to encourage each one of them to the development of his own peculiar qualities and to the avoidance of mere imitation.

Dickens's readings were as original and peculiar in their style as Dickens's writings. I have never heard any public reader who could display a dramatic vividness, variety, and power such as Dickens could show at all times and without any apparent effort when he read to some great audience. It really was not mere reading—it was the impersonation, or rather the calling into life, of each character whose words he spoke. It ran through all the moods of human feeling, was high tragedy or broad comedy, pathetic appeal or exalted contemplation, according as the subject gave opportunity, and yet it was never in any sense mere stage-play. Dickens had a voice of marvellous compass, depth, and variety of tone; some of its chords were perfect music; and although he had often to pass in a moment from the extreme of one mood to the extreme of another, there was never the slightest strain or effort or struggle after effect; all seemed to come with perfect ease from the instinct and the inspiration of the man. I remember well that there were some daring critics at the time, even among the most devoted admirers of Dickens, who ventured to challenge the common verdict of absolute approval as to Dickens's manner of illustrating this or that character in his readings. For instance, there were those among us who fearlessly maintained that Dickens had not done full justice to Sam Weller in his manner of rendering the utterances of that remarkable personage. He did not quite bring out, it was contended, all the full significance of this or that remark made by Mr. Weller the younger. But let us think for a moment what a tribute this was in itself to the genius of the author and the powers of the reader. All the disparaging criticism which the audacity of such critics could venture upon only went to argue that Dickens had created for us a living character of such odd and various humor that even Dickens himself was not quite able to read up to the level of his own creation. We used to dispute over the point as if it were some great question of faith or politics, and I remember well that I wondered much at the time whether Dickens himself would not regard the criticism as only a new and splendid tribute to his genius.

Dickens was superb as an after-dinner speaker, and was, I think, the greatest master of that modern form of eloquence I ever remembered to have heard. But he was a great master also of the eloquence which belongs to the public platform, and proved himself so on the rare occasions when he took a leading part in some popular movement. During the course of the Crimean War there was an effort made to get up a great agitation in favor of administrative reform, with the view of bringing about some better system of management in the War departments under the government. It was some such popular movement as might have been set on foot during the course of the South African campaign, for instance, when public attention had been directed to cases of gross maladministration in some of the War Office departments. Dickens threw his whole soul into the enterprise, and in the speech I heard him deliver he made a powerful attack on the weaknesses of the administrative system which led to so much useless and avoidable waste of life among the British troops engaged in service against Russia. He touched most effectively every note of feeling in his thrilling speech—the indignant, the pathetic, and the humorous—and every touch told with irresistible effect upon the crowded meeting. He was especially happy in his allusion to Lord Palmerston as the "comic old gentleman" of the administration, and the phrase lived for long after in the current speech of political and social life.

There is a common belief that Dickens never had any inclination for a parliamentary career, and would not have listened to a suggestion inviting him to become a member of the House of Commons. We know, however, from some of Dickens's published letters that he had, at least at one time, a strong desire to offer himself as candidate for Parliament. The desire soon passed away, and none of his admirers can feel regret that it was never carried into action. The world of literature must have suffered severe loss if the temporary impulse had found satisfaction, for it is utterly impossible to imagine Dickens becoming a mere casual attendant to his parliamentary duties if once he had accepted such responsibilities. Nothing can be more certain than that Dickens would have given a close attention to any work he had voluntarily taken upon himself, and if he had consented to accept a seat in the House of Commons he would unquestionably have given to his parliamentary duties much of the valuable time which the world expected him to devote to his calling as a writer of novels. The House of Commons would have gained a brilliant and powerful speech now and then, and the reading public would have lost much of delight and of instruction. The House of Commons never wanted for men who could make eloquent and powerful speeches in great parliamentary debates, but for the world outside there was only one Charles Dickens, and he could not be spared from his own peculiar and appointed work. He accomplished enough as a public speaker to prove the marvellous versatility of his talents.

I cannot call to mind any other instance of a really great author in modern times who displayed such a capacity for success in fields of competition which were not especially his own. He might have been a great actor, he might have been a great orator—he made proof of this over and over again—and he was in more instances than one a thoroughly successful editor. We owe directly to him the creation of a whole school of modern periodical literature, and we know that he was the first editor of the *Daily News*. The world feels nothing but gratitude to him for the steady resolve with which he kept himself mainly to his work and did not allow himself to be tempted into any prolonged excursion from it. It is curious to observe how little his style as a novel-writer owed to any recollections of other men's writings. That he was a reader of books may be taken as certain, but I can only call to mind at the moment one instance in which he pointed his meaning by a poetical quotation. The novels of Walter Scott are studded everywhere by such citations; they are common in the pages of Bulwer Lytton and George Eliot; and many of Thackeray's reflective passages gleam with allusions drawn from the literature of various countries and periods.

The one poetic quotation in a novel by Dickens to which I have made allusion is to be found in *Martin Chuzzlewit*, and is taken from a poem written by Thomas Moore, when he was in the American States. Moore was a very popular author even among Englishmen at that time, and it may be remembered that Mr. Richard Swiveller indulges in several reminiscences of the Irish minstrel's lines. But I am concerning myself at present only with the passages in which Dickens is speaking for himself, and in these, so far as I can remember, the one poetic quotation is from Thomas Moore. Dickens quotes four lines in which Moore speaks dismally of the inborn dangers threatening the young American republic. But for some few of her nobler citizens he declares that "Columbia's days were done"; he describes her growth as "rank without ripeness, quickened without sun"; and augurs that only for these guardians of her true civilization "her fruits would fall before her spring were o'er." It is easy to understand how Moore and Dickens in their different days came to be filled with such gloomy forebodings. Each man was overborne by his detestation of the slavery system and his dread of the corrupting effect it was likely to have on the growth of American civilization. Neither Moore nor Dickens quite foresaw the turn events were destined to take and the rising of that great antislavery movement which was ordained to end in a national convulsion and in the complete overthrow of the corrupting system.

We must all admit that from their point of view Moore and Dickens were alike in the right, and that if the slavery system had not been crushed by a great national uprising the social life of the young republic might have proved but an unwholesome growth. It is not without interest that Dickens's one poetical quotation is in itself another tribute to his love for humanity, and to the same spirit in the poet whose lines he feels called upon to cite in support and illustration of his devotion to the cause of man's freedom. Even those among us who at the present day on this side of the Atlantic hold a full faith in the great future of the American republic, even those who like myself own a love for America only second to the love for their own country, and who cherish the most delightful memories of its people, its homes, and its scenery, must well understand the sensations of disappointment and pain which the toleration of slavery aroused at one time in men like Moore and Dickens. The portrait of Dickens in this chapter seems to me to picture him in just such a mood of melancholy contemplation as that which must have possessed him when he introduced into the pages of his novel that memorable quotation from the poem by Thomas Moore.

CHAPTER III

W. M. THACKERAY

We cannot think long over Charles Dickens and the place he held in English literature without finding our thoughts turn to his great contemporary and, according to common acceptation, his great rival, W. M. Thackeray. There was at one time a school of Thackeray and a school of Dickens. Thackeray was born about a year earlier than Dickens, but Dickens made his mark in the *Sketches by Boz* some four years before the publication of Thackeray's *Paris Sketch Book.* Thackeray was becoming known to readers as a brilliant and original writer of magazine articles before Dickens had made his sudden uprising to the front rank in literature. Dickens must have still been a reporter in the House of Commons press-gallery while Thackeray was beginning to make a certain reputation for himself among the readers of magazines. But did Thackeray achieve, even by his first published book, anything like the reputation instantaneously accomplished by Dickens on his first venture in the form of a volume? My own recollections of my boyish days make it clear to me that Dickens was recognized as a great author before those of us who lived far away from the centre of England's literary life had come to know anything about the rising genius of Thackeray. I can even remember that we were all in those days so completely possessed by our admiration for Dickens as to feel a kind of resentment when we read in London papers that a new man was coming to the front who threatened a possible rivalry with the author of *Pickwick* and *Nicholas Nickleby.* I had the great good fortune at a later period of meeting both men several times in London and the honor of some slight acquaintanceship with each of them. My life holds no clearer memories than those which it treasures of Dickens and Thackeray.

In appearance and manner Thackeray was as unlike Dickens as in his literary style. Thackeray was very tall, standing quite six feet four inches in height, and was built with a broad framework. His great, massive head and expansive forehead were crowned with a covering of thick and prematurely white hair. He did not live to be what we should now call an elderly man, and the first time I ever saw him, which was many years before his death, his hair was snowy white. He always wore spectacles, and his eyes never gave out the penetrating flash-lights which Dickens could turn upon those around him. Thackeray's manners were in general quiet, grave, and even gentle, and his most humorous utterances, which were as frequent as they were delightful, had an air of restraint about them as if the great satirist wished rather to repress than to indulge his amusing and sarcastic sallies of wit.

The first time I ever saw Thackeray, except as the solitary figure on a lecturer's platform, he wore a thick mustache, and the mustache was of a dark color, contrasting oddly with his white locks. That first sight of him thus unusually adorned was on the platform of the Lime Street Station, Liverpool, when he came down from London to go on board the Cunard steamer on his way to deliver his course of lectures in the United States. There were a few small groups of people gathered on the platform to get a glimpse of the great author as he passed out, and I well remember that one enthusiastic young lady, who was personally quite unknown to him, went boldly up and pressed a bunch of roses into his hand. Nothing could be more graceful and genial than the manner in which Thackeray accepted this unexpected tribute, and took off his hat with a benignant smile in acknowledgment of the gift. I know that that young woman was made happy for long after by the memory of the silent welcome which was accorded to her votive offering.

I had heard most of Thackeray's lectures before that time, and had, like all his hearers, been fascinated by their manner as well as by their matter. Thackeray had, indeed, none of the superbly dramatic style of delivery which made Dickens's readings and speeches so impressive. His voice was clear and penetrating and his articulation allowed no word to be lost upon his listeners, but he never seemed to be making any direct appeal to the emotions of the audience. No accompaniment of gesture set off his quiet intonation, and he seemed, indeed, to be talking rather at than to the crowd which hung upon his every word. He did not act his part as Dickens did, but merely recited the words he had to give out as one might have done who was simply expressing his own thoughts as they came, without any effort to arouse the susceptibilities of those who filled the hall. It was not exactly a reading, although he always had his manuscript laid carefully out on the desk behind which he stood, for he only glanced at the manuscript every now and then to refresh his memory, but it was certainly not the speech of an orator who appeals with impassioned force to the sympathies of his listeners, and it was not in the slightest degree endowed with dramatic effect. Even when his audience broke into irrepressible applause at some passage of especial beauty and power the lecturer did not seem to gain any fresh impulse from the plaudits which broke forth, but went on to his next sentence with the same self-absorbed composure as though he were only thinking aloud and were unconscious of the presence of listeners. None the less the very manner of the lecture as well as its literary style had an intense fascination for all who came to listen. I observed on many occasions that the audience seemed to become possessed by a common dread lest anything, even an outburst of premature applause, should interrupt the discourse and cause a word to be lost. I noticed this especially in some of the more pathetic passages, as, for instance, in the closing sentences of the lecture on George the Third—that marvellous description of the blind, deaf, and insane old king as he wandered through the halls of his palace and bewailed to himself the deplorable conditions of his closing days. The most studied dramatic effects of voice and action could not have given to those passages of the lecture a more complete and absorbing command over the feelings of the listening crowd. Every one appeared to hold his breath in fear that even a sound of admiration might disturb for an instant the calm flow of that thrilling discourse. If there were art in that manner of delivery it was assuredly the art which conceals art. I have heard many great orators and lecturers in my time and in various countries, and I never made one of an audience which seemed to hang upon the words of the speaker more absolutely than did the men and women to whom Thackeray delivered the finest passages of his many lectures.

I can well remember the effect which was wrought upon the public mind when the yellow-covered monthly numbers of *Vanity Fair* first began to make their appearance. There were some distinguished literary men in England who had long entertained the belief that if Thackeray were to devote himself to the novelist's work he would prove himself a rival to Charles Dickens. Some of these men had actually expressed such an opinion in published articles, and the immediate effect was only to impress the general body of readers with the idea that an absurd attempt was made by a small group of admirers to start a sort of opposition to the great author who up to that time had held an undisputed sway over the living public. Thus from the very beginning of the serial issue of *Vanity Fair* there were already formed two sets of disputants as to the merits of the new model. By far the larger number was made up of those who were disposed to regard with indignation anything like an effort to make too much of the new writer, while by far the smaller number felt the full conviction that a great new literary chapter was opening on the world, and that Charles Dickens had found his rival at last. Even when *Vanity Fair* had compelled the public in general to recognize the fact that an entirely fresh force was coming up in novel-writing, there was still a large portion of readers who resented the idea that any one could come into rivalry with Dickens, and who felt disposed, out of sincere partisanship, to depreciate Thackeray because of what they held to be the extravagant admiration of those who spoke his praises.

I only allude to this contest of opinion as an interesting historical fact which has almost faded out of memory at the present day, but is curious and interesting enough to be brought under the notice of the present generation. I am not inclined to trouble myself much about any comparison between the relative places in literature of Dickens and Thackeray. I have an intense admiration for both men; I regard them not in any sense as rival forces, but as the creators of two different forms of novel-writing, and I see no necessity for endeavoring to exalt the one by depreciating the other. But my mind still retains a very vivid recollection of the ardent discussions which used to go on in those days, and of the rival schools of admirers then formed to carry on the debate. I do not remember anything quite like it in more recent years, and I therefore describe the phenomenon merely as a matter of historical interest without the slightest wish to revive that futile, fierce, and wellnigh forgotten controversy.

I feel no regret now that Thackeray did not succeed in his one attempt to obtain a seat in the House of Commons. At the time when the contest took place I was, of course, in the youthful glow of my ardent admiration of Thackeray, an intense partisan of his candidature, and I looked upon it as nothing but the height of audacity on the part of his opponent, Edward Cardwell, afterwards Lord Cardwell, to contest the seat against such a man. The contest took place in 1857 and the constituency was the city of Oxford. In after years I felt nothing but satisfaction that Thackeray had not succeeded in his unexpected and, as one cannot help thinking, uncongenial ambition to become a member of Parliament. We may take it for granted that he would not have made a success in the House of Commons. It would have been different in the case of Charles Dickens if Dickens had succeeded in obtaining a seat there. Dickens would unquestionably have delivered some speeches which must have impressed and delighted all the occupants of the green benches in the representative chamber. He was, as I have already said, a public speaker of extraordinary powers, and he would assuredly have wakened up the House, even in its dullest moods, by his voice, his manner, and the happy originality of his illustrations and his phrases. He would have got off some words of sarcastic allusion to his opponents in debate which must have lived long in public memory and passed into incessant quotation. But Thackeray was a poor speaker whenever he attempted to go outside the range of his prepared lectures. He never, indeed, made a speech which had not in it some telling and suggestive sentences, but his manner was ineffective; he had no aptitude for public debate; he would have been regarded in the House as merely a curiosity, and I cannot bear to think of the author of *Vanity Fair* submitting himself to be regarded by any assembly as a mere curiosity and out of his place.

I can well remember Alexander Kinglake, one of the most brilliant writers of his time or of any time, when he had a seat in the House of Commons and occasionally took part in a debate. The general impulse of listening members was to ask themselves whether this ineffective and labored speaker could really be the author of the famous *Eothen.* I can remember that another writer of books which were immensely popular in their day, Thomas Chandler Haliburton, the author of *Sam Slick,* when he was in the House made a very poor figure there, and was once turned into ridicule—fancy Sam Slick being made ridiculous—by a happy sentence or two from Mr. Gladstone. It would, indeed, have been a subject for regret to all lovers of literature if Thackeray had been permitted by unkindly fate to run the risk of becoming, as I feel sure he must have done, a mere parliamentary failure. I presume that Thackeray must himself have felt a certain sense of relief when his sudden impulse to enter the House of Commons was not allowed to go any further than a candidature and a minority at the poll. So far as I know he never again thought of making an attempt in the same direction. A leading article in the *Times* observed after the result of the Oxford contest that Thackeray might find consolation for his defeat in the reflection that the Houses of Lords and Commons put together could not have produced *Barry Lyndon* or *Vanity Fair.*

I am far from countenancing the idea that men of great distinction in letters, science, or arts should resolutely keep themselves aloof from parliamentary life if they have a calling that way, or feel that there is some great cause to be advocated towards the success of which they are especially qualified to contribute. I joined in the general rejoicing which filled the minds of all his admirers and followers when John Stuart Mill consented to give up for a time the quietude and retirement of his thoughtful life and accept a seat in the House of Commons. At that time there were especial reasons why all genuine Liberals and lovers of political progress felt that it would be an immense advantage to their cause if Mill were to present himself as its advocate and its expounder in the great political assembly. Mill, although not qualified by aptitude or training to become a great parliamentary debater, was yet able to impress the House and to command its attention on the rare occasions when he took part in its debates, and on one occasion at least he was listened to with profound and breathless interest. But then Mill was a leading advocate on many important public questions, and his mere presence gave a new strength to the rising and enlightened minority in the House of Commons.

Thackeray had never taken any part or shown much interest in political controversy and could not have been regarded in the House as the recognized advocate of any political doctrine. It would, therefore, have been a mere throwing away of his literary influence if he had been compelled to devote any considerable part of his time to the business of Parliament. One does not want to think of Tennyson, or Robert Browning, or Richard Owen, or Herbert Spencer as a mere member of a political party in the House of Commons delivering every now and then an ineffective speech, spending futile hours in waiting for the division bell, and only tolerated in the House because of the respect men felt for the work he had done and the success he had accomplished in very different fields of intellectual achievement. From the few speeches which Thackeray delivered during the Oxford contest one does not obtain the impression that he would have been a steadfast champion of the more advanced ideas which since then have become recognized principles among all parties in the House of Commons. Literature might have lost much and political life could have gained but little if Thackeray had abandoned, though only for a time, his yellow-covered monthly numbers and devoted himself to the study of parliamentary blue-books.

Thackeray was easy of access in private life to all at least who had any claims upon his attention. He was one of the principal founders of the Garrick Club, the object of which was to bring young literary men into habitual association with the leaders of the profession. The foundation of the Garrick Club was the cause of a literary dispute which led to a great deal of public discussion at the time and something like an animated controversy in literary circles. Thackeray objected to the manner in which one member of the club, the late Edmund Yates, was in the habit of describing its social meetings and its leading men in some of the newspapers to which he was a contributor. The controversy itself does not call for much comment now, and the only fact that gave it any biographical interest was the position in which, for the moment, it placed Dickens and Thackeray as the leaders of opposing sides. I do not intend to enter into any of the personal questions involved in the dispute, and I only introduce the subject because it illustrates what may be called an opening chapter in the development of that order of journalism which finds its main business in depicting the ways and manners of social life. At that time it was not quite understood that such distinguished personages are not supposed to have any private life so far as the observation of the newspaper correspondent is concerned. Thackeray strongly resented the descriptions of his own personal appearance and manners which were printed in certain journals and were known to be the work of Edmund Yates.

Nobody at the present day would think it worth his while to raise an objection, sure to be futile, to any descriptions of himself or comments on his way of living in the London or provincial newspapers. It is now thoroughly recognized that there are journals which make writing of this kind the main business of their existence, and are read all the more by the public according as their descriptions are more and more intimate and free. Journalism of this kind has long been a settled institution among us. Few public men think about it at all, and the few who might feel inclined to complain of it are perfectly well aware that open complaint would only render them more and more liable to disparaging comment, and that no combination of complaint could be of any avail for the suppression of the practice so long as there are to be found a vast number of readers who delight above all things in personalities and gossip. There was nothing said about Thackeray in the newspaper paragraphs I have referred to which could be compared for freedom of speech with some of the personal paragraphs we may now read every day in London newspapers of accredited position. But at the same time I cannot help thinking that Thackeray might well be excused for expressing an objection to the practice when it invaded what might have been considered the private intercourse of a literary and artistic club. Thackeray's main purpose in helping to found the club was, as I have said, to bring the young literary and artistic beginner into habitual association with the leaders of these crafts, and it may have seemed to him hardly fair that a member of this private association should make use of his position there to indulge in more or less satirical accounts of those whom he met within its walls. No such controversy could have arisen in our days, but I am not quite certain whether this fact in itself is to be regarded as an evidence of an improved tone in journalism and in public opinion.

Thackeray's was a familiar figure in some of the London streets, and no one who had ever seen him or read any descriptions of him could fail to recognize that tall, swaying form, half a head above most other pedestrians, that white hair and those eyes that beamed with a penetrating light even through the spectacles. He could be met with in the Strand, or Piccadilly, or St. James's Street, or in the Temple Gardens. I do not remember to have ever met him in the vicinity of Westminster Palace even at the time when he was a candidate for a seat in the House of Commons. I associate him especially with the Temple Gardens for the perhaps quite insufficient reason that my first sight of him in London was in those historic enclosures, and it was there, too, that I saw him for the last time not many days before his death. Thackeray's figure seems to me appropriately associated with the Temple Gardens. There are many allusions to them in some of his books which one always loves to remember, and the recollections they gather around them from history and romance form a fit setting for his picturesque figure. Sir Roger de Coverley and Will Honeycomb must have loved to ramble in the Temple Gardens; and one cannot help thinking that the age of Queen Anne, to which Thackeray's mind always turned with so much interest and sympathy, left some of its lights and shadows over the place.

When Thackeray's library was sold in March, 1864, I bought his volume of Smollett. The title-page of the book describes it as containing "The Miscellaneous Works of Tobias Smollett, Complete in One Volume." A memoir of Smollett, by Thomas Roscoe, is prefixed to the works, and the volume is "Printed for Henry Washbourne, Salisbury Square, London, 1841." I need hardly say that the volume is a precious treasure in my household and an object of intense interest to my friends. It obtains a priceless value from the fact that some pencilled notes in Thackeray's own handwriting are scribbled on the margins of two or three pages. The notes are written in a faint and delicate but clear and legible hand. I quote one of them which appears on a page of *Humphrey Clinker,* because it seems peculiarly characteristic of the writer: "As Smollett forgave his enemies in life, he made amends to his opponents in his history; in this he compliments Lyttelton, whom he had lampooned."

CHAPTER IV

THOMAS CARLYLE—ALFRED TENNYSON

In the early sixties Thomas Carlyle was commonly accepted as the despotic sovereign of thought. Even those who remained in an attitude of uncompromising resistance to his sovereign authority could not deny the extent of his domination. Those of us who did not fully acknowledge his rule were somewhat in the position of living Russians who will not recognize the authority of the Czar, but do not pretend to deny or ignore the fact that the Czar is a mighty monarch. There were some of us in the sixties who preferred to take our thinking from John Stuart Mill, for instance, but we did not affect to deny the power of Carlyle, and we could be as rapturous as his own professed disciples in our admiration for many of his writings. Darwin's great work on *The Origin of Species* had but recently been published; the philosophy of natural selection had not yet spread its influence over the general community; and the teachings of Herbert Spencer had not reached the ears of the groundlings.

Carlyle, therefore, as the leader of an order of thought may be said to have had it all to himself even among those who could not always be loyal to his leadership. I am stating a mere fact and not designing any disparagement of the present day's intellectual development when I say that there is no man just now who has anything like the influence over readers and thinkers which was exercised in the sixties by Thomas Carlyle. That influence was the greater because, as I have said, it met with so much resistance. We sometimes find that the leaders of certain schools in thought do not extend their influence outside the limits of their avowed and acknowledged pupils. The followers of the one school accept to the full the doctrines of their teacher and do not trouble themselves about the doctrines or the teacher of any other school. This was not so with Carlyle. We all discussed him, followers and rebels alike.

When I think of Carlyle himself—the man and not his books—I always think of him as a moving figure on Cheyne Walk, Chelsea. This is not because I first saw Carlyle in the Chelsea region, but because my recollection of him during all the later years of his life brings him back as a resident of Chelsea, whose form was familiar to those of us living in that picturesque and historic quarter. The only occasions when I had the good fortune to be in his company are associated with friendships formed in Chelsea. I had but few opportunities of being in Carlyle's society, and my acquaintance with him was very slight indeed, but I must always retain a vivid impression of his manners and his conversation. I may say at once that he impressed me rather too much for my own ease and comfort. I was only beginning my life as a worker in London just then, and I was naturally shy and diffident in the presence of a man whose intellectual greatness I so thoroughly recognized. His manner seemed to me to have something overpowering in it. Whatever he said he said with emphasis and with earnestness, and it appeared to me as if I could hardly summon up courage enough to offer any opinion which was not likely to commend itself to his approval. I felt quite sure that my views on most subjects could not possibly commend themselves to him, and yet I was sometimes beset with the thought that it was a sort of cowardice on my part to sit and listen to his laying down of the law on several great subjects without venturing to interject a word of remonstrance. If only the conversation would have turned on Goethe or on Schiller, or even on Mirabeau and Robespierre, I could have listened forever in unfeigned delight and reverence, and might have had no occasion to utter any words but those of modest and humble agreement and admiration. But it unluckily happened that just about the time when I had the good fortune to meet Carlyle there were great questions stirring the world on which Carlyle held the most definite opinions one way, while I could not help holding opinions which put me on the opposite side of the dispute.

The great American civil war was then going on, and Carlyle was ever ready to give judgment against the Northern States. I was at that time one of the writers for the *Morning Star,* the daily newspaper which represented the views of Bright and Cobden, and was naturally a strenuous and consistent advocate of the Northern cause. The *Daily News* and the *Morning Star* were the only London daily papers which held firmly to that side during the whole of the long struggle. Carlyle, in a short, sharp essay of his called, if I remember rightly, "The American Iliad in a Nutshell," which appeared in one of the magazines, had summed up the whole controversy to his own complete satisfaction as merely a question between the right to hire one's servants by the week or for life. Some of us still persisted in thinking that servitude enforced for life was a very different thing from servitude hired by the week or by the month, and we continued to regard slavery just as we had done before. At the time every

THOMAS CARLYLE

From an unfinished Painting by Sir John E. Millais, in the National Portrait Gallery

one was naturally talking of the American war, and it was not pleasant for those who thought as I did to draw out Carlyle on the great question. Nor did he always wait to be drawn out, for he frequently expressed his opinions and denounced his opponents without any challenge or provocation on their part. Under these conditions it will readily be understood that an obscure and modest young man who did not happen to agree with the sentiments of the orator was not likely to find himself quite comfortable in the presence of Carlyle. I did not, therefore, seek for opportunities of possible dispute, and my slight acquaintanceship with him soon came to an end. I had no excuse for endeavoring to press myself on Carlyle's notice after the whole question had been settled, and I never afterwards saw him except when I happened to meet him in the highways and byways of Chelsea. But I still hold it as a privilege to have been admitted to his society even on the few and rare occasions which I have described, and the mere fact that I did actually meet him and listen to his talk must ever be one of my cherished memories.

I knew intimately many of his friends, and I knew from them how little the whole character of the man could be judged from the manner in which he sometimes loved to bear down all opposition. No man had friends more thoroughly appreciative of him, more grateful for his friendship, and more entirely devoted to him. Some of those friends were Americans from the Northern States, avowed and complete adherents of the Northern cause, but of course they knew the man well, and were not affected in their admiration of him by the fact that he held views opposed to theirs on the one great question, and that it was his habit to express his views occasionally without overmuch regard for the feelings of all his listeners. His presence still haunts that Chelsea quarter for me whenever I find myself in the neighborhood of the house which was so long his home and must forever be associated with his fame.

We had one great poet in those days of the sixties, and his name was Alfred Tennyson. Now I hasten to rescue myself from any possible mistake on the part of my readers by announcing at once that we were quite aware of the existence of other poets as well. Some of us had lived in the later days of Wordsworth, were devoted admirers of his poems, and had passed many times before his home in the Lake country with the hope of getting a glimpse of the poet himself; but Wordsworth lay buried at Grasmere many years before the sixties set in and Tennyson had succeeded him as Poet Laureate—a title which in those days at least was understood to confer upon its bearer the highest place in the living poetic order. Perhaps I may also observe in vindication of the early sixties that we were most of us not unfamiliar with the works of a poet named Robert Browning, and of those of a poetess named Elizabeth Barrett Browning, who died at the opening of the period which I am now recalling to memory. But the appreciation of the Brownings was as yet confined to the few, and it had not yet become the fashion to give to Robert Browning his due place in the foremost order of English poets. Tennyson, therefore, was the acknowledged king of living poets, and it did not occur to the general public to admit any rival to the throne.

My first sight of Tennyson was obtained under very striking and appropriate conditions. It was during the visit paid by Garibaldi to London in 1864, and I was one of those who were invited by the hospitality of the late Mr. Seeley, a member of Parliament, with whom Garibaldi was then staying at his home in the Isle of

Wight, to meet the Italian visitor. There were many Englishmen of great distinction there, and Tennyson was the most conspicuous among the guests. Tennyson's appearance was very striking, and his figure might have been taken as a living illustration of romantic poetry. He was tall and stately, wore a great mass of thick, long hair—long hair was then still worn even by men who did not affect originality — his frame was slightly stooping, his shoulders were bent as if with the weight of thought; there was something entirely out of the common and very commanding in his whole presence, and a stranger meeting him in whatever crowd would probably have assumed at once that he must be a literary king. I met him several times after that, although I never came to have the honor of a close acquaintance with him. I saw him once, and once only, in the House of Commons. He occupied a place in the seats which are known as "under the gallery," and are reserved for members of the House and for distinguished strangers. His appearance there attracted the attention of every member, and I do not think that so long as he remained any close interest was taken in the debate then going on.

Though I never had much acquaintance with Tennyson, it is something to have met him occasionally, to have heard him talk, and to have exchanged a few words with him now and then. His manner was singularly impressive, and a stranger might sometimes have thought that there was a half-conscious display of lyrical authority about him. There was a certain eccentricity in his ways and his manner of expressing himself, and one could never tell how he might suddenly bear down upon the subject which happened to be the topic of conversation and compel the company to give up all idea but that of listening in eager silence for anything he might happen to say. Those who knew him well knew that there was no artificiality about him, and that the simplicity of genius was at the heart of his mystery. I met many of his intimate friends, and heard from them that he was a most delightful host and a congenial companion. He loved to enter into discussions on poetry, and would sometimes recite passages from his own poems with natural and incomparable effect. When he happened to be in London he was a familiar figure in some of the quieter recesses of the parks, more especially of St. James's Park, and nobody to whom he was personally unknown could have passed him without turning to look back upon him and without taking it for granted that he must be a man of distinction and importance. Those who knew him only by sight and happened thus to meet him were sure to tell their friends that they had just seen Tennyson in the park.

In ordinary society Tennyson seldom spoke unless when he had something to say which he felt inspired to utter, and then the company listened as if he were some monarch delivering a speech from the throne. Now and then he disappointed his host and the rest of the company by indulging in long intervals of absolute silence until some sudden thought suggested itself to his mind, and then he came out with a burst of natural eloquence. I have read many anecdotes of his spending a whole evening alone with some honored guest, and of the host and guest sitting and smoking in silence, each finding companionship enough in the presence of the other and the interchanging clouds of smoke, without needing any spoken utterances to express their sense of good-fellowship. One such anecdote is told of Tennyson and Carlyle, but I must own that I have never been able quite to realize the idea of Carlyle thus

LORD TENNYSON

submitting himself to unbroken silence. There was evidently in Tennyson a certain shyness which held him back from ordinary conversation, and it is possible that among his intimate friends he felt at liberty to indulge to the full his humor of silence whenever the humor took him. I have heard, on the other hand, many accounts of his delightful adaptability to the ways of those who happened to be with him, of the pleasure he took in making young women feel quite at home with him, and in drawing them out on whatever happened to be their own familiar topics. But I think he must sometimes have felt the poetic dignity accorded to him an oppressive influence, and must occasionally have envied those commonplace persons who were liable to be interrupted in the flow of their conversation. Certainly wherever Tennyson went in the social world he was sure to be regarded as the most conspicuous and commanding figure in the company. There might have been a prime-minister present; there might have been a great parliamentary orator; there might have been a foreign diplomatist accustomed to rule in state affairs; there might have been an archbishop or two; there might have been a soldier who had led great armies and won victories on the battle-field—but Tennyson at that time was always Tennyson, and everybody else was a secondary figure. I do not know that in the present day we have any poet or scholar, or leader in art, science, or literature, who holds the sovereign place which in the sixties was accorded to the author of "Locksley Hall." I have often in later years been led to make comparison between the position accorded by every one to Tennyson and that given to Robert Browning, even among Browning's most devoted admirers. Browning was a thorough man of the world in the best and happiest sense. He enjoyed society and unaffectedly welcomed the companionship of his friends and of those whom his friends introduced to him. He was a brilliant talker, and could talk with ease to every one. I had the honor of knowing him well, and loved him, as all did who knew him. But he never attempted to hold the place of literary monarch among men and women, and without any effort on his part he prevailed upon us all to think that we were, for the time at least, among his peers. There was nothing eccentric about him, and we came to accept him as one of ourselves who happened also to be a great poet.

So far as I can remember there was no proclaimed anti-Tennysonian school. No rival to Tennyson was set up. There was always an anti-Byronian sect, and in much more recent times there was a school of indignant anti-Swinburnians. But even among those who were most strongly opposed to some of Tennyson's utterances on certain public questions, when the Poet Laureate felt himself drawn into utterances on such questions, there was no impulse to rebellion against his poetical supremacy. At one period English society was divided into two hostile camps on the subject of the methods which had been used to suppress the supposed rebellion in Jamaica, and when Tennyson took up the championship of Governor Eyre there was a cry of lamentation and of anger sent forth by many even among his most devoted admirers. A satirical ballad was published at the time in one of the London daily newspapers concerning the views which Tennyson maintained with regard to the sudden condemnation and execution of Gordon, who was accused of having fomented the supposed rebellion. Chief-Justice Cockburn, it will be remembered, had denounced this execution as an act committed in defiance of all law and all evidence. The satirical ballad took the form of a parody on Tennyson's touching poem, which begins with the line:

> "Home they brought her warrior dead."

The satirical balladist thus began his verses:

> "Home came news of Gordon dead,
> But the poet gave no sigh.
> Mill and Bright indignant said
> 'Twas a crime that he should die."

I am sorry to say that I have forgotten the lines which followed, and do not even remember how the parody worked itself out and what was its climax. It had a certain run at the time among those who upheld the views of Chief-Justice Cockburn, but even those who quoted it and cordially welcomed it were not driven into any overt act of rebellion against the supremacy of Tennyson the poet. We were sorry that such a man should have taken up that side of the controversy, and we much wished that he had let the whole matter alone, but we did not feel the faintest desire to question his right to regal state among England's living poets.

The last time I saw Alfred Tennyson was, like the first, an imposing and unique occasion. That last time was on the day when Tennyson, just endowed with a peerage, was formally introduced to the House of Lords. I watched the ceremonial from the bar of the House of Lords, the place where members of the House of Commons are privileged to stand. The whole ceremonial is a severe trial for the nerves and the composure of even the most self-possessed and most self-satisfied among newly created peers. The new-comer wears for the first time his robes of state, and these robes make a garb in which it is hardly possible for any novice not to appear somewhat ridiculous. The new peer is formally conducted by two of his brother peers into the House of Lords, is presented with due ceremony to the Lord Chancellor and other leading members of the House, and has to make many genuflections and go through many forms which bear, to irreverent eyes, a suggestion of theatricality and masquerade. I must say that Tennyson comported himself with modesty and dignity throughout the whole of this peculiar ordeal, and the general feeling was that even if the performance had been carefully rehearsed, which we assume it certainly was not, Lord Tennyson could not more successfully have got through his part in the dramatic exhibition. I am not disposed to enter into the question whether it is the most appropriate tribute to the genius of a great poet that he should be created a member of the House of Lords. But it is something to remember that when England's great poet thus received a state recognition he should have shown himself equal to the occasion and should not have broken down into awkwardness under the unusual robes and made the grand ceremonial seem needlessly ridiculous. It is something certainly for me to remember that I was one of those who beheld the introduction of Alfred Tennyson to his place in the House of Lords.

CHAPTER V

RICHARD OWEN—THE BROTHERS NEWMAN

THE great struggle between two rival schools of scientific thought may be said to have begun with the sixties. Richard Owen represented what was called the older school, the orthodox school, while men like Charles Robert Darwin and Thomas Huxley were the leading apostles of the new school. Darwin's *Origin of Species by Means of Natural Selection* had been given to the world in 1859, and the controversy was thus fairly opened for the sixties. I do not propose to enter upon any task so superfluous as that of describing the controversy which formally opened a new era in the history of scientific development. My object at present is nothing more ambitious than to accompany the portrait of Richard Owen by some personal recollections of the great man himself. I have one relic of Richard Owen which I especially desire to bring under the notice of those who read this volume. That relic is the peroration of one of Owen's lectures. The peroration is written out in Owen's own hand and is the only part of the long discourse which was thus written. The accompanying facsimile will put it almost as much in the possession of my readers as the actual pages of writing are in my own possession.

Richard Owen was one of the most effective public lecturers to whom I have ever listened. His presence was stately and effective, while at the same time he showed no consciousness of personal stateliness and there seemed in him no striving after effect. His face was expressive, his eyes were luminous with meaning, sincerity, and a desire to come into complete understanding and sympathy with whose whom he addressed. The most difficult questions of anatomical science were made intelligible by the simplicity and clearness of his language, by the unadorned precision of his style, and by his faculty of addressing himself directly to the comprehension of his audience. His discourse never passed over the heads of his listeners; the listeners were taken along with him and were carried away by what might fairly be described as his unadorned eloquence. It was on the occasion of a lecture delivered by him in Liverpool, where I had been living for some years before the sixties set in, that I had the opportunity of obtaining from him the valuable manuscript reproduced for the illumination of this chapter. It was as one of the reporting staff attached to a Liverpool daily newspaper—the first daily newspaper set up in an English provincial town—that I found my opportunity. Owen spoke the greater part, and indeed nearly the whole, of his address without reference to manuscript or to notes of any kind. But I observed, while he was speaking the concluding sentences of his address, that he had a page of paper before him both sides of which were covered with manuscript, at which he glanced from time to time. More than one great speaker to whom I have listened in the House of Commons and outside it had the habit of writing out some particular passages in a speech in order that no sentence and no word might fail of its due effect, might be inadequate to express its precise meaning.

I was then a very young man and had the audacity of youth to support me, and I ventured, when the lect-

RICHARD OWEN

ure was over, to ask the great lecturer to allow me to take possession of the sheet of paper which contained his written words. Owen was most kindly and gracious, appeared to be pleased by the boldness of my request, and made me the owner of this inestimable sheet of autograph composition. He was even more gracious than this, for he kindly invited me to call upon him during his stay in Liverpool, and I need hardly say that I gladly availed myself of this unexpected invitation. I went to see him next day, was received with courtesy and kindness, and was, in fact, encouraged to consider myself as one of his personal acquaintances. At a later period, when I had settled in London, I had the happy chance of meeting him occasionally while he was engaged in his work at the British Museum, and I never met him without being impressed more and more by the unaffected sweetness of his manners and by the readiness with which he seemed to tolerate my obvious admiration. Owen was undoubtedly a great man, was probably the greatest scientific anatomist since Cuvier; but, like many other great men, and unlike some, he assumed no airs of greatness and was ready to put himself for the time into full companionship with those who were admitted to his society. I shall never forget the evidences he gave me of his willingness to keep up the acquaintance, and I remember with a peculiar sense of gratification that to the end of his life he continued to send me, now and then, printed copies of some discourse which he had delivered, or some work in pamphlet form which he had published.

At that time Owen was commonly regarded as the leader of the old school of scientific philosophy. The old school and the new school fought out their battles just then with energy, and sometimes, it must be allowed, with considerable acrimony. But Owen at least was not very acrimonious in his part of the controversy, and he took the assaults of his opponents with remarkable composure. The public in general divided itself between the two schools and followed the teachings of the leaders on either side with deep and sometimes impassioned interest. I do not know whether at the present time there are any two such schools of scientific philosophy, and can only say that if any such controversy now goes on its echoes do not reach my sequestered ears. Perhaps the older school died out with the life of Richard Owen and the whole controversy with the lives of such great controversialists as Huxley and Tyndall. Perhaps the older school has vanished altogether from the living history of scientific dispute. Both schools professed to found themselves on actual scientific facts, but the older school assumed the principle that all new discoveries must be in accordance with established and orthodox faith, while the new school proclaimed that the discovery of scientific truths must be followed out with no regard to the consequences to accepted revelation. The new school acted no doubt, whether consciously or unconsciously, on the general principle laid down by Auguste Comte, who had defined the growth of human thought as destined to pass through the stages of the mythical, the metaphysical, and the scientific.

I had the honor in later days of becoming acquainted with Thomas Huxley and having many opportunities of meeting him and conversing on all manner of subjects. I am now, however, only dealing with the early sixties and with Richard Owen, and I did not believe myself at that or after endowed with sufficient knowledge of scientific questions and evidences to entitle me to form any very clear opinion as to the general bearings of the controversy. I admired Richard Owen

In the survey taken in the prest. brief course on the characters, succession & geogr. distn. of the M. cl. if I have succeeded in demonstr. the adaptation of each varying form to the exigences & habits & well-being of the spec. I have fulfilled one object I had in view, viz to set forth the wisdom intelligence & beneficence of power the Creator.

So far as I have shown the uniformity of plan pervading the osteological structure of so many diversified animated forms, I must have enforced, were that necessary, as strong a conviction of the unity of the Creative Cause.

If, in all the striking changes of form & proportion which have passed under review, we could discern the results of minor modifications of the same few osseous elements — we must be the more strikingly impressed with the wisdom & the power of that Cause wh. could produce so much variety, & at the same time, such perfect adaptations & endowments, out of means so simple.

For in what have those mechanical implements — the hands of the ape, the hoofs of the horse, the wings of the bat, the trowels of the mole, the uprooting paws of the Megatherium — so variously formed to obey the behests of volition in denizens of diff. elements — in what way, have they differed from the artificial instruments wh. we ourselves plan with foresight & calculation for analogous uses, save in their greater perfection, & in the unity & simplicity of the elements wh. are modified to constitute those several locomotive or prehensile organs

FACSIMILE OF OWEN'S MS.

[See page 46

Every where, in organic nature, we see the means not only subser to an end, but that end accomplished by the simplest means. Hence we are compelled to regard the Gt. Cause of all, not like certain philosophic ancients, as a uniform + quiescent mind, - as an all pervading anima mundi, - but as an active + anticipating intelligence.

By applying the laws of Comp. Anat. to the relics of extinct races of an.^l found in diff.^t strata of the Earth's crust + corresp. with as many epochs in the earth's history, we make an important step in advance of all preceding philosophies, and are able to demonstrate that the same active + beneficent intelligence which manifests his Power in our times, has also manifested that power in times long anterior to the record of our existence. But we, likewise, by these investigations, gain a still more important truth, viz., that the phenomena of the world do not succeed each other with the mechanical sameness attributed to them in the cycles of the Epicurean philosophy, for we are able to demonstrate that the diff.^t epochs of the Earth were attended with corresponding changes of organic structure; + that, in all these instances of change, the organs, as far as we could comprehend their use, were exactly those best adapted to the functions of the being. Hence we not only show intelligence evoking means suited to the end; but at successive times + periods producing a change of mechanism adapted to a change of ext.^l condi

then, as I afterwards came to admire Thomas Huxley, for his splendid intellectual gifts, for his genial manners, and for his extraordinary powers of eloquent exposition. The impression then made upon me by Richard Owen has never faded. He was the first great scientific man I had the good fortune to know personally, and my acquaintance with him formed an epoch at the opening of my literary career which must always live in my recollection. Huxley and Tyndall were both eager controversialists even on questions which had nothing to do with scientific development, and each of them went out of his way now and then to advocate some political or social cause which was arousing deep emotion throughout the whole country.

I do not remember that Owen ever allowed himself to become involved in any public debate which was not directly associated with his own sphere of strictly scientific study. Owen kept himself to his minute study of physical organization, and he took the facts as he found them, but he evidently reconciled them with his great faith in the organizing Cause. He seems to put this forth in the concluding sentences of the peroration reproduced in this chapter. "Everywhere," he says, "in organic nature we see the means not only subservient to an end, but that end accomplished by the simplest means. Hence we are compelled to regard the great Cause of all not, like certain philosophic ancients, as a uniform and quiescent mind—as an all-pervading *anima mundi*—but as an active and anticipative intelligence. By applying the laws of comparative anatomy to the relics of extinct races of animals found in different strata of the earth's crust, and corresponding with as many epochs in the earth's history, we make an important step in advance of all preceding philosophies, and are able to demonstrate that the same active and beneficent intelligence which manifests His Power in our times has also manifested His Power in times long anterior to the records of our existence." "If," he goes on to say, "I have succeeded in demonstrating the adaptation of each varying form to the exigencies and habits and well-being of the species, I have fulfilled one object I had in view—viz., to set forth the intelligence and beneficence of the Creative Power. So far as I have shown the uniformity of plan pervading the osteological structure of so many diversified animated forms, I must have enforced, were that necessary, as strong a conviction of the unity of the Creative Cause." And thus he declares "we must be the more strikingly impressed with the wisdom and the power of that Cause."

I have said in a preceding chapter that I must always associate the memory of Thomas Carlyle with the streets of Chelsea. In the same way I must ever associate the figure of Richard Owen with the neighborhood of the British Museum, with that region where he accomplished so much of his great work and where it was often my good fortune to meet him in days long gone by, which can never pass from my recollection.

I have heard many interesting accounts from friends in London of the great kindness which Richard Owen was in the habit of showing to children, and of the exquisite sympathy with which he could enter into all their ways and draw them into unrestrained converse with him. Only the other day a friend of mine was telling me that in her childish years she and her brothers and sisters were brought into acquaintanceship with Richard Owen when they were at school in the neighborhood of the British Museum, and she gave me many instances of his kindness to them, and mentioned the fact that when sometimes they met him in the street and he appeared to be wrapped in profound contemplation, they thought it right to pass on without disturbing him, but that he was sure to see them and would stop in his walk, enter into conversation with them, and even turn out of his way to escort them to their home. The anecdote came out unexpectedly, and was only occasioned by some talk about the interest which many great men, who seem to live above the clouds of common life, have taken in the companionship of children. I had not happened for a long time to hear any one speak of Owen, and her reminiscences of him were a new and a welcome contribution to my own impressions of his sweet and winning nature. I think that feeling of companionship with ordinary humanity pervaded all Owen's teachings and suffused his conceptions of the Eternal Cause. William Blake, the painter, poet, and mystical dreamer, has declared that "the Eternal is in love with the productions of Time." There would not seem to be much affinity between the character and studies of Richard Owen and those of Blake, but I have often thought that the words I have just quoted might be taken as a brief embodiment of the spirit that breathes through that passage of Owen's discourse reproduced in this chapter.

Among the portraits from the sixties about and around which I am writing in this volume is one of Cardinal Newman. It has seemed to me that in the grouping of these portraits there might be a certain appropriateness in setting the pictures of Owen and of Newman, metaphorically at least, side by side. The two men had, indeed, very different spheres of thought and action, but each was alike devoted to what he believed to be his supreme mission in life, and each lived above the clouds of ordinary and worldly existence. Cardinal Newman's was a life of absolute austerity, but there was a certain sweet simplicity in his manner which reminded me sometimes of Richard Owen. My personal acquaintance with Cardinal Newman was very slight, but I had many opportunities of listening to him and of observing his bearing and his ways. I saw him for the first time before the opening of the sixties. While I was living in Liverpool, just before the Crimean War, Newman delivered there his famous series of lectures on what was then regarded as the Eastern Question, the existence of the Ottoman power in Europe. There is no need to go very deeply into that question at the present time of day; we must all of us have made up our minds long ago on the whole subject, whatever our conclusions may happen to be. I need only say that Newman's views might have been regarded just then as a prophetic protest against the policy which was leading to the Crimean War. Newman regarded the settlement of the Ottoman Turk in Europe as, from first to last, a mere calamity to Christian civilization. A man of Newman's character and training could not make himself the advocate of any policy designed to expel the Turks by force from the European territories they had occupied, but he made himself the earnest and uncompromising opponent of any policy setting itself to maintain and strengthen the ill-fated dominion of the Ottoman power. Newman's expositions and warnings had, it is needless to say, no effect whatever on the majority of Englishmen at the time, but he uttered no warning which subsequent events did not fully and strictly justify. The lectures were singularly impressive, although they made no pretension to the graces and the thrilling tones of eloquence. The language seemed unstudied, but was always exquisitely chosen, every word expressing precisely the idea it was intended to convey, and no more, and there were many passages

JOHN HENRY NEWMAN

[*See page* 51

FRANCIS WILLIAM NEWMAN.

[*See page* 53

which lived long in the memories of those who heard them spoken. The lectures were delivered with perfect ease, and the voice, although not powerful, could make itself heard without effort in any ordinary assembly. It had certain tones of melancholy reflectiveness which seemed appropriate to a warning only too certain to be made, for the time at least, in vain.

No man was a more accomplished master than Newman of all the resources the English language can command. I heard him speak and preach on many later occasions, and he always seemed to me to have a certain distinct faculty of eloquence which has nothing to do with mere rhetoric, but is sincere and lofty thought embodied in the most appropriate form of phrase. In some of the arts and the gifts that go to make a great orator or preacher, Newman was strikingly deficient. His bearing was not impressive; his gaunt, emaciated figure, his sharp eagle-face, his eyes of quiet meditation, were rather likely to repel than to attract those who heard and saw him for the first time. But the matter of his discourse, whether sermon, speech, or lecture, was always captivating, and if the language had any defect it might be that it was perhaps a little overweighted with thought, and thus might seem hardly suited to attract from the beginning a popular audience. But in speaking, as in writing, he soon made it evident that he was an influence—I do not know how better to express my meaning—which must command attention by its own force. Both as a speaker and as a writer he showed himself richly endowed with a keen, pungent, satirical humor, while there was, on the other hand, a subtle vein of poetry and of pathos suffusing all his argument, his illustration, and his appeal.

Newman's brother Francis was led away, as most of my readers will remember, into a field of thought and activity strangely unlike that into which faith and destiny had conducted him who was to become a cardinal and a leading spirit in the Church of Rome. I cannot think of the brothers Newman without recalling to memory a deeply interesting passage in Thackeray's *Pendennis.* Arthur Pendennis and his comrade George Warrington have a dispute about men and beliefs. "The truth," Pendennis asks—"where is the truth? Show it me. I see it on both sides. I see it in this man who worships by Act of Parliament, and is rewarded with a silk apron and five thousand a year; in that man, too, who, driven fatally by the remorseless logic of his creed, gives up everything—friends, fame, dearest ties, closest vanities, the respect of an army of churchmen, the recognized position of a leader—and passes over, truth-impelled, to the enemy in whose ranks he is ready to serve henceforth as a nameless private soldier; I see the truth in that man as I do in his brother, whose logic drives him to quite a different conclusion, and who, after having passed a life in vain endeavors to reconcile an irreconcilable book, flings it at last down in despair, and declares, with tearful eyes and hands up to heaven, his revolt and recantation." Of course every reader of *Pendennis* knew at the time when the book was published who were the two brothers of whom this touching description was given. *Pendennis* made its appearance in volume form some ten years before the period which the portraits in this book are intended to illustrate. But the parting of the two brothers only grew wider and wider as time went on, and they never can be said to have worked together during the remainder of their lives.

About the time with which this book opens I became acquainted with Francis Newman and was brought much more into intercourse with him than it was ever my fortune to be with the great Cardinal. The reason for this was that John Henry Newman kept, as a rule, quite apart from political movements, and that Francis Newman took an active share in the conduct of many political organizations. I was then beginning to be much engaged in English political life as well as in journalism, and I thus had many opportunities of meeting with Francis Newman. He was a man of great intellect and of very noble purpose, but he never acquired in his own sphere anything like the influence his brother exercised in the sphere to which his conscientious convictions had called him. I am sure my readers will quite understand that I am not now entering into any comparison or contrast of these two far-divided spheres. With questions of religious faith these chapters have nothing to do. My endeavor is to put myself for the time into the position of Arthur Pendennis, and to regard the two brothers as equally sincere followers of that which each believed to be the truth. But I have always thought that Francis Newman, while acting with the most sincere and unselfish motives, never succeeded in accomplishing as much by his intellect and his perseverance as might have been expected from one so richly endowed with noble qualities of mind and heart.

Francis Newman lent his best energy to the support of many a great political cause which time and events have since proved to be right, in the judgment of most thinking men at home and abroad. But unquestionably he sometimes wasted too much of his intellectual capacity on what might be called the eccentricities of political and social endeavor. There were all manner of new questions, political and social problems as they would now be called, coming up at the time, and Francis Newman did not always seem able to distinguish between a creed and a crotchet. The mere charm of novelty appeared to have an undue fascination for him. He was tempted too often into the frittering away of his remarkable intellectual powers over some new idea, as it was called, which turned out to be merely an old and exploded idea, recalled to a semblance of cohesion and reality by the futile energies of some sect or group of belated reformers. There was a time when nine out of ten men in London who took any interest in public affairs were apt to set down Francis Newman as hopelessly given over to crotchets, while the tenth man, admiring however much his character and his capacity, was sometimes grieved and sometimes angry that both together did not make him a greater power in the national life.

The last time I ever heard Francis Newman address a public meeting was at a small gathering of men and women in London who were engaged in organizing an opposition to some measure before Parliament, the purpose of which has long passed out of my memory. The meeting was held in Exeter Hall, not in the vast room where oratorios were performed and huge public assemblages are gathered together to discuss some question of national or international importance, but in a little, subterranean room. The attendance was not nearly up to the size of the room itself, limited though that was. There on the platform sat the good and gifted and fearless Francis Newman, and immediately around him were some dozen embodied and living crotchets and crazes. There was this learned physician who had renounced his medical practice and was holding communication regularly with the spirit-world. There was that other eminent personage who had long been trying in vain to teach an apathetic government how to cure crime on purely phrenological principles. There was Smith, who was opposed to all wars; Brown, who firmly believed that every disease known to poor humanity came from the use of salt; Jones, who had at his own expense put into circulation thousands of copies of his work against the employment of medical men in cases where the ailments of women were concerned. We just wanted, on this memorable occasion, the awful persons who proved to you that the earth was all a flat, and the indefatigable ladies who expounded their claims to the British crown, then feloniously usurped by Queen Victoria.

Nothing came of the demonstration, whatever it was, and I have only mentioned it here just to illustrate the extraordinary contrast between the commanding position to which Francis Newman, with his intellect, his energy, and his lofty purposes, might have attained, and the position to which from the highest and most unselfish motives he had allowed himself to descend. I could not help admiring the man, as much in these later days of his career as in that earlier time when he stood forth the great and recognized advocate of so many a noble cause. Surely the parting of the ways had brought these two gifted brothers very far apart. John Henry Newman had by this time become a prince of the Church of Rome, and was one of the most conspicuous and, in the strictest sense, one of the most influential men of his age. Yet every one who knew the two brothers must have known that mere personal ambition had influenced no more the one, who had obtained so lofty and commanding a position, than the other, who had fallen away from public life and become merely the futile advocate of so many a lost and unimportant cause. Both brothers had eminently the genius of the controversialist, both followed alike faithfully the light of the guiding star which his conscience recognized, and it is something of comfort to feel sure that both will alike have a place of honor in the history of England's intellectual development.

May I be allowed to say that I think Cardinal Newman did much good even to that Church from which he withdrew? He was really the main-spring of that movement which proposed to rescue the Church from apathy, from mere quiescence, from the perfunctory discharge of formal duties, and to quicken her once again with the spirit of a priesthood, to arouse her to the living work, spiritual and moral, physical and mental, of her ecclesiastical mission. Throughout the English Church in general there has been surely a higher spirit of work since that famous Oxford Movement, in which John Henry Newman took so influential a part. I think the influence of that English Church has been more active, more beneficent, more human, and at the same time more spiritual since that sudden and startling impulse was given. The story of these two brothers is, on the whole, as strange a chapter as any I know in the history of human intellect and creed. It may at least teach us a lesson of toleration, if nothing better. The very pride of intellect itself can hardly pretend to look down with mere scorn upon beliefs which carried off in contrary directions these two Newmans. The sternest bigot could hardly refuse to admit that truthfulness, self-sacrifice, and devotion might abide outside the limits of his own creed when he remembered the high and noble example of pure, true, and disinterested lives which John Henry and Francis W. Newman have alike given in their different ways to their fellow-men.

CHAPTER VI

RICHARD COBDEN

This volume has for its frontispiece the photographic reproduction of a picture which has not, so far as I know, been ever before thus brought to the notice of the public at large. The picture represents the principal framers of the famous French commercial treaty with England—the treaty brought into existence in 1860—seated around the table of a great salon — a picture drawn from the imagination, we may assume—and the most celebrated figures in which are Cobden, Michel Chevalier, Bright, Gladstone, Palmerston, Milner Gibson, Persigny, Fould, and many other of the eminent public men who were engaged in the negotiations which led to the treaty. The present chapter contains also a portrait group of Cobden, Bright, and Milner Gibson. Even at the present day readers will remember that Milner Gibson was one of Cobden's most earnest and capable supporters in the early English struggle for free-trade. Thomas Milner Gibson was a man of high social position, and was returned to Parliament so early as 1837 by the conservative party, to which he then belonged. He soon, however, saw reason to renounce his conservative opinions, and on one memorable occasion he boldly proclaimed in the House of Commons his conversion to the liberal doctrines, and he actually crossed the floor of the House and took his place among the free-traders. In 1841 he was elected from Manchester as a free-trader, and from that time forth he was, during the whole of his public career, one of the most consistent, persuasive, and distinguished champions of the free-trade cause and of every other doctrine of genuine liberalism. He held office more than once in a liberal government, and took a leading part in the repeal of the advertisement duty on newspapers, of the newspaper stamp-duty, and the paper duty itself. I used to meet him often in those days, and I felt the highest admiration for his sincerity, his great political capacity, his parliamentary eloquence, and the unaffected geniality of his manners. Cobden, Bright, Charles Villiers, and Milner Gibson were the apostles of free-trade, and may justly be said to have created a new chapter in English history. So far back as 1835 Cobden had published his first pamphlet advocating free-trade, and within a few years the Anti-Corn Law League was established in Manchester, with Cobden for its leading member. Sir Robert Peel afterwards acknowledged that to the agitation carried on by Cobden and the League was due the measure for the abolition of the Corn Laws which Peel carried in 1846. Charles Villiers, a member of the great Clarendon family, had been elected to the House of Commons for Wolverhampton as a declared free-trader in 1835, and used to bring forward every session a motion in favor of free-trade before the principle was adopted by any statesman in office. When Peel carried his measure for the abolition of the duty on the importation of foreign corn the general belief prevailing all over the country was that the question of free-trade had been settled forever in England.

There is a peculiar appropriateness in the reproduction of this picture of the three great free-trade apostles at the present time. During all the years which intervened between 1846 and this present

BRIGHT, COBDEN, AND MILNER GIBSON

year nothing was heard of any serious purpose on the part of a responsible English statesman to introduce a financial policy which could in any sense be held to repudiate the principle of free-trade. There were always some tory members in the House of Commons and some old-fashioned persons here and there in country districts who cherished a sort of ancestral and feudal homage for the old doctrine of protection. There were still men to be met with in and out of Parliament who insisted, with an almost touching devotion to the financial creed of their forefathers, that no matter what statistics and Board of Trade returns and parliamentary blue-books might say to the contrary, the country was positively going to the dogs because of free-trade, and that the sun of England's prosperity had set forever. England went on, however, perversely prospering in spite of all their protestations and predictions, and the professed protectionist came before long to be regarded as a mere curiosity, the late surviving symbol of a past age. No political or financial organization of the slightest influence attempted during all these years to bring about a reversal of England's commercial policy, and that a statesman in office should ever attempt such an undertaking seemed as little likely as that a statesman in office should undertake a crusade against the election of members to Parliament by a popular majority. It has been reserved for our times to behold the appearance of such a strange and unexpected phenomenon. We have lately heard from the lips of a statesman holding high office the proclamation of a resolve to bring up the whole question once again for national judgment, and to invite a reversal of the policy originated by Cobden, Bright, and Villiers, and carried into legislation by Sir Robert Peel.

I do not propose to enter into any discussion here as to the principle of free-trade, and I am well convinced that so far as England is concerned that question is settled forever. Nor do I intend to offer any arguments designed to show that the doctrine of preferential tariffs is merely another form, a somewhat diminished form, of the doctrine of protection. We may take it for granted that some questions at least in financial as well as in constitutional policy have been settled once for all. There need be no fear that any subtlety of plausible argument will ever induce England to return to what used to be called the principle of divine right in government, and we have just as little reason to fear that any such argument can prevail upon her to make at this time of day a reactionary experiment in the way of protective tariffs. There is a fashionable and self-opinionated lady in one of Molière's comedies who declares that she never could, even after the fullest consideration, see any reason why a woman should not change her husband as often and as freely as she changed her undergarments; but the lady would no doubt have admitted that with all her influence she was never able to get her theory adopted by the ruling powers of France. In the world of fashion it might be possible for some ruling queen of society to bring about for a time a new reign of the crinoline, but we do not reconstitute our financial system at the mere dictation of some adventurous and self-confident member of a divided government. I cannot help thinking with keen and curious interest of the effect which might have been produced on that triumvirate of English free-traders if it could have been foretold to them that before very many years an English statesman, who had during the greater part of his life professed complete devotion to their doctrine, should suddenly come forward with the proclamation that he was determined to lead a crusade against the principle of free-trade. Each of the three men, Cobden, Bright, and Villiers, had in him a genuine faculty of humor, and I can imagine any one of them adopting the words in which Scott's Antiquary comments on the pretensions of the German adventurer Dousterswivel who figures in the novel. Dousterswivel professes to have magical ways of discovering buried treasure, and thus enabling people at a small pecuniary sacrifice to become possessed of indefinite and ever-increasing wealth. The Antiquary declines to discuss the question, but he makes an appropriate quotation from our great Elizabethan dramatist, and closes with the words—his own words—" Ah! rare Ben Jonson! Long peace to thy ashes for a scourge of the quacks of thy day! Who expected to see them revive in our own?"

I made, for the first time, the personal acquaintance of Richard Cobden when he was conducting the negotiations for a commercial treaty between England and France. That was not, however, the first time I came to know Cobden as a public man and a public speaker. I had heard many of his great speeches in Manchester, in Liverpool, in Rochdale, and other places before I came to know him in private. That was a remarkable and a peculiarly interesting period of modern English history when I first made Cobden's personal acquaintance. He was then closely engaged with the preparations for the treaty, and was going to and fro between London and Paris, between the English government, for whom he was acting as unofficial representative, and Louis Napoleon, then Emperor of the French. Louis Napoleon was at the zenith of his power, and had succeeded in completely dazzling the minds of most persons in England as well as in France, and making them believe that he had founded an imperial system which was destined to have the control of France during an indefinite time. Many of those who had opposed his dictatorship in France were exiles, and some of them were settled in London. One of these was my friend Louis Blanc, who was not able to return to his own country until the war with Prussia had led to the overthrow of the empire and the establishment of that republic which has already lasted for a longer time than any system formed in France since the outbreak of the great Revolution.

When I first met Cobden he had as his colleague in the work of preparing the treaty the celebrated French political economist and statesman Michel Chevalier, who was acting on behalf of the French government. I had the advantage of being admitted to some of their conferences, of listening to the views they interchanged, and of seeing the documents they were engaged in drawing up. I could not help thinking at the time how strange it was to remember that the last great attempt to establish a commercial treaty between England and France was the work inspired by Bolingbroke, a man whose whole character was as unlike that of Richard Cobden or Michel Chevalier as could well be imagined. There was nothing showy, nothing that could even be called brilliant, about the style and the achievements of Cobden or Chevalier. One must describe Cobden as a great orator, if by oratory we mean the art of persuading, of convincing large bodies of men, whether in Parliament or outside it. But Cobden did not belong to that order of eloquence in which Bolingbroke must ever be remembered as one of the greatest masters. Oratory has been defined by Macaulay as the blending of reason and passion, and this we may assume to be a perfect description of Bolingbroke's brilliant and overwhelming style. Cobden made no appeal to the passions of men, but, on the other hand, he made constant appeal to those higher and nobler feelings with which Bolingbroke never proved himself to have much sympathy.

It would be a great mistake to suppose that Cobden's eloquence only addressed itself to man's reasoning faculties. Cobden accomplished some of his greatest effects by his frequent appeals to the eternal sentiments of equity and justice, to the exalted principles of peace among nations and brotherhood among men. He did not confine his arguments in favor of the commercial treaty to mere questions of tariff, to the commercial and individual advantages of an interchange of products on convenient terms, and to the individual benefits which must come from a treaty enabling each nation to have cheap possession of the articles produced or manufactured by the other. He preached the gospel of universal peace and friendship while illustrating the benefits of unrestricted commercial intercourse. He was not an orator in the ordinary sense of the word. He did not indulge in any splendid flashes of dazzling declamation. There are few passages in any of his speeches likely to be preserved as illustrations of the highest effect the English language can be taught to create. There are few sentences to be found in his public speeches which English school-boys would be enjoined to get by heart as models of successful declamation. His style had little in it that could even be called ornamental. His speeches were intended to convince the reason and, at the same time, to call into activity the purest and the noblest feelings.

I have heard Cobden's speeches described, even by some who express entire admiration for them, as the utterances of a man who is merely thinking aloud while he holds in profound attention a great, listening assembly. The description has always appeared to me curiously inadequate. In the House of Commons and on the public platform Cobden was always addressing himself directly to those whom he endeavored to persuade, was in close and constant touch with them. He was ready to reply to any word of interruption which suggested an opposition to his argument, and was able to supply on the spur of the moment any gap in his process of reasoning which even the doubtful glances of his listeners might remind him that he had left unfilled. Not the most fluent of the great debaters in the House of Commons was more quick than Cobden to take advantage of any sceptical or hostile interruption by turning it to his own account, and pouring forth upon those who had interrupted him some new or fresh argument or illustration intended to bear down upon the suggested criticism or dissent, and to report him and his cause aright to the unsatisfied. Even if one happened to have no particular views of his own on either side of the actual subject under discussion, it was a positive treat to listen to a speech of Cobden's in the House of Commons and observe the unfailing readiness with which he could bring forth new arguments in support of his pleading.

Cobden was remarkably fluent as a speaker; never seemed to want a word, and, what was better still, never seemed to want the precise word which most strongly and lucidly expressed his meaning. His voice was not great in volume—at least it did not seem so to those who only heard him addressing an assembly of limited extent, such as that which he had to address in the House of Commons. It was clear and liquid and even, and seemed admirably adapted in its compass to a full effect in a parliamentary assembly. But it had a power and a range which one only came to appreciate fully when he heard Cobden speaking from the platform of some great open-air meeting. Then the listener was filled with the satisfying conviction that Cobden could make himself easily and thoroughly heard at the farthest limit of the greatest public gallery. I have listened to speakers, renowned for the strength and volume and range of their voices, who could not have succeeded more completely and with less apparent effort in holding the attention of the largest crowd. Not one of these could accomplish with less suggestion of straining a more complete mastery over his audience than Cobden, whose voice was never regarded as one of his especial oratorical endowments.

Every one knows how it tries an audience to be compelled to make a continuous effort in following the argument of a speaker whose sentences are likely to lose some part of their meaning by an occasional failure in the reach of the orator's utterance. A certain lack of attention is sure to follow in a great assembly, especially an open-air assembly, when even the most convincing and rousing appeal is thus sometimes marred by a defective power of sustained elocution. No one ever felt any of this irritating strain when listening to Cobden. Every one settled down to the comfortable conviction that he had only to listen and no word could fail to reach his ears. Men like Gladstone, like Bright, like the anti-slavery orator Wendell Phillips, had magnificent voices, which were able to command any assembly by the mere charm of their musical intonation. But the wonder of Cobden's voice was that it could always exercise the same command, although it did not seem to be endowed with any such extraordinary power. His voice was like his eloquence, which had nothing in it showy, nothing that appealed to the musical sense, but could always captivate, arouse, and hold in silent, rapt attention.

There was something in it essentially characteristic of the man himself—it was plain speaking, a constant appeal to the reason, the judgment, and the better qualities of men, without any proclaimed right to control by mere rhetorical display. This was Cobden all through. It was an eloquence entirely his own, peculiar and self-possessed, but never self-assertive.

Cobden was unquestionably a great man, a great political and intellectual influence, but he seemed modestly unconscious of his own splendid powers, and never gave one the idea that he felt himself endowed with the heaven-born right to dictate and to command. His manner in private was simple, modest, and companionable. We felt perfectly at ease in conversing with him, and were never impressed with the humbling consciousness that we stood in the presence of a superior mortal. He lifted us up to his own level without any apparent effort to bring himself down to ours. He had had experiences and opportunities of observation which were far from common in his days. At that time great statesmen were not much in the habit of improving their minds by extensive and varied foreign travel. The leaders of parliamentary and public opinion were not then accustomed to go far beyond the range of that limited amount of travel which, at one time, used to be habitually described as the *grand tour.* Lord Palmerston, Lord John Russell, and other statesmen had never extended their wanderings beyond the easily attained reach of conventional European travel. They knew nothing, from personal experience, of England's foreign and colonial possessions. Even men like Gladstone and Disraeli had not accomplished much in this way beyond the familiar regions of the Continent, and Gladstone's experiences of Greece and Disraeli's visit to the Holy Land were beyond the ordinary reach of a statesman's journeyings. I remember hearing it remarked at one period that the late Lord Stanley was the only member of his administration who never having held the office of Viceroy was personally acquainted with India. Cobden had made himself familiar with all parts of the European Continent, including Russia; he had travelled all over the United States and Canada, and during debates in the House of Commons on any great foreign or colonial question he was able to strengthen his arguments by his own personal knowledge of the condition of the various populations in the countries whose affairs were the subject of discussion. Wherever he travelled he was on the lookout for the best and most trustworthy information to be had from all quarters, and he was not content to take his impressions of a foreign state or a distant colony from the views which prevailed at the British Embassy or at the headquarters of the colonial governor. He spoke and wrote French with fluency and accuracy, and I often observed that Michel Chevalier and he carried on their conversation on questions of tariffs and the interchange of commodities and other intricate and essentially technical subjects in Chevalier's own language.

My acquaintance with Cobden was kept up at intervals to the close of his life, and I was only more and more impressed each time I met him with the sweetness of his nature, the modesty of his manners, and his utter freedom from that overbearing or even self-asserting quality which is so commonly and excusably the attribute of those who come to know they have achieved greatness. He had that faculty which belonged also to Gladstone, of finding something to learn from every one with whom he came into contact. However limited and commonplace might have been the experiences of some who had the good fortune to make Cobden's acquaintance, we always found him inclined to bring each of us into conversation on subjects personally familiar, and thus to make even the slightest addition to his own extensive stores of knowledge.

The country lost much by the fact that Cobden never held high office, or office of any kind, in an administration. Every one remembers that Lord Palmerston invited him to accept office in the government of 1859. Palmerston then offered him the position of President of the Board of Trade, a place which would exactly have suited his inclination, his knowledge of commercial affairs, and his wide and varied experience as an observer and a traveller. I have personal reasons for remembering the occasion well. Cobden was in the United States on a second visit at the time when Palmerston was forming his government. The offer was made known to Cobden's friends and political colleagues, and it so happened that Cobden's return to England was just then expected. He was to land at Liverpool, where I was then living, attached to the literary staff of a daily newspaper. Some of Cobden's friends engaged a small steamer to take them out of the Mersey, in order that they might meet the vessel which was bringing Cobden home, and thus let him know at the earliest possible moment the offer Lord Palmerston was about to make. I was given the opportunity of accompanying the party of friends, an opportunity of which I availed myself most gladly. I had at that time no personal acquaintance with Cobden, and was merely an observer of the meeting which took place between him and his friends. Cobden acted with his usual composure and discretion when he received the news. He told his friends that he could not make any statement off-hand as to the course which he should pursue with regard to the invitation, or give any answer until the time came for delivering his reply to Lord Palmerston himself. I can remember that most of his friends already anticipated the answer which was to be given, and had, indeed, anticipated it even before they had an opportunity of telling the news to Cobden. Lord Palmerston's offer was refused, and every one capable of forming an impartial judgment felt that it would have been impossible for a man of Cobden's sincerity and consistency to give any other answer to the proposal.

Cobden had always publicly and privately condemned the general principles of Palmerston's home and foreign policy. He took it for granted, no doubt, that even though he were to occupy a seat in the cabinet, which, of course, was part of the proposal, he could not hope to overrule the influence of the prime-minister to any degree which would make it worth his while to associate himself with a Palmerstonian administration. Many of Cobden's warmest admirers and most devoted followers, even in the north of England, were strongly of opinion that he ought to accept the opportunity of bringing his influence to bear upon the new administration for the advancement of liberal principles and for the good of the country. At the very time when Cobden received at Liverpool Lord Palmerston's letter containing the offer, he received also a very urgent letter from Lord John Russell, pressing him to accept it; but Cobden's resolution was formed; his conscientious course was clear; and I may add that his determination had the absolute approval of John Bright. The whole story is told by Cobden's own letters, published in John Morley's *Life of Richard Cobden,* which has now become an English classic. I must confess to having brought up this chapter of Cobden's life chiefly for the selfish reason that it is associated with my own personal recollections. I look back upon that day in the Mersey, when I had the good fortune to take part in the welcome given to Richard Cobden, as one of the bright memories of my life.

Thomas Carlyle is rather severe on persons who waste any time in speculating on what might have been. I am much disposed, however, to yield to this natural inclination just at present. Suppose Cobden could have seen his way to enter the cabinet of Lord Palmerston, and suppose—a still more difficult supposition—that he could have exercised any real influence over the self-asserting nature and the perverse policy of Palmerston, how many troubles might have been averted for England during the few years that preceded Cobden's death! Let us speak of one subject only. The great American civil war was then just about to open, and Palmerston led that large majority of Englishmen in high social position who firmly believed that the Southern States were destined to win, and that the Northern States were sure to make but a poor figure, and even a ridiculous figure, in the struggle. Cobden had a living acquaintance with all parts of the American republic, and could make sound calculation as to the comparative resources on both sides of the great quarrel. Naturally, Cobden's whole sympathy went with the cause of the North, just as Palmerston's sympathies went with the cause of the South, but Cobden's cool judgment was never likely to be overborne by his sympathies, and he was able to make quiet comparison of the forces arrayed on either side. Cobden was convinced that the Federal States were destined to be the victors; Palmerston took it for granted that the Federal States were sure to be the vanquished.

Palmerston's whole policy during all the earlier part of the civil war was conducted on the assumption that the North was simply playing the part of a braggart and a coward and a bungler, and that no English government was called upon to show anything but contempt for so sorry and hopeless a performance. This was not only the meaning of his policy, but it found expression in many of his speeches in and outside the House of Commons. His tone was taken up by many public speakers and by most of the daily and weekly journals, by whom the cause and the statesmen, the generals and the armies, of the North were held up to incessant ridicule. Before the Federal States were able to prove their capacity for carrying on the war to a successful issue a strong feeling of hostility had already been excited among Americans of the Northern States, and at one time it seemed as if a lasting enmity were doomed to prevail between England and the victorious North. If it were possible that even so great a man as Cobden, holding a seat in the English cabinet, could exercise a restraining influence over Lord Palmerston and some of his colleagues, the country might have been saved from the *Alabama* trouble, from the payment of the heavy damages decreed by the Geneva Convention, and from the humiliation of having to make a public apology. But we may take it for granted that not even Cobden could have exercised such a restraining influence over Palmerston, and that the great free-trader, if he had accepted office, would have sacrificed his conscientious scruples to no good purpose whatever.

We know only too well from documents afterwards published with authority that Queen Victoria herself was entirely opposed to the tone and policy of Lord Palmerston in dealing with the American question, and that her influence, limited as it was by her fidelity to constitutional principles, was not strong enough to bring the prime-minister to a better mood. The course taken by Cobden when he positively refused, under whatever persuasion, to accept office in Palmerston's cabinet must have the full approval of history. We know that in this case the might have been would not have been. Cobden was as true a lover of his country as ever lived or died for her service. He loved her so well and so fearlessly that he never shrank from telling her when he believed her to be in the wrong. His death cast a profound gloom over the sixties, not only in England, but throughout the whole civilized world.

CHAPTER VII

JOHN BRIGHT

THE first time I saw John Bright was at a great public meeting in the Free Trade Hall, Manchester—a very appropriate place in which to have one's first glimpse of such a man. That was before the opening of the sixties and when I was still a resident of Liverpool. Much as I had heard of Bright's eloquence, I was not quite prepared for the splendid intellectual treat which I enjoyed on that memorable evening. Bright's speech seemed to me a perfect combination of argument, eloquence, and music of voice. Often as I heard him through a long series of succeeding years, I never found any change made in the impression wrought on me by his speech of that evening. He could not have added to the estimate I then formed of his oratorical powers, and in no important speech of his to which I afterwards listened did he ever lessen that first estimate. I have heard many orators of the highest order who sometimes even on great occasions did not show to their best advantage, but John Bright was certainly not one of these. Perhaps one reason for this was that Bright seldom made a speech unless on some important occasion. Until towards the close of his life he never was a member of an administration, and thus was not compelled to address the House of Commons on mere questions of departmental work. He took no pleasure in the making of speeches except for the mere sake of the influence he could exercise on behalf of some great cause in which he had a heartfelt interest.

It seems strange that a man so richly endowed with the gift of eloquence and with a voice whose clear, various, and musical tones might make even the commonplace seem eloquent, should have found no personal gratification in the delivery of a speech. The natural sense of satisfaction springing from success of any kind might, one would think, make such a man welcome any fair opportunity of displaying his remarkable power. But I had Bright's own assurance more than once that he never would have made a speech if he had thought it consistent with his sense of duty to remain silent, and, of course, I fully believed his assurance, as every one must have done who knew him. In truth, Bright always seemed to me to be as devoid of any sense of personal vanity, even artistic vanity, as it is possible for a man to be. He threw his whole soul into the advocacy of the cause he was striving to promote, and always devoted the highest resources of his intellect and his eloquence to the promotion of that cause; but his own personal success was to him a matter of little or no consideration. Nor does he appear to me to have felt any of that joy in the political strife which is common among great parliamentary debaters. It was impossible not to feel the conviction that Gladstone thoroughly enjoyed the mere excitement of encountering and bearing down his opponents in a parliamentary discussion; and with Disraeli, when he had to deliver his closing reply on some momentous occasion, the rapture of the battle was even more apparent. I am disposed to regard John Bright as the greatest orator I have ever heard, but not as the greatest debater. Perhaps the very peculiarity of his temperament, which I have attempted to describe, may account for the fact that he never seemed to give himself entirely up to the splendid business of debate. To be a consummate debater, one must be inspired by the joy of the strife.

I came to know Bright personally very soon after I had settled in London in 1860, and my acquaintance with him lasted until the close of his great career. Bright took a close, personal interest in the conduct of the *Morning Star,* the London daily newspaper with which I became associated, first as reporter in the press-gallery of the House of Commons, then as foreign editor, and afterwards as editor-in-chief. Bright used to visit the editorial rooms of the *Morning Star* very often during the parliamentary session; used to tell us how things were going in the House, offer suggestions and advice, and talk over all manner of interesting subjects. We had then a five-o'clock-tea arrangement in our editorial rooms, and those who formed the editorial staff sat down together every evening to discuss the arrangements for leading articles and other contributions, and to talk over the events of the day. The editor of the *Morning Star* at that time was Mr. Samuel Lucas, a brother-in-law of Bright, a man of great intellectual faculties and charming conversational powers. Bright often took part in our evening gatherings, gave us his advice on the manner in which passing political events ought to be treated, discussed with imperturbable calmness this or that question on which difference of opinion existed among us, and entered very freely into all our talk. His brother Jacob Bright sometimes, but not so often, made one of our little gathering. Most of the men who sat round that table in the early sixties have passed out of this world.

John Bright was in the habit of coming down to the *Star* office from the House of Commons at any hour of the evening or night when he had something to tell us which it was important that we should know at the earliest possible moment. Thus began my close acquaintance with Bright—an acquaintance which is one of the most treasured memories of my life. I do not know that I have ever experienced a higher sense of personal gratification than that which came to me one evening during the first few days after my election to a seat in the House of Commons. Some debate was going on having to do with the condition and the government of Ireland —such debates came on rather often then as now in that assembly—and Bright took part in the discussion. In the course of his speech he made passing reference to the recent election for an Irish constituency, and in the kindliest words offered his genial welcome to me on my introduction to the House, and expressed a hope that I might often be heard in its debates. I felt then and feel now that I could not have received a higher recommendation.

During my long intimacy with Bright I had, of course, ample opportunity of becoming acquainted with his simple and noble nature, his opinions on all manner of subjects, his likings and dislikings, his tastes and his aversions. I never knew a man who had less of personal vanity, less of ambition, less of self-seeking. He understood and appreciated the value of his own speeches on great occasions, but he regarded them with no more feeling of personal pride than a man might take in his physical health and his power of enduring fatigue. He was keenly interested in the eloquence of other men, but I think he could hardly bring himself to a thorough admiration of any eloquence which was not inspired by absolute sincerity. Thus it did not seem to me that he ever quite appreciated the marvellous powers of Disraeli as a debater, and that his judgment was always somewhat biassed by the conviction that Disraeli was striving for his own personal success rather than for the success of any great political cause. I think if he could have believed that Disraeli was a sincere and convinced Conservative he would have thought more highly than he did of the tory leader's oratorical capacity. This was, in fact, his way of estimating all public men —he demanded integrity of convictions first of all, and gave to other qualifications, however great, an inferior place in his estimate. His intense admiration of Gladstone had its first impulse in his recognition of Gladstone's absolute sincerity. With that conviction to start from, he came to have the most exalted opinion of Gladstone's eloquence in debate.

He was on one occasion positively angry with me because I happened to say that I regarded him, John Bright, as a greater orator than Gladstone, although not perhaps so great a debater. He told me, in his blunt, good-humored way, that I could hardly have been thinking of what I was saying, because nobody with any judgment could set him up as a rival in eloquence to Gladstone. He spoke with absolute earnestness, and not in the least with the manner of one who modestly affects to disclaim some words of praise implying the disparagement of another orator. He was merely angry with me for what he evidently considered an inexcusable defect of critical judgment, and he went on to illustrate his meaning by referring to various passages in some of Gladstone's speeches which he declared that no living man but Gladstone himself could have spoken. Perhaps I may have thought, when offering my opinion, that the superior place I had given to Gladstone as a debater would have disarmed his opposition, but if I had any thought of the kind he soon convinced me that I had not thoroughly appreciated his admiration for

Gladstone's surpassing qualities. I may say, too, that Bright especially admired in Gladstone the quality which made him direct all his intellectual and oratorical powers to the promotion of some definite and practical end.

It was, perhaps, one of Bright's characteristic weaknesses that he was apt to undervalue mere intellect, however great, which did not devote itself to the accomplishment of some direct and substantial, some immediate and palpable benefit to humanity in general. His sympathies and his admiration did not find themselves much attracted by mere thinkers, however exalted their thoughts might be, and however just their conclusions. He never fully appreciated, for instance, the intellectual powers of John Stuart Mill until Mill had come out from his habitual seclusion and made himself an active worker in political life. From that time Mill had no warmer admirer than Bright, although even then he was sometimes a little impatient of Mill's theories about representation of minorities, which Bright considered to be rather out of the way of immediate and practical reform. This tendency of his mind was effectively expressed in his resolute refusal, on one important occasion, to take any part in discussing the relative advantages of the monarchical and republican system of government. There were at that time among the most advanced of the younger Liberals some able men who were inclined to favor republican principles on the ground that they represented a more true and just idea as an ultimate theory of government than that represented by the monarchical system. Bright merely declared that the republican question had not come up for England, and with that declaration he put the whole argument aside and would have nothing more to do with it. His conviction was that the business of the hour was enough for practical men, and that mere theories had better be left for the time when a change of conditions might bring them within the range of practical statesmanship.

Bright loved reading, but his range of reading was limited. He was an intense and even impassioned admirer of some poets, but there again his critical judgment was influenced by his inherent conviction that the tone of the poet must be absolutely pure. Among the books inspired by mere human genius he gave the highest place to Milton's *Paradise Lost* and *Paradise Regained.* He could declaim from memory long passages of *Paradise Lost,* and I have never heard poetic lines delivered with more true and exquisite effect. He never felt drawn in the same manner towards Shakespeare, although he was quite willing to admit Shakespeare's supreme place among English poets. But his intense love of purity shrank from the Cleopatras and the Iagos and the Falstaffs as much as from the Ancient Pistols and the Doll Tearsheets. He had an abhorrence of sensuality and coarseness even when these formed essential parts of the character which had to be described. "Why describe such characters at all?" he asked, and this was a great part of his critical theory.

Bright was a master of genuine Saxon humor. Some of his unprepared replies to the interruptions of political opponents in the House of Commons were marvellous examples of this faculty, and are frequently quoted even now in speeches and in newspaper articles. But there was nothing whatever of levity in Bright's humor, and his most effective satirical touches seemed as if they were intended rather to rouse into better judgment than to wound or offend the man at whom they were directed. I think the one defect which Bright could not fully forgive in any man was want of sincerity.

I have heard him again and again in private conversation enter into the defence of some extreme political opponent on the ground that the opponent, however mistaken, aggressive, and even unjust, was acting in accordance with his sincere convictions. I can remember many instances in which Bright strongly objected to certain criticisms of political opponents, criticisms appearing in the newspaper representing his own political creed, on the ground that they were not quite fair and would be likely to give pain. Most of the men who wrote for the *Morning Star* in those days were young and had their fair share of youth's audacity and recklessness, and when they got a good chance of holding up some political opponent to ridicule or contempt they were not slow to avail themselves of the opportunity, and were not always over-scrupulous in their manner of using it. Bright always objected to any criticism which seemed to him unfair or exaggerated. He did not object to hard hitting—he was himself the most splendid of parliamentary hard-hitters; but he would give no sanction to anything that seemed like hitting below the belt. He was "ever a fighter," like Robert Browning's hero, but it was always in open fight and in honorable adherence to the rules and traditions of the game.

The mention of Robert Browning's name reminds me that Bright was a personal friend of the great poet. To the ordinary observer these two men might seem to have very little in common, but each had a high and just estimate of the other's greatness in his own field, and each found much that was congenial in the society of the other. I have been told lately that Browning once objected with good-humored earnestness to the manner in which Bright gave serious consideration to the theory of collaboration between Shakespeare and Bacon. Browning said to a friend of mine that it particularly distressed him to hear Bright lending the aid of his noble voice and his marvellous elocution to the wrong side of such a controversy. But I do not think that Bright ever went any further than to claim a fair hearing for the theory, and I am happy to believe that the friendship of Bright and Browning was not seriously affected by Bright's theoretical views on the subject even if we suppose his views to have been heretical. I am always glad to remember that for my first introduction to the personal acquaintance of Robert Browning I was indebted to John Bright. The acquaintance was a very happy one for me, and it lasted while Browning lived.

Bright was in one sense a sort of human paradox. I never met a man more liberally endowed with that delightful gift, a sense of humor, and yet I never knew a man more profoundly serious in his views of life. We have all been made quite familiar in poetry, in fiction, in biography, and in actual life with the men who always present an outer surface of jocularity, wit, and humor while the hearts that lie beneath are ever steeped in gloom and melancholy. But Bright did not belong in any sense to that order of mortals. His was not a melancholy or a gloomy, but a calm and even a hopeful temperament. His nature was cheerful, and was full of faith in the ultimate purposes of life and in the final triumph of the rightful cause. In the darkest times of outer depression for the men and the movements holding his sympathy he always looked steadily forward to the sure coming of the brighter day. He had not the moods of the satirist and the scorner any more than he had the moods of the sceptic. Under all his jocularity and his delight in humorous forms of expression he was intensely serious, and he regarded even trivial things from a serious point of view. This was the peculiarity in him which I have hardly ever observed in other men, and it made him sometimes seem what I have described as a human paradox. Many of Bright's finest and most effective oratorical hits were made when he dealt with some serious argument of an opponent as if it could best be demolished by a mere flash of humor, and yet all the time he was considering the subject with the utmost seriousness, and only made use of the jest as the most prompt and complete method of demolishing a hostile argument.

This was the characteristic quality of Bright's ordinary conversation in private life. It was his way to illumine the gravest subject by this light of humor, but those who knew him understood well what a depth of seriousness—not gloom, not despondency, not satirical scorn—lay beneath his lightest and most jocular expression. He was not an extremist in any of his political views, and there was nothing of the destructive in his political projects, although many years of his public life he passed among most of his opponents for a man whose chief desire was to pull down all existing systems. He had little or no sympathy with mere revolution of any kind, and there was much of true conservatism in all his plans of political and social reform. He occasionally disappointed some even of his warmest admirers by the steadiness with which he distinguished between reform and revolution. He was willing to accept the existing system anywhere so long as it was susceptible of gradual improvement, and his object was to develop whatever was good in the existing conditions and not to pull down the whole fabric and then begin building all over again. For this reason he had but little sympathy with continental revolutions, and he seldom warmed into genuine enthusiasm even for the most sincere among continental revolutionists.

JOHN BRIGHT, M.P.

[See page 75

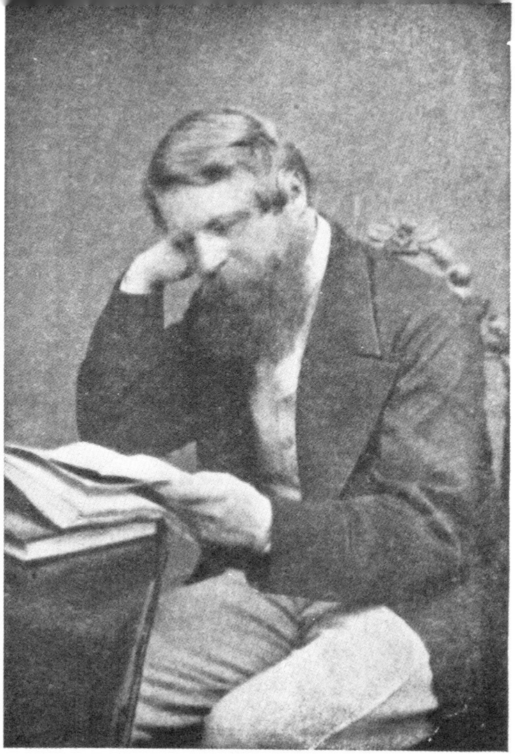

SIR STAFFORD NORTHCOTE, M.P.

[See page 88

Bright had little opportunity of proving his capacity for official administration. He held office three times in a liberal government, but not long enough at any time to give him a chance of showing what he could do in a working department. When he first took office under Gladstone in 1868 he gave a remarkable proof of the rigid conscientiousness which belonged to his character. He withdrew from all share, direct or indirect, in the conduct of the *Morning Star,* because he believed that a minister of the crown would be open to the charge of exercising an undue influence if he kept up any control over a newspaper. This may seem a mere scruple, but it was an honorable scruple, and entirely in keeping with Bright's code of principles and of honor. There is a common belief that he resigned the last office which he held under Gladstone because he could not accept Gladstone's proposal for the restoration of the Irish national Parliament. I have seen this erroneous opinion set forth again and again by writers who ought to have known better, and might have had a better memory of the actual facts. Bright resigned office at that time because he could not support the policy of the government with regard to Egypt, and would not have anything to do with the course of action which ended in the bombardment of Alexandria. Bright was not a man pledged to the doctrine of "peace at any price," but he could not lend himself to a policy of war which was not strictly defensive and was not the last available recourse.

Bright was not a member of the government which, under the leadership of Gladstone, brought in the first measure of Home Rule. Bright was opposed to the principle of a separate Parliament for Ireland; but although I must ever regret that he should have opposed it, I cannot but admit that he was acting with perfect consistency. Bright was the friend of Ireland when she had hardly any other friends among leading English statesmen. He had been entertained at a national banquet in Dublin given to him in recognition of the splendid services he had performed in defence of Ireland against unjust and oppressive legislation. He had declared his guiding principle with regard to the government of Ireland again and again. That principle was that the imperial Parliament ought to do for Ireland exactly what Ireland would have done for herself —that is, what the great majority of the Irish people would have done—if she had been able to accomplish a successful revolution. To that principle he ever held with unflinching consistency. But it was his belief that the work could be accomplished by the imperial Parliament, and would be accomplished, in course of time, by the force of argument, by increasing knowledge of Ireland's wants, and by the growth of enlightened public opinion. He did not believe that a national Irish Parliament was needed for the purpose, and he was opposed to the breaking-up of the central Parliament into separate parliamentary systems. We need not discuss that question now and in these pages, but I am anxious to record my conviction that Bright was consistent in his whole course of action towards Ireland, and that he did not, as others did, become a sudden convert to the doctrine of what now would be called imperialism. He had been denounced more than once by his political enemies as the friend of Ireland, and even those Irishmen who, like myself, cannot believe that he came to a wise conclusion on the subject of Home Rule are ready to admit that he remained, according to his lights, the friend of Ireland to the last.

At one period of Bright's career — indeed, at its zenith—a high-toned and fastidious London journal, having given him much commendation for his eloquence, declared that it was a pity Mr. Bright had never quite caught the tone of the House of Commons. The immediate and obvious comment made by other writers on this declaration was that it was a much greater pity the House of Commons had never quite caught the tone of Mr. Bright. Such may be set down as the decisive comment of history at this day. No House of Commons has ever caught, or is ever likely to catch, the tone of Mr. Bright. We cannot expect to have large popular assemblies made up of great orators like John Bright.

CHAPTER VIII

SIR STAFFORD NORTHCOTE

In writing about the public man who was the original of the portrait illustrating this chapter, I have preferred to call him by the name which was for so many years familiar to us. I write of him as Sir Stafford Northcote, although we all know that towards the close of his career he was raised to the peerage and became the Earl of Iddesleigh. Those who knew Sir Stafford Northcote as a leading parliamentary debater holding high office in successive administrations never could have known the man at his best. I have always regarded Stafford Northcote as a genuine statesman, but of course an outsider cannot know how far the policy of a ministry or a party is originated or guided by any particular one of its leading members. Sir Stafford Northcote was not the self-asserting personage who is always sure to proclaim in some way or other that his is the guiding influence and the mainspring of every movement made by those associated with him.

Stafford Northcote was an effective and a ready parliamentary debater, but he had nothing of the orator in him, and even among the parliamentary debaters of his time he did not take a commanding place. A stranger visiting the House of Commons might have heard him speak night after night and have only got the impression that he was a ready and fluent speaker who could put his arguments with clearness and with force.

Those who came to know the man himself in private intercourse soon found that he was a thinker, a scholar, and a humorist, who had a keen artistic appreciation of pictures and statues, of books and music, and was a close student of many literatures, a shrewd and penetrating observer of men and life. I had the good fortune to be brought soon after my election to Parliament into a friendly personal relationship with Northcote which lasted during many years. I met him often in private society, and have the most delightful recollections of long talks with him on all manner of subjects.

Northcote was a great lover of books, and was especially well acquainted with that literature which too many Englishmen neglect—the literature of Shakespeare's time which is not the creation of Shakespeare—the works of Ben Jonson, Beaumont and Fletcher, Massinger, and the rest. He was familiar with all the great English novelists, and appeared to have a wonderful memory for every book he had read with interest. For him nothing in literature was old-fashioned or new-fashioned; he was just as much at home with Fielding and Smollett as Dickens and Thackeray. He had a charming vein of humor, and could illumine any subject in conversation with his bright flashes of playful wit. He was glad to escape as much as possible in private life from the serious business of politics, and seemed never more at his ease and happy than when the conversation turned wholly on books or pictures or the drama. He was fond of theatrical performances, and the opening night of a new piece at any of the great London theatres was almost certain to have him and Lady Northcote among its audience. When the talk was on political questions it was delightful to observe how, by a few easy and humorous phrases, he was able to touch off the weaknesses and foibles of some pretentious personage who had chosen to fancy himself an important figure in the House of Commons. His satire was not unkindly, had nothing in it of bitterness, but it was apt and bright and penetrating. He could take the measure of a man with a readiness and a precision which I have seldom found equalled, and he was as quick and as willing to recognize real merit as to analyze self-satisfied pretension. Northcote never allowed political antagonism to influence his personal relations with other men, and this habit in him seemed to come not from any studied resolve to cultivate impartiality, but to be the result of his natural kindness and the liberality of his mind. Whenever I had a fortunate opportunity of talking with him our talk generally turned on books and on literature, and I have never heard more interesting and suggestive criticisms than some of those which came from him. Even while some exciting debate was going on in the House of Commons I have often noticed that if we happened to meet in one of the dining-rooms, Northcote could at once detach his mind from the strife of politics and show himself thoroughly interested in some new book or some new theory of art. I have often thought that if the force of events and habitudes had not impelled him into political life he might have made for himself a distinguished name in literature. He did, in fact, publish a work on financial policy and a volume of lectures and essays which find their readers still, but the fates had ordained that he was to be a political leader, and we may assume that the kindly fates knew what was best for him and best for us.

During his Oxford career Stafford Northcote won high distinction in classics—the classics which in his busy after-life he always loved and often studied. In his early manhood he became private secretary to Mr. Gladstone, who was then, it need hardly be said, a conservative politician, and one can well understand how such an occupation under such a man must have served him as the most valuable training for that work of financial administration in which he afterwards came to hold so high a place. He was called to the Bar, but never really took to the profession, and in 1855 he entered the House of Commons for the first time. Some of my readers will probably remember that in 1871, when the *Alabama* had led to serious difficulties between England and the United States, and the arrangements were in progress for the Geneva Convention, which was to settle the dispute, Sir Stafford Northcote was one of the three commissioners sent by the British government to Washington for the purpose of conducting the negotiations. The other British commissioners were the Marquis of Ripon and Professor Mountague Bernard, of Oxford. I happened to be in New York at the time, and I well remember seeing Sir Stafford Northcote and his colleagues at a great banquet given to them by my late friend, Cyrus W. Field. It is certain that Northcote rendered the most valuable services in the negotiations which brought that memorable dispute to a satisfactory conclusion. His appointment to the commission took place under the administration of Mr. Gladstone, and Mr. Gladstone no doubt had the best reason to know how well fitted by his ability, his thorough impartiality, and his genial temperament Sir Stafford Northcote was for so delicate and difficult a task.

I need not follow in systematic detail the progress of Northcote's subsequent parliamentary career. He remained always a member of the conservative party, although there were many questions on which so advanced and enlightened a thinker could not always have been in complete sympathy with some of his colleagues and a large proportion of their followers. On subjects belonging to foreign policy, where the party lines of English public life could not be rigidly maintained or even traced out, Northcote made many a speech which might have come as appropriately and as effectively from the liberal as from the conservative benches. He held the office of Chancellor of the Exchequer in Disraeli's government, and when Disraeli went to the Upper House he became leader of the party in the House of Commons. He was raised to the peerage in 1885, and then was made First Lord of the Treasury. When Lord Salisbury came into office for the second time Northcote was induced to accept the position of Foreign Secretary, but he held that position only for a short period, and then suddenly resigned office. Every one must remember his sudden death at Lord Salisbury's official residence in Downing Street on January 12, 1887.

Stafford Northcote's death was in every sense a tragedy. It was well known that new influences were coming into power among the conservative leaders at that time, and that Northcote's friends believed him to have been treated unfairly by his party, or at least by those who were then put in control of the party. The general impression was that Northcote had been pushed aside on the coming of Lord Randolph Churchill to hold a high place in the party, and we who were then in the House of Commons well knew that Lord Randolph Churchill and Northcote were not likely to work together harmoniously under such conditions. It is an old and a sad story of which we shall probably never know the whole truth until some coming Greville Memoirs shall give us the whole story. I was then in the United States, and only read of these events in the newspapers, and I felt the thrill of a most sincere grief when I learned that such a career had been closed so suddenly and unexpectedly and under such conditions. He was still regarded as a man well qualified to exercise a healthful influence over the political life of his country, and his sudden death seemed to leave a blank not likely soon to be filled up. A conservative government was then in the very nature of things called upon to be an active, watchful government, and under these circumstances it appeared to all impartial observers that a man like Stafford Northcote would have been of inestimable value in the education of his party to meet the new and changed conditions of political life. Northcote was much in advance of his party in what may be called general political intelligence and instruction, and if he had lived and been allowed to exercise his due influence, he might have been able to bring that party into a better understanding of the popular demands which were coming up for settlement. His death, though sudden and at the time quite unlooked for, could not be called premature, but the wish of the whole country would have been that the close of his life should be crowned with a distinct success and should not have been associated with misunderstanding, disappointment, and failure.

Northcote could not have been called a great statesman any more than he could have been called a great parliamentary orator. But his disappearance from life was unquestionably a great loss to Parliament. No man in either House enjoyed more fully the confidence and the respect of all political parties. I cannot believe that he could ever have made a personal enemy, or that he could ever have lost a sincere friend. No man could have been more truly considerate in his dealings with his political opponents. During the fiercest controversies he never lost his self-control, his good temper, or his courteous way of meeting his antagonists. In the House of Commons it had been well known for some time that Lord Randolph Churchill and his immediate followers had grown impatient of Northcote's want of initiative, his willingness to listen to compromise, and his lack of the genuine fighting spirit. When Lord Randolph was still leading his followers of the small Fourth party we were all allowed to see the evidences of this growing impatience. Lord Randolph was in the habit of describing, after his characteristic fashion, Northcote and certain other members of the conservative administration as "the old gang," and there could have been little doubt that if Lord Randolph should come into power he was not likely to get on very well with such a man for his leader. Lord Randolph's own administrative career came to an end soon after, and indeed the whole of his active career in Parliament did not last long, but was brought to a premature close by his too early death. It is only right to say that during his short period of administration Lord Randolph developed qualities which showed that he might, under happier auspices and with better health, have come to be a financial minister of a very high order.

I have, of course, been anticipating events and have wandered far away from the days of the early sixties, but the mere study of Sir Stafford Northcote's portrait has led me naturally into a consideration of the man's whole career and the futile thought of what might have been under different conditions. I may now, however, retrace my steps and return to that period of Sir Stafford Northcote's life which is illustrated by his picture, and in which he made so conspicuous and so attractive a figure in the House of Commons. My own impression at that time was that Northcote seemed qualified and destined either to lead his own party into a recognition of the growing changes in political life which were making the old-fashioned toryism a thing of the past, or to become a leading influence among the Liberals who were determined to go forward and to accept the real principles of political freedom. One can well understand why the Conservatives of the older school, the school which would not be educated, should have found little satisfaction in the leadership of so thoughtful and so far-seeing a statesman as Northcote, and even in the early sixties many evidences of this fact were already making themselves apparent. Northcote had little or no respect for the antiquated forms of partisan administration; he did not pledge his faith to any traditional policy; and the inherited war-cries of his party could never have inspired him with a combative enthusiasm. He was above all things a thinking man, and a thinking man was not just then well qualified to command the allegiance of the Conservatives who represented county constituencies. On the other hand, he had evidently not the power of initiative which enables a man to dictate a new policy and create a new party.

It must be borne in mind that for many years after his first entrance into Parliament there were in the House of Commons many men among whom it was very hard for a new-comer to make a distinguished name. This will account for the fact that even after he had come to hold important office in an administration his name was but little known to the general public outside. It must have been a clear appreciation of his actual capacity for a high office in parliamentary work which inspired the leaders of his party to accept him, in advance of the public judgment, as one well fitted to hold the place of minister of the crown. Knowing what we now know of him as an administrator, we are not surprised that some at least of his leaders and his colleagues should have discerned his genuine capacity, but it is certain that surprise was felt by the general public when he was raised to a place in the ministry. That was a time when the House of Commons had reached its highest position as a chamber of debate. We have now no such array of eloquent and powerful speakers in the House as those who were then in rivalry night after night for the highest honors in parliamentary debate. The liberal benches have now no orator to compare with Gladstone; the tory benches do not make the slightest pretension to any such mastery of debating powers as those which were displayed by Disraeli. Palmerston had reached the highest point of his success as a party leader and as a man who could play upon all the moods of the House with the skill of an accomplished artist. The independent Liberals were represented by Cobden and Bright—Cobden, whose eloquence had a persuasive charm of argument, illustration, and telling phrase which went home to the reasoning faculties of his audience; Bright, who was probably, on the whole, the greatest orator whom the House has known in modern times. Then there were such men as Roebuck and Horsman, as Cockburn and Whiteside, as Sir Hugh Cairns and Lord John Manners, and many others who must have been regarded as brilliant debaters in any parliamentary assembly. The level of political eloquence was then beyond question much higher than it has been in days nearer to our own, and it is not surprising that under such conditions Sir Stafford Northcote should have failed, during the earlier years of his parliamentary career, to win for himself a distinct and a distinguished reputation.

In the sixties, therefore, Northcote was still only a man with a name to make, and the portrait of him which is seen in these pages must be regarded as that of a beginner whose intimate friends alone could foresee his ultimate success. That success was never won by splendid and sudden displays, but was the gradual result of steady work and unpretentious administrative capacity. But it must be owned that Northcote always proved himself eminently qualified for every task he set himself to accomplish, and even on occasions of great debate he never failed to secure a fair and full appreciation from the House of Commons. I was a close and constant observer of parliamentary life for many years before I had a chance of obtaining a seat in the House, and there were few men whose speeches I could follow with deeper interest than those delivered by Northcote. He never threw away a sentence; he never wasted his debating power in mere redundancy of words. The listener was afraid to lose a single word, lest by its loss he should miss some important link of the argument. He could illustrate even the most prosaic subject by his apt and happy comparisons drawn from the most varied sources of history and literature and keen, practical observation. He had a marvellous skill in appropriate quotation, and I do not remember to have ever heard him introduce any citation which was not new, fresh, and precisely adapted to give point to his argument. He never overdid anything; never strained after effect; and always gave one the refreshing idea that the resources of the speaker were not exhausted. No one needs to be told how the attention of the listener begins to flag from the moment when he finds that a speaker is overtasking his powers, and is continuing his speech only because he fancies it is due to the occasion that he should endeavor to make a great display. The listener never felt any such uncomfortable sensation while Northcote was addressing the House, and, on the contrary, the general feeling was that he might have gone farther and fared even better. We may hope to have greater orators than Sir Stafford Northcote in the time to come, as we had in the time which is passed, but we shall not have many men who could better command on an important occasion the unbroken attention of such an assembly as the House of Commons.

CHAPTER IX

A PARLIAMENTARY GROUP

Edward Baines was a typical figure in the days which the portraits in this volume bring back to memory. He was a hard-working, most attentive, much-respected member of the House of Commons. I can well remember his pale, clear-cut face, his white hair, and his expression of earnest and unchanging purpose. He belonged expressly to that body of men who were known in the sixties, and for long after, as the "private members." That was, of course, but the colloquial description of this class of representatives. If any one were writing about the men who made up that class or were speaking about them in a formal way, he would have described them as independent members in the language which would be applied to them at the present time. These men may be classified as members of the House of Commons who, although belonging consistently to the one great political party or to the other, were yet each of them resolved to maintain the interests of some particular cause no matter whether it were supported by the government or by the party in opposition. One man had pledged himself heart and soul to some great political reform, such as an extension of the franchise, for instance; another was above all things a champion of religious equality; a third was "peace at any price," or, at all events, an opponent of all wars not purely and strictly defensive; a fourth was for additional legislation to restrict the power of the Papacy and the Jesuits in the British empire. Such men might be found at either side of the House, although of the types which I have mentioned, the first, second, and third might be looked for with greater certainty among the ranks of the Liberals, and the fourth among the ranks of the Tories.

But on whatever side the independent member sat, it might be taken for granted that he had come into the House of Commons with the view of making the advocacy of some particular cause the main business of his parliamentary life. If he belonged politically to the party in power, and the leaders of that party would not give any help to his cause, then he was prepared to vote against them in any division which turned upon that particular question. If the party in opposition suddenly professed a favoring inclination for his cause, he would be ready to vote with them even though the division might involve a possible defeat of the ministry. This devotion of the independent member to his cause or his crotchet or his craze, according as it might happen to be described from different points of view, was thoroughly understood by all parties in the House, and the independent member was regarded even by the party leaders and Whips with a certain amount of toleration as one of the unavoidable inconveniences attaching to the representative system. There are many independent members in the House of Commons to-day, but they do not seem to me to constitute so distinct and peculiar an element of parliamentary life as they did in the good old times when national representation and national education still had to find their most persistent champions among the men who preferred the promotion of some particular cause to the political interests of either party. The independent member at his highest level was then the far-seeing advocate of some great reform which had yet to be accepted and adopted by the leaders of either the government or the opposition, and in his lowest degree he was no worse than the representative of some new-fangled crotchet or some form of antiquated fanaticism.

Edward Baines was one of those who belonged to the best order of the independent member. He came from the north of England, and was educated at one of the schools of the dissenting bodies in Manchester. His father was one of the most influential men of his time in the north of England, and was owner and conductor of the *Leeds Mercury,* then as now a powerful organ of public opinion. Edward Baines, the son, was known as the author of some important works on the history of the cotton manufacture and the woollen manufacture of England, and he did not enter the House of Commons until comparatively late in life. He was in his fifty-ninth year when he became one of the members for Leeds. It used to be a sort of axiom at one time that no man ever made a success in the House who had reached his fortieth year before obtaining the right to occupy a seat there. Most assuredly Edward Baines never gained a distinguished position as a debater in the House, but I do not believe he could have acquired any such reputation even if he had obtained a seat at as early a period of life as that of Charles James Fox when he first entered Parliament.

Edward Baines never, so far as I have heard or known, had the slightest ambition for the renown of a great parliamentary debater. He came into Parliament for the especial purpose of advocating certain reforms which he had deeply at heart, and he never took the trouble to make a speech on any subject which did not come within his own particular and practical sphere.

He was a clear and argumentative speaker, and any one who took the slightest interest in the subject on which he was addressing the house could not fail to be impressed by his earnestness, by his well-ordered array of facts and arguments bearing on that question, and by the directness of his appeals to the intelligence of his listeners. It would be rather too much to say that he could always hold the House, because for one reason a large number of the members then attending the House took no manner of interest in any of the subjects on which he spoke, and never would have thought of leaving the dining-room, the smoking-room, or the library to go in and listen to one of his speeches. But it may fairly be said of him that he could always command the close attention of that proportion of the members who felt any genuine interest in the measures of reform which he was especially concerned in advocating.

Tuesday was then the only day when a private member had any chance of bringing a motion of his own before the House. It required courage, perseverance, and a devoted sense of duty to keep a man up to the work of bringing such motions forward with the certainty before him that he must be defeated by a large majority, even if he could prevail upon his friends to rally round him at the critical moment and save him from the humiliation of a "count-out." The private member, if he were also an independent member, has been through whole generations the pioneer of every great measure of reform in political, municipal, industrial, and educational affairs afterwards adopted by a ministry in power and carried into triumphant legislation. There were some men in the House during the early sixties who were only known because of their persistent advocacy, year after year, of some such reform, and for many sessions each annual motion and the speech which introduced it seemed to be little more than the "calling aloud to solitude" which Cervantes has described in his thrilling words. Edward Baines was for a long time one of the most conspicuous and the most patient among the small number who were thus devoted to the persistent, and as many thought the hopeless, advocacy of reforms which have long since been brought to success by some powerful ministry, and are now regarded as integral parts of the British Constitution.

From my earliest observation of the House of Commons I always felt an admiration of Edward Baines for his unfailing devotion, amid whatever depressing conditions, to the work which he had accepted as his business in Parliament. He was but a short time in the House of Commons when he attempted to bring in a bill for the reduction of the franchise in boroughs to a six-pounds qualification. Need I say that his motion was rejected by a large majority? Again and again in succeeding sessions he renewed his effort, and with the same result. Only a short time had to elapse before a much wider measure of reform than any which Baines had ever attempted to introduce was competed for, if I may thus express it, by the two great rival parties in the state, and was actually carried by Mr. Disraeli and the tory government. The truth is, that the advanced Radicals whom Edward Baines represented in the House of Commons had a much larger following outside, and more especially among the manufacturing districts, than was suspected by many of the unconcerned legislators who never troubled themselves to go into the debating chamber when Baines was bringing forward his annual motion. Baines took a leading and an active part in opposing the church-rates system and the imposition of university tests. I suppose even steady-going Tories are now willing to admit that the British Constitution is none the worse for the sort of legislation which Baines was accustomed to advocate.

Edward Baines had in temperament and in manner nothing whatever of the enthusiast, so far as a mere observer could discern. We generally associate the idea of a political or religious reformer with that of passionate advocacy and thrilling eloquence. Baines seemed to go at his parliamentary work with a sort of chill pertinacity which never allowed any expression of emotion to escape from him. The fire of an orator could no more be expected from him than it might be expected from an iceberg. Not even a flash of humor ever came from him in his parliamentary speeches, although his personal friends well knew that he was not austere in nature and that his heart was full of human sympathy. By most members of the House of Commons he was regarded rather as an influence than as an individual. The general public has probably for the most part already forgotten to associate the name of Edward Baines with some of the great reforms which he helped to carry to success, but in the history of England's political and educational progress during the nineteenth century his name must ever have an honorable mention. I am glad to have an opportunity of paying my poor personal tribute to his character as a man and his services as a reformer.

Let me now turn to the portrait of a very different personage, a man who had, perhaps, nothing in common with Edward Baines but sincerity. Baines represented ideas which were then new and have since found almost universal adoption; G. M. Whalley represented one idea which was becoming antiquated even in his day—and is now only preserved as a curiosity in mem-

EDWARD BAINES, M.P.

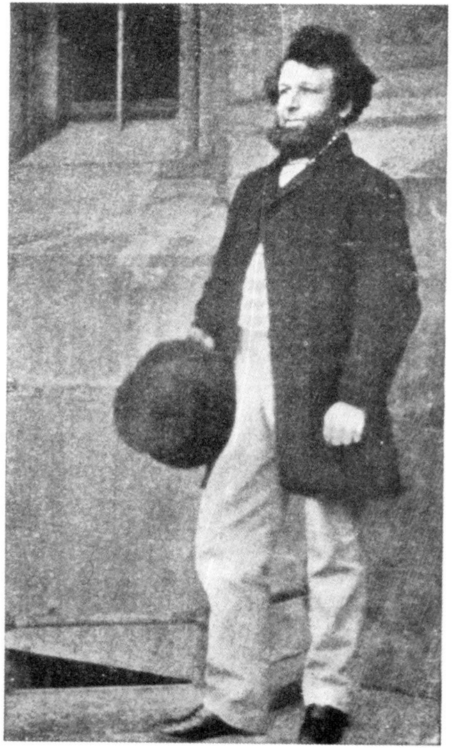

G. M. WHALLEY, M.P.

ory's museum. Whalley devoted his whole parliamentary career to a war against popery in general and the Jesuits in particular. The receptacle which I suppose must be described as his mind was entirely occupied, to all seeming, by this one idea. I cannot say that he never made a speech in the House of Commons on any other subject, but I can positively assert that if he ever did deliver such a speech I had not the good fortune to hear it. Whalley was absolutely and inextricably associated in the thoughts of the House and the public with the machinations of the Jesuits. Whalley's eloquence and the Jesuits' craft floated double in the parliamentary stream like the swan and shadow of St. Mary's lake. He had always some new question to put to the government with regard to the latest plots of the Jesuits for the overthrow of the Protestant dynasty in England and for the subjection of every English household to the dictation of the Church of Rome. He was ever seeking and planning for some opportunity to bring before the House a formal motion on the subject, and when he did secure a hearing for his motion the debate was generally brought to a premature end by a "count-out," this being no doubt, in poor Whalley's mind, another successful stroke of policy on the part of the malignant Jesuits.

I need hardly say that the House of Commons paid but little attention to the warnings, the arguments, and the appeals of Whalley. The moment he rose in his place everybody knew already what he was going to talk about, and this of itself was enough to settle his chance of a good audience. "I fear the man of one book" is a classic proverb, but "I fear the man of one topic" would express, although in a somewhat different sense, the general sentiment of the House of Commons. Whalley, however, did not seem to care whether the

House paid any attention to what he was saying or not, and indeed I do not know how he could ever have had any experience of an attentive audience, at least in the House of Commons. Most of the members left the debating chamber as a matter of course the moment Whalley rose to offer his observations on the familiar topic, and I have heard him more than once as he delivered his speech to the Speaker, the clerks at the table, one or two members, and the visitors who happened to be in the Strangers' Galleries. It was all the same to Whalley—he believed that he had a duty to do, and he did it without regard to persons.

On one occasion while the Conservatives were in power Whalley put a question to Disraeli, then leading the House, calling on him to say whether her Majesty's ministers had lately received any new information with regard to the present machinations of the Jesuits against the Established Church of England. I may be allowed to quote from my own *Reminiscences* my recollection of what followed the question. "Disraeli arose, and, leaning on the table in front of him, began with a manner of portentous gravity and a countenance of almost funereal gloom to give his answer. 'Her Majesty's ministers,' he said, 'had not been informed of any absolutely new machinations of the Jesuits, but they would continue to watch, as they had hitherto watched, for any indication of such insidious enterprises. One of the favorite machinations of the Jesuits,' he went on to say, with deepening solemnity, 'had always been understood to be a plan for sending into this country disguised emissaries of their own, who, by expressing extravagant and ridiculous alarm about Jesuit plots, might bring public derision on the efforts of the genuine supporters of the state Church. He would not venture to say whether the honorable member had knowledge of any such plans as that—' but here a roar of laughter from the whole House rendered further explanation impossible, and Disraeli composedly resumed his seat."

I had many talks with Whalley in private, and I always found him good-humored and companionable. He knew, of course, that my religious and political views were entirely out of accord with his, but he did not on that account refuse to interchange friendly words now and then. Perhaps he did not think that nature had provided me with intellectual gifts likely to make me a very dangerous emissary in the service of the Jesuit plotters, but whatever may have been his reason I can only say that I always found him tolerant and agreeable. I had, indeed, a sort of personal liking for Whalley, and I never felt any doubt of his simple sincerity in the cause to which he devoted such a large proportion of his laborious days and nights. I do not suppose there is any member of the House of Commons now who holds a like position. One can hardly help feeling a certain sort of admiration for the man who could thus go on session after session delivering speeches to which no one cared to listen—speeches to which he could but know that no one cared to listen—merely because he felt himself compelled by a perverse sense of duty to proclaim his opinions on every possible opportunity to an empty House and an unconcerned public. I have thought it well to put these two men, Edward Baines and G. M. Whalley, into immediate contrast. Both men were sincere and both were acting alike in obedience to an unselfish sense of duty. But the one man was born to be the advocate of great reforms, and the other was but the belated exponent of a forgotten policy. Edward Baines had remedies to offer for the evils which he sought to remove; poor Whalley could only bring for the removal of what he believed to be the perils of the state a sort of mediæval incantation.

I ought to say that in arranging this parliamentary group I am not assuming or suggesting that any bond of sympathy, or even of habitual association, brought together the men whom I am now describing. I do not know that these men were ever brought into comradeship of any kind beyond the comradeship created for them by the mere fact that they all happened to be members of the House of Commons at the period with which I am now dealing. I have chosen the figures in this group because each had an individuality peculiarly his own. The first thought which the name of any one of them brought up to the mind of an observer at the time was not that of a man identified with any of the great political parties, but rather that of a man who had a cause of his own, or it might be a crotchet of his own, or at all events a peculiar and separate identity which marked him out. Nor am I suggesting by any means that the men stood upon a level in the estimation of the House of Commons. Edward Baines had a great cause to which he was devoted, but it had not at that time been officially adopted by any of the recognized parliamentary parties. Whalley had his crotchet about the Jesuits and their machinations, and although he never could have held that place in the estimation of the House which was deservedly owned by Baines, he was at least a peculiar and almost isolated figure. The one common characteristic of my group is that those of whom for my purposes I have composed it were men who had each a distinct individuality and were not lost in the crowd.

I am afraid that the portrait of "J. A. Blake, M.P.," will not bring to my readers in general any immediate and accurate recollection of the man whose picture was taken in the early sixties. I may ask those whose associations with the House of Commons belong only to the present not to confound him with my friend Mr. Edward Blake, who for many years held a commanding position in the Dominion Parliament of Canada and at the Canadian Bar, and is now a member of the Irish national party. The late John Aloysius Blake was an Irish member of Parliament in the early sixties when I first came to know him, and retained that position until his death many years after. J. A. Blake was an Irish national member in the quiet days when the late Isaac Butt led the Irish nationalist party, before the strong, stern rule of Charles Stewart Parnell had made that party a power in the displacement of English governments and the cause of Home Rule a question of paramount interest in the House of Commons. J. A. Blake was a man who had acquired large means in business, and devoted time, for the most part, to his parliamentary work as an Irish representative, and the remaining part to the gratification for his love for travel. He had gained experiences in travel unusual for a member of Parliament in those now distant days before world-wandering had become part of the ordinary education of men who could afford to spend a little money. He had made himself acquainted with Canada and the United States, with the Australasian colonies, and with many parts of Asia and Africa. I remember that in later years his attention was much attracted by some descriptions of the Cabul expedition in the early part of Queen Victoria's reign, long before he himself had come to the age of travel, and he made it his business to survey the regions of disaster. His especial desire was to see and study the historic Khyber Pass, and he devoted his time and energy to a long journey over the whole historic region.

Blake was a humorist in many ways, a most delightful companion, and a genial host who loved to entertain his friends in the true spirit of Irish hospitality. He did not often speak in the House of Commons, but when he did speak he was always listened to, for he was sure to entertain the House with some amusing and original contribution to the debate. I remember that on one occasion the House was engaged in discussing some question which brought up the subject of racing and hunting, and Blake suddenly enlivened a somewhat dull interchange of views by his unexpected way of dealing with the question. He told the House that he had only once, since he had come to mature years, taken part in a fox-hunt. Then, he went on to say, he was lucky enough to have the swiftest horse in that part of the country, and he kept well at the front of the field. The House listened without much interest to his narrative up to this point. It was not surprising to the members in general to hear that an Irish member should make a boast of having had the best horse on the country-side at a fox-hunt, and that he had kept well in front of all rival riders. "But, Mr. Speaker," Blake suddenly exclaimed, "I rode on that occasion entirely in the interest of the fox!" Then he went on to explain that he was, on principle, a resolute opponent of all cruelty to animals; that he regarded the hunting even of the fox as mere cruelty; and that on this great occasion of his exploit in the hunting-field he had made use of his horse's fleetness and of his own riding powers merely in order to take care that the persecuted Reynard should have an opportunity of escaping from his pursuers.

The tory members from the hunting shires broke

into furious groans of wrath at this unexpected declaration; the members who did not hunt gave way to bursts of laughter over the audacious humor of Blake's intervention in the debate, as he had intervened in the hunting-field purely for the sake of defending the cause of the fox. Some members in the House quite understood that Blake was a sincere even if a somewhat eccentric representative of the principle which protests against civilized and responsible human beings seeking and finding pastime in the destruction of dumb animals. This was, indeed, a part of Blake's conscientious convictions. He had many ideas which divided him from the ordinary and conventional opinions of society at that time. He had a curious combination of qualities—I had almost said of characters. He was, politically, a typical Irish member of the old-fashioned order, which was content to go on quietly bringing forward a motion every session demanding national government for Ireland, and another motion claiming that justice should be done to the cause of the Irish tenants. When the debate and the division had been taken on these motions the national work of the Irish member was supposed to be done for the session, and it was not customary for Ireland to show any interest in the general business of the House.

John Aloysius Blake was, however, a thorough humorist as well as an Irish national member, and he had a keen perception of the absurdity of the whole situation and the futility of endeavoring to arouse the attention of the British public to a national cause thus represented twice a year by a mere ceremonial performance. He made many good jokes in private conversation about the tremendous effect which the quiet speech of some colleague, delivered during one of these debates to an almost empty house, was sure to have upon the feelings and the conscience of the British nation. Blake was in a certain sense what might be called a sentimentalist as well as a humorist. This peculiarity has been already illustrated by the part he took in the debate which brought up the fox-hunting question. There was a tenderness of feeling in him, a quality of compassion which often swayed his practical judgment in the business of life. I have heard it said of him that while acting as a magistrate in his native county he could never be brought to pass any severe sentence on a juvenile delinquent no matter what the juvenile delinquent's offences might have been, and indeed he lived to see a time when even the criminal law itself consented to embody some of those sentiments of compassion in the treatment of the young which were always cherished by him.

Blake was an anti-vivisectionist in days before the question of vivisection had come to be the subject of serious public agitation. He was a shrewd observer of life, of men, and of manners, and one who had only met him in private society and had been much in conversation with him there, might well have wondered how a man of his wide travel, his varied experiences, and his quick, sharp power of criticism should have failed to make any mark in parliamentary debate. But, in truth, Blake had no ambition for success as a speaker, and with his clear, good sense he had thoroughly taken the measure of his own capacity, and felt quite sure that nature had not created him to be a power in the House of Commons. He was well known and very popular in the House, but he was liked only for his private qualities, and was never taken into account when people talked about the rising debaters of the different political parties. I have never known any one who illustrated more aptly in his own person the

J. A. BLAKE, M.P.

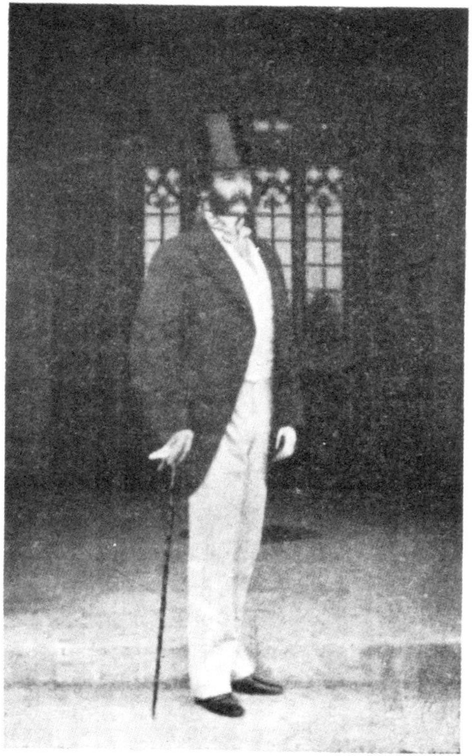

LORD DUNKELLIN

saying that a man may be in Parliament but not of it. He was, as I have said, a most genial host, and I have enjoyed many of his delightful dinner-parties at Queen Anne's Mansions, at the Langham Hotel, and at the Star and Garter in Richmond. I have met many conspicuous members of Parliament there and many distinguished foreigners, for Blake had the amiable weakness—if it be a weakness—of loving to gather around him guests who had made a reputation or who had, at all events, something to say for themselves which it would interest others to hear. My closer acquaintance with Blake did not begin until after the early sixties had passed away, but I knew him even in the early sixties, and he remained much the same man all the time. He followed the guidance of his own tastes, inclinations, principles, and sentiments, and he must have led, on the whole, a happy, and for him a satisfying, life. These pages I have written about him may, I hope, bring a kindly memory of him to some at least among the older living members of the House of Commons.

The portrait of Lord Dunkellin recalls to my mind a remarkable parliamentary episode. That episode, indeed, contains the only associations I have with Lord Dunkellin's parliamentary career. It occurred in the new Parliament of 1866 when Mr. Gladstone brought in his first Reform Bill. That was the measure which led to the famous Adullamite secession led by Robert Lowe, afterwards Lord Sherbrooke. Never perhaps was there heard in the House of Commons more brilliant debating than in that session and on that measure. Gladstone, Bright, and Lowe rose to the very height of their powers, and although Lowe was not an orator in the higher sense of the word, and although his very articulation was against him, and his voice had no musical thrill in it, yet it must be owned that his mastery of bitter sarcasm and telling illustration enabled him to hold his own fairly against the two great masters of parliamentary debate with whom he had to contend. The Conservatives and the Adullamites, as they were called from a happy phrase of Bright's — the "Cave of Adullam" is still quoted in speeches and leading articles—were united in opposition to the reform measure, which was, after all, but a very moderate scheme of suffrage reform, and would seem rather like old-fashioned conservatism to politicians of our day. The bill at last got into committee, and it was then that Lord Dunkellin became for the first and, so far as I know, for the last time a personage of parliamentary importance.

Lord Dunkellin brought forward a motion to the effect that the proposed franchise of seven pounds in boroughs be a qualification founded on rating and not on rental. The effect of this amendment, if carried, would have been to raise the qualification for a vote a little above the limit which the liberal government proposed to establish. It would appear that houses are usually rated at a lower figure than the actual rent which the tenant has to pay. To require, therefore, a rating franchise of seven pounds a year would have the practical effect of making it equal to a rental of about eight pounds a year. It seems to us now rather hard to understand how even the most conservative minds could have thought that a difference of one pound a year or so in the qualification for a voter could have formed anything like a substantial barrier against that invasion of democracy which the Tories and the Adullamites professed to regard with so much dread. Lord Dunkellin's amendment, however, was taken with absolute seriousness by the opponents of the Reform Bill, and the discussion was carried on with as much fervor on both sides of the House as if it were the last stand made by the devoted defenders of order against the champions of anarchy, the apostles of red ruin, and the breaking-up of laws.

Lord Dunkellin was successful with his amendment, and became the hero of the hour among the opponents of reform. He carried his proposal by a majority of seven, and that success sealed the fate of the reform measure. Lord Russell and Mr. Gladstone felt that under all the conditions there was no further use in their trying to carry the measure. The secession of the Adullamites had clearly made the success of the bill impossible. Russell and Gladstone and their colleagues tendered their resignations to the sovereign, and the resignations had to be accepted. That was, in effect, the close of Lord Russell's great career. The Conservatives came into office, and in the following session introduced to the House of Commons, under the guidance of Disraeli, a reform bill of their own, which they allowed to be expanded into a much more extensive improvement of the parliamentary suffrage than anything which Lord Russell and Gladstone had proposed. Not often, perhaps, in the parliamentary history of England has so trivial an amendment on one of the provisions of a government measure brought about so sudden and so momentous a parliamentary event as that which was accomplished by Lord Dunkellin's proposal. Not within my recollection, certainly, has a man so suddenly sprung into parliamentary importance as Lord Dunkellin did in that session, and so completely faded away from political notice during the remainder of his public career.

Daniel O'Connell, M.P., is the name belonging to another portrait which I have thought it well to include in this somewhat peculiar parliamentary group. A glance at the portrait will possibly for a moment puzzle many a reader. Daniel O'Connell, M.P.! The ordinary reader knows, perhaps, of only one Daniel O'Connell, M.P., and his fame hardly belongs to the early sixties. Then the portrait itself would not recall to mind any recollection of the many pictures, statues, and engravings which represent the great Irish tribune. There is a portrait of Daniel O'Connell, for instance, in the Reform Club which many of my readers may have seen, and it does not seem quite like the face of the man with the trim mustache who is pictured in this parliamentary group. But the momentary puzzle will soon come to an end. Those who read these pages will begin to remember that Daniel O'Connell had a younger son, another Daniel, who sat in the House of Commons at one time. I have but faint recollections of the great orator and agitator, the Liberator, as he was called by his countrymen. He died while I was only in my seventeenth year, and up to that time I had never seen the House of Commons. I saw O'Connell but once, in fact, and that was in the closing days of his life. He attended on that occasion a gathering held at one of the schools of my native city Cork, and delivered an address. He was seated in an arm-chair, an old, outworn man whose voice was hardly heard through the greater part of the hall, and this is my only personal recollection of the orator and national leader whose magnificent voice could reach with thrilling effect to the farthest extremity of some vast open-air meeting, and who was universally regarded as one of the greatest speakers the House of Commons had listened to in modern times.

But Daniel O'Connell had sons, three of whom had seats in the House of Commons, and the Daniel O'Connell whose portrait is given here was one of these. I

DANIEL O'CONNELL, M.P.

THOMAS CHANDLER HALIBURTON, M.P.

met him during the sixties, and in later years I was often in his society, and was counted, I hope, among his friends. He had been appointed British consul at various foreign ports, and towards the close of his life he held some civic appointment under the government—I think as one of the Commissioners of Income Tax. He then lived in London, and we had many opportunities for meeting. He was a very interesting man to talk with, because he had had a large and varied experience of life and of travel, and he had a pretty wit of his own. But he had none of his father's great gifts, and he took but little interest in political affairs. Of the three sons who sat in Parliament, Maurice was the ablest; John remained in Parliament for a considerable time but without making any decided mark there, and will probably be best remembered by his countrymen because of his compilation of his father's speeches accompanied by a well-arranged memoir. The name of the younger Daniel has almost entirely ceased to be even a memory in the House of Commons. I have included his portrait in this volume, believing it may have an interest for many of my readers, if only as a link with a thrilling past and as the shadow of a great name.

I must add to this group of members one whose short parliamentary career came to a close in the early sixties, and whose death followed not long after. This was Thomas Chandler Haliburton, a Canadian by birth and bringing up, who had been called to the Bar in Canada, made a successful career there, became a judge of the Supreme Court, and then settled in England, where he died and was buried. I am inclined to believe that the name of Thomas Chandler Haliburton will not at once bring to the minds of all my readers any clear idea as to the personality of the man whose picture I now bring under their notice. I am afraid that even when I describe Haliburton as the author of *Sam Slick* some at least of my readers will not at once remember who Sam Slick was. Sam Slick was supposed to be a Yankee clock-maker, who, after various experiences and adventures in his own country, obtained promotion to the rank of an attaché to the United States minister at the Court of St. James's, and who gives us his observations upon English life and his experiences of English society in the same style as that which had pictured life in his own land. Sam Slick has been described as a sort of American Sam Weller, and it is not too much to say that Haliburton's Sam might fairly rank for drollery, for keen observation, and for genuine humor with the Sam who was the creation of Charles Dickens. *Sam Slick* was at one time, and for a long time, a book of immense popularity among English as well as among American readers. I greatly fear that it has now passed out of the memory of most readers in this country, and that to declare one's self an admirer of the work and of its hero is an admission that one has left one's youth a long way behind.

I can remember the days when Sam Slick was as well known in England as Sam Weller, and when his sayings and doings, his odd, original humors, and his vivid pictures of eccentric figures were the subject of frequent allusions and quotations in English books and newspapers, and in the conversation of all who had a genuine relish for fiction of the comic order. There was much in Sam Slick not merely comic; he had many touches of deep feeling and of keen pathos which we do not associate with the peculiarities of Sam Weller. Indeed, one of the defects of Sam Slick was that he too often indulged in serious meditations on the graver side of life, and even preached us occasional sermons when we should all have preferred his more habitual rattle of jokes and quaintly satirical sayings. Most of the readers, even among those who felt a warm admiration for the Yankee clock-maker, were apt to skip the sermons and to give their whole attention to the comicalities. It is certain, however, that the book was a great success on this side of the Atlantic as well as on the other, and that for a long time it continued to have its numberless admirers. Haliburton, although he won his fame as the creator of an American character, was at heart a very devoted subject of the British crown, and was delighted when the opportunity came which allowed him to settle in England and become absorbed in English life. When he succeeded in obtaining a seat in the House of Commons, the British public regarded his appearance in that assembly with the keenest interest and expectation. Everybody was eager to know how the author of *Sam Slick* would comport himself, and whether he was likely to enliven the House by the humors and drolleries which had made him such a favorite in fiction. I am afraid there was a certain disappointment experienced by the public in general when Haliburton turned out to be very much like an ordinary member of Parliament belonging to the somewhat old-fashioned school. When he did speak in a debate he addressed himself with unmitigated gravity to an argument on the subject under discussion. He spoke but seldom, and he might but for his accent have been an ordinary British representative from one of the conservative counties, and might never have had anything to do with the Yankee clock-making trade.

My first opportunity of hearing Haliburton was not in the House of Commons, but at a dinner given on the occasion of some great agricultural celebration in Killarney, within sight of those lakes which can challenge comparison with Windermere and Grasmere, with Geneva and Lucerne, with Como and Maggiore, with Lake George and Lake Champlain. In the speech he delivered on that occasion Haliburton indulged in his humorous style, and described himself as coming from Pumpkinton county, Ohio, a place famed for its "gals, geese, and onions." I heard him afterwards in the House of Commons, and my memory especially goes back to a debate he took part in, and in which he was made the victim of a rather happy stroke of satire by no less a person than William Ewart Gladstone. Haliburton had been expressing his views on some subject then before the House—the subject, I must admit, has wholly passed out of my memory—and he was severely condemning in solemn and almost funereal tone the manner in which the members of the liberal government had endeavored to throw ridicule on their opponents. Gladstone was a leading member of the administration, and it became part of his duty to sum up the case on behalf of the ministry. In the course of his remarks he made allusion to Haliburton's speech, and declared that nothing in all his parliamentary experience had given him greater surprise than to hear the author of *Sam Slick* object to the use of ridicule. The retort was fairly invited and was very happy. Even Haliburton's political associates were rather pleased with it, because they, too, could not help feeling a certain sense of disappointment when the author of *Sam Slick* refused to give the House some taste of his genuine quality.

I do not now remember whether Haliburton ever made a really humorous speech in the House, but I am quite sure that if he did I had not the good fortune to hear it. After the first sensation of interest and curiosity caused by his introduction to the House had passed away, the parliamentary career of Haliburton remained entirely undistinguished. His career could hardly be called a failure, because he made no effort at success; but I always thought that there must have been some lack of nervous energy, some curious, morbid shyness in Haliburton's temperament, which kept him from trying to find any field in parliamentary debate for the wonderful qualities of shrewdness, keen observation, original humor, and high moral purpose which characterized all his best writings. Haliburton's figure is not the least remarkable in that parliamentary group whose pictures belong to this chapter.

CHAPTER X

ANOTHER PARLIAMENTARY GROUP

Many of the portraits around which, if I may so express myself, this volume is constructed bring back to my mind figures which, although not coming under even the shadow of a great name, may recall distinct and interesting memories to readers of the present generation. The men with whom I dealt in the last chapter had each of them a distinct career or purpose of his own, and they may be regarded as in a certain sense historical personages. But there were others associated with the Parliament, and especially with the House of Commons, of those far-off times who made a distinct impression on the attention of every one familiar with that House, although none of those I am about to mention in this chapter had made any mark upon public life by his eloquence, by his political influence, or even by his fanaticism or eccentricity. One man, indeed, with whose portrait this chapter is illustrated, was not even a member of the House of Commons, and never, so far as I have heard, showed or felt the slightest desire to become the representative of any constituency. Yet this man had a seat in the House of Commons for many years—a seat from which he could not have been ejected by the vote of any political majority. Even the Speaker of the House of Commons has to be elected to a place in that House by the vote of a majority of his constituents, and if at any general election he should fail to obtain that majority or a majority in another constituency, his place in the Speaker's chair is vacant, and some duly elected member of the House must be chosen to fill it. But the man about whom I am going to speak did not owe his seat in the House to the favor of any constituency, and could not have been displaced from it by the verdict of any number of successive general elections. For this fortunate man was the Sergeant-at-Arms.

The portrait of Captain Gosset will bring back many pleasant and kindly memories to those whose recollections extend, as mine do, back to the parliamentary life of a past generation. Captain Ralph A. Gosset held for many years the office of Sergeant-at-Arms in the House of Commons. Now, as most of my readers know, the Sergeant-at-Arms is a very important functionary. He wears a court suit, is girt with a sword, and his duty is to carry out, and, if necessary, to enforce all the directions of the Speaker for the maintenance of order in the House. He sits in a little chair, or box, or throne of his own, near the entrance to the House from the members' lobby, at the right side of the Chamber as you advance towards the Speaker's chair. He sits quite close to the benches of the members on that side of the House, and he faces Mr. Speaker. He has a Deputy Sergeant-at-Arms and an Assistant Sergeant-at-Arms, who relieve him of his duties during a great part of each sitting, and, indeed, if he had not such relief his life would be sadly monotonous during his hours of official attendance. The Sergeant-at-Arms is not allowed to beguile the time by reading a book or a newspaper. No man may read a newspaper within the House of Commons. I remember that in one of Thackeray's novels the great author makes some passing reference to Sir Robert Peel, and describes the statesman as rising from his place on the treasury bench, and proceeding to read certain passages from a copy of the *Times* which he holds in his hands and concerning which he proposes to offer some observations. It is strange that so observant a man as Thackeray, who might have been expected to know all about the ways of that House in which at one time he strove to obtain a seat, should have made such a mistake. No member can rise in the House and read extracts from a newspaper. If there are any passages in a journal on which he desires to comment he must have them copied out from the newspaper, and he will then be in order if he reads from the copy, but he must on no account presume to take the newspaper itself in his hand and read from its columns. Such at least were the strict rules of order up till the time when I resigned my seat in the House of Commons, and as that was only at the last general election I do not suppose any change in this old-time rule has since been made.

All this, however, is merely a digression into which I was led in explaining the fact that the Sergeant-at-Arms is not allowed to amuse himself by reading a newspaper while he occupies his official seat. The Speaker himself is restricted in a like way, and he, too, is not permitted to while away a dull hour by reading from a book or a newspaper while he occupies his throne of office. But then there is a difference. The Speaker is the guardian of order in the House. No matter how dull, tame, and prosy a debate may be, the Speaker can never feel certain that at any moment something may not be said or done which would constitute a breach of order and call for his prompt and peremptory interference. Therefore he has to keep his attention as closely fixed as he can upon the speeches of right honorable and honorable members, and he probably has the well-founded conviction that the moment he allowed his attention to wander some encroachment on the rules of order would be certain to occur.

But the Sergeant-at-Arms has no such strain imposed on his intellectual faculties. His duty is merely to see that the commands of the Speaker are promptly and effectively carried out, and that the well-known and long-established regulations of the House are not infringed upon by careless members or ignorant or obtrusive strangers. If, for instance, a member were to begin reading a newspaper or writing a letter while occupying his seat in the House, the Sergeant-at-Arms would promptly and of his own motion inform the erring member that he was committing a breach of order. If a stranger were to walk in from the lobby and attempt to take a seat on one of the benches of the debating chamber where only members sit, the Sergeant-at-Arms would not have to wait for any direction from the Speaker, but would at once conduct the intruding personage back to the lobby again. But in the ordinary course of things while a debate is going on the Sergeant-at-Arms has no particular motive for fastening his attention on the speeches which are delivered. That is the business of the Speaker, and the thoughts of the Sergeant-at-Arms are free to wander whither they will. I remember being greatly amused once while Captain Gosset himself was endeavoring to impress on some of us in a private conversation that the lot of the Sergeant-at-Arms was even harder during a long and dull debate than that which official duties imposed on Mr. Speaker. Captain Gosset contended that if you have to keep your attention fixed on what is said during even the dullest debate you must be inspired with a certain kind of interest in what is said, and that this in itself helps to make the time pass more quickly than if you have to sit out the whole performance but are not compelled to listen. I commend the question as one well worthy the attention of those who make the operations of the human mind a subject of habitual study.

I must now return to my portrait and its subject. Captain Gosset was one of the most good-humored and genial of men. He was on the most friendly terms with every member of the House. But no doubt he had his preferences and his feelings of companionship like most other mortals, and these he was enabled to manifest in a very satisfactory way without the slightest sacrifice of that official impartiality which was one of the duties of his position. He had private rooms within the precincts of the House, and one of these rooms he used as a place of social reception for members whose company he found congenial. There, while he was off duty, he used to have pleasant gatherings of his friends during the evening hours, and much delightful talk and gossip and cheery criticism used to go on. It was a privilege and a pleasure to be invited to join in some of these friendly gatherings in the sergeant's room. Men of all political parties met and talked there in the friendliest fashion, and it often happened that two members who had been denouncing each other and each other's party and each other's politics an hour or two before during a debate in the House met in the most companionable terms in the sergeant's room, smoked their cigars, refreshed themselves with his liquids, and chaffed each other about their recent performances on the parliamentary field.

One of the portraits in this chapter is that of Sir Patrick O'Brien, an Irish member who was often to be met with in Gosset's social gatherings. The present generation, I am afraid, has forgotten all about Sir Patrick O'Brien, but he was a man of note in his day

CAPTAIN GOSSET, M.P.

SIR PATRICK O'BRIEN, M.P.

among all who took any interest in the sayings and doings of the House of Commons. I have seldom met a man who had in him a better capacity for success in political life, and who turned his abilities and his opportunities to less permanent account. He was a man of humor and of wit, had an original way of looking at things, could make a rattling speech in debate, and could say something fresh and telling even on the most outworn subject. The House has always some one or two odd humorists at least who can put life into the dullest debate, and whose rising commands immediate attention because every one knows that something is about to be said which will be original in its way and is sure to amuse the listeners. Such a man, for instance, was Bernal Osborne; such a man, although perhaps not quite with equal gifts, was Patrick O'Brien; and I could mention one or two men of the same order in the present House of Commons, but that these latest specimens would hardly have an appropriate place in my collection of portraitures from the past. Everybody liked to meet Sir Patrick O'Brien because he was sure to say something peculiar and amusing, and when there was no question of an interchange of mere drolleries he could make himself interesting in any conversation about politics or literature or conspicuous figures in the living world. Such a man was sure to be welcomed among those who frequented Captain Gosset's room, where political opinions counted for nothing, and, indeed, Sir Patrick O'Brien's political opinions were not of a sharply defined order. Sir Patrick was understood to accept in general the political creed of the majority of his countrymen. But it was not quite easy to know where to have him even on Irish questions, and he certainly would not have been regarded as an advanced Irish Nationalist of that order which was called into existence by Charles Stewart Parnell. I have many pleasant memories of him, but I am not concerned with any criticism here of his political career.

I remember a story which Captain Gosset once told about another Irish member belonging to the past, whose name it is not necessary to set down. This unnamed Irish member was often in Gosset's room and spent as much time there as he could. His convivial habits belonged to a still earlier time, and his friends regretted the fact all the more because he was known to have a loving and devoted wife, admired by every one who knew her. Captain Gosset was once giving some kindly advice to this member, and was urging him to keep earlier hours and not to sit in the smoking-room of the House, as might have been done in those days for an indefinite time after the Speaker had announced the close of the sitting. My countryman listened to the advice with perfect patience and then said, "Look here, Gosset, I tell you that if you had a wife who always sat up for you to give you a dismal lecture, you wouldn't be in quite such a confounded hurry to get home."

Another of Captain Gosset's stories concerned an English member whose name I also omit to record. An all-night sitting was expected—this was in the earliest times of the all-night sittings—and as it was already very late the honorable member had, contrary to the regulations of the House, found a comfortable arm-chair in the library for the reception of his wife, who had been sitting in the ladies' gallery until all the other ladies had left the gallery and gone to their homes. The debate, however, broke down for some reason or other, and the Speaker proclaimed the adjournment of the House. In the excitement caused by the sudden close of the debate the English member forgot all about his wife, and straightway drove home. He let himself in with his latch-key, and he always had a bedroom arranged for himself on the ground floor in order that after a late sitting of the House he might avoid disturbing his wife and his family by his return to his home at break of day. This considerate arrangement proved unsatisfactory on the occasion I am describing. The honorable member went to bed and fell fast asleep. A little later some of the attendants in the House of Commons found the poor lady seated in her arm-chair in the library and fast asleep also. I do not care to speculate as to the scene which may have taken place when the lady and her husband met for the first time in their home on that memorable morning.

I pass from these memories pleasant and yet melancholy of Captain Gosset and his semi-official gatherings to say a few words about my old friend Thomas Bayley Potter, who was in his time one of the best-known members of the House of Commons. Thomas Bayley Potter was a man of influence in his way and was absolutely devoted to the cause of advanced liberalism represented by Bright and Cobden. He was also a man of means, and he lent effective help to the maintenance of liberal organizations and liberal movements in his part of the country, Lancashire, and indeed wherever his help was needed and could fairly be claimed. He was absolutely one of the most unselfish men I ever knew. He was rigidly attentive to his duties in the House of Commons, and the whips of the liberal party could always count on his presence at any division, no matter how other men might feel self-excused for their occasional absence. He was not a devoted ministerialist when the Liberals were in power, and would oppose a measure introduced by a liberal government if it seemed to him to run counter in any, even of its minor provisions, to the true principles of the liberal cause. He had absolutely nothing to get so far as I can see by his steadfast attention to his parliamentary duties. He was not an effective speaker, and he was quite aware of his want of eloquence and hardly ever obtruded himself on the attention of the House. He had absolutely no ambition. He had not the slightest desire or inclination to obtain a place in any administration, and was never inspired by the faintest wish to make his way in what is called society. Cobden and Bright were his life's leaders, and so long as he could help to forward the principles which they represented he had no further ambition to gratify in parliamentary and public life.

During many periods when the liberal party was occupying the benches of opposition I used to sit near to Potter—" Tom Potter," as he was commonly called —and had many long talks with him. I used to meet him at public gatherings and at the dinners of the Cobden Club, which he had helped to found. His nature was curiously blended of plain common-sense and an almost romantic enthusiasm. Now, it must be allowed that we do not often meet with such an admixture in one man, for your enthusiast is seldom found to have in his temperament a basis of what is called common-sense, and your man of practical common-sense is rarely touched with the divine fire of enthusiasm. But in Tom Potter's case I could never quite decide for myself which quality held the more controlling place. One might talk to Potter again and again on the ordinary topics of the day, and never draw from him a sentence which spoke the possession of anything beyond the most practical and prosaic common-sense. But when you came to converse with him on some of the

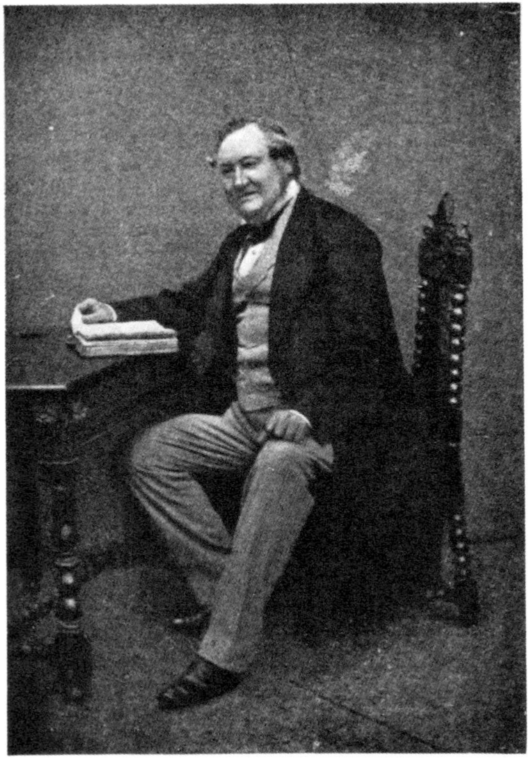

THOMAS BAYLEY POTTER, M.P.

JAMES WHITE, M.P.

great public questions which occupied so much of his life, you could not help seeing that he was inspired by an almost uncalculating enthusiasm for the cause he believed to be right. His physical conformation, solid, broad, and square-built, seemed the very impersonation of prose, and I do not know whether he ever read a poem or a romance in his life, and yet his absolutely unselfish devotion to his leaders and their cause had in it something that was essentially poetic.

It could hardly be said that Tom Potter was very popular in the House of Commons, for he had not the attractions of manner, of talk, or of mind which win popularity in such an assembly. But the House in general liked him, and while some of his own party seldom spoke of him without a half-amused, half-compassionate smile, yet all who knew him well, no matter what their political opinions might be, gave him full credit for his steadfast and disinterested course of life. Potter was endowed with a genuine gift of admiration, and although he could not well be described as a man of intellect, he had a singular faculty for the discernment of noble qualities in others wherever these existed. Strong, definite, and unalterable as were his political opinions, he had an instinct for recognizing the higher qualities even of those whose political views were most odious to him, and the worst fault a man could have in his eyes was a lack of sincere attachment to the principles he professed and proclaimed. Insincerity and self-seeking were the defects Tom Potter could not tolerate, and where he believed these to exist no gifts of eloquence, no success in statesmanship, could extort any praise from him. There was much of the heroic in the spirit which animated that most unwieldy figure.

James White was a sturdy Radical — one of the

sturdiest Radicals in those days when radicalism had more to do with the unmaking than with the making of administrations. He was not by any means so completely devoid of personal ambition as Thomas Potter, and he had to all appearance a fair estimate of his own capacity for debate. He spoke often, and he sometimes spoke well—just well enough to provoke criticism, but not nearly well enough to disarm it. He was a very tall man, with rather an imposing presence and something self-asserting in his demeanor, which made some of his political opponents anxious to depreciate his efforts at success in debate. He had a way of sitting on one of the front benches below the gangway with his head resting on the back of the bench and his long legs stretched out to their full extent in front of him and half across the floor of the House. Some reckless political enemy it must have been no doubt who, writing in a newspaper, once described his habitual attitude by quoting certain words from Milton, telling how "stretched out huge in length" a certain very objectionable being lay. Disraeli once got off a joke against Mr. White which stuck to his victim for a long time. White had been making a speech into which he introduced several allusions to the late Mr. Sheridan. The speech was somewhat ponderous and uninteresting, and perhaps Disraeli's sense of the ridiculous was aroused by the formal manner in which the great orator and wit of an earlier day was always described as "the late Mr. Sheridan." Disraeli had to make a speech during the course of the debate, and he found occasion to refer to the speech of James White, whom he described as "the successor to the late Mr. Sheridan in this House." This was not perhaps a great stroke of wit in itself, but it told immensely on the House of Commons. The contrast presented to every mind between the late Mr.

Sheridan and his newly created successor brought out Homeric laughter from all parts of the House, and for some time after James White was constantly referred to inside and outside Westminster Palace as the successor to the late Mr. Sheridan.

The portrait of Edward Knatchbull-Hugessen brings to my mind many recollections, and suggests what might seem to be a paradoxical reflection. Knatchbull-Hugessen the politician is, I fear, all but forgotten by the younger generation, but, on the other hand, Knatchbull-Hugessen the literary man has passed from the memory of the elders in general, and is only known to their children or grandchildren. For Knatchbull-Hugessen was a writer of stories for the young, and wrote, indeed, some of the most delightful tales for children published in the England of Queen Victoria's reign. He wrote *Stories for My Children, Crackers for Christmas, Moonshine Tales, Whispers from Fairyland, Puss-Cat-Mew,* and numbers of other stories and sketches which were the delight of young people who had long emerged from the nursery. I remember Knatchbull-Hugessen very well in the House of Commons, where he became Under-Secretary for the Home Department and afterwards Under-Secretary for the Colonies in a liberal administration. He was not, however, what would at any time have been called a very robust Liberal, and I believe that after he had been raised to the peerage as Lord Braybourne he settled down into quiet conservatism. He never made any impression on the House of Commons, although when he had occasion to speak he always spoke clearly and to the purpose. To look at him there he seemed about the least likely man in the world to be capable of writing stories which could amuse the young folks, for he always wore an aspect of intense and even dismal gravity, and gave the idea of one who had been sentenced to imprisonment in the House for some offence of which he was not guilty. On the other hand, one who read his stories for children, and knew nothing of the author's personal career, would never have dreamed of associating such bright and lively writing with the grim-looking personage who seemed to put in an unwilling appearance in the House of Commons.

We have grown of late somewhat accustomed, at least in literature, to these living contrasts in one frame. We have, indeed, come to assume almost as a matter of course that the maker of perpetual jokes is a gloomy pessimist at heart, that the professional mute at the funeral is the merriest of creatures when he is out of business hours, and so forth. I remember once hearing two young men discussing some great question of world philosophy after a pleasant dinner-party. One was dark-haired, with sallow complexion and an aspect of intense melancholy. The other was fair-haired, with fair skin, bright eyes, and a smiling countenance. The company was much taken by two sentences which came from the lips of the disputants. "You see," the fair-headed, beaming youth observed, "I am a thorough pessimist." "And I," his gloomy comrade replied, with brows growing darker than ever, "am in all things a thorough optimist." The humorous incongruity brought sudden laughter from all the listeners, and the dispute came to an end. I have always thought that Knatchbull-Hugessen the parliamentary politician and Knatchbull-Hugessen the writer of stories for the young formed as effective an illustration of this living paradox as ever came within the range of my observation.

There seems something peculiarly appropriate to the time when my present chapter comes to be written in the portrait of the Right Honorable William Francis

E. H. KNATCHBULL-HUGESSEN, M.P.

(Lord Brabourne.)

RIGHT HONORABLE WILLIAM FRANCIS COWPER, M.P.

Cowper. Mr. Cowper was better known to later years as Mr. Cowper-Temple, having been allowed to assume the family name of Lord Palmerston after the death of that statesman, who had become the second husband of Mr. Cowper's widowed mother. The appropriateness of which I have just spoken would require some words of explanation for the ordinary reader of the present day. During the winter in which I have got thus far with my volume the whole time, or very nearly the whole time, of the parliamentary session is occupied in debates on the education bill. Every day's papers contain long reports of these discussions, and leading articles of considerable length for or against this or that particular clause in the bill. It may be of interest at such a time to point out that much of the discussion turns on the question whether the government ought or ought not to stand by the terms of what was called the Cowper-Temple amendment to the education measure introduced by Mr. W. E. Forster. I can assure my readers that I have no intention to discuss in these pages either the education measure of 1870 or that of 1902, and only make this brief reference to the two measures with the selfish object of giving my portrait of Mr. Cowper-Temple an additional touch of living interest by its association with an important event in our past history which is making its mark on the events of the present day.

I remember seeing and hearing Cowper-Temple many times in the House of Commons before he had received that addition to his name by which he is best remembered now, and I cannot say that he impressed the House as a brilliant debater. He held office in several administrations. I remember him best as First Commissioner of Public Works. In this capacity he distinguished himself on one occasion and outside the

House of Commons more than he ever had done by any of his speeches within the House. He had introduced some measure for the limitation or regulation of the right to hold public meetings in Hyde Park. There was a great deal of alarm felt in those days as to the possible consequences which might arise to the cause of law and order, crown and constitution, if radicals and freethinkers and such like disorderly persons were to be allowed the full liberty of holding their meetings and expounding their doctrines at any time they thought fit, and to any numbers they could gather around them, in the great metropolitan park. I do not remember the exact nature of the limitations or regulations which Cowper-Temple proposed to introduce, but I believe that they were in themselves reasonable and not illiberal. Much indignation, however, was aroused by Cowper-Temple's measure among the classes who usually got up and attended the meetings, and an extravagant notion was formed as to the limitations which the author of the measure intended to introduce. Cowper-Temple acted promptly in a manner which amazed some of his graver colleagues, but which roused much admiration in many minds, and I am free to say in my own, by its spirit and its pluck. He attended a meeting called in Hyde Park to denounce his measure; he mounted one of the platforms and boldly delivered a speech in its defence; he insisted on arguing that it interfered with no genuine public right, and he succeeded in winning not only the attention but the confidence and applause of most of those to whom he addressed his courageous words. I had never before thought of Cowper-Temple as the possible orator of a platform in Hyde Park. He had always seemed to me an entirely formal, methodical, and somewhat self-centred sort of person, and I must confess that my estimate of him was greatly changed by his remarkable open-air performance. Such a performance was certainly not quite in keeping with official rules and ministerial etiquette; but I could not help thinking at the time that it was exactly the sort of enterprise which Lord Palmerston would in his heart have highly approved, and would have liked, if he might, to commend in public. I have no doubt that Cowper-Temple's unofficial exploit did much to abate the hostility which the promoters of Hyde Park meetings were stirring up against the new methods of regulation. With that odd incident the name of Cowper-Temple is associated in my memory.

Gathorne-Hardy was, in the early sixties, one of the most conspicuous men on the conservative side of the House of Commons. He was educated at Shrewsbury and at Oxford, won some distinction at Oriel, and entered Parliament for the first time in 1856. He rose rapidly in the House of Commons, and was almost from the very first recognized as an influence in his party. At that time the Conservatives in the House of Commons had not much to boast of for intellect and for debating power, so far as the rank and file of the party were concerned. The leader of the party, Disraeli, was, of course, well able to hold his own against any rival in debate, and he had among his leading colleagues two or three men of genuine capacity who would have reckoned for much in any parliamentary assembly. But these leading men were not well supported by many of their followers, and it soon came to pass that Gathorne-Hardy was regarded as a genuine strength to the Conservatives in debate. He was not an orator in the higher sense of the word, and he could not be called a brilliant debater. He had no gift of humor, and his argument was rarely brightened by anything like a flash of eloquence. But he was a fluent speaker, he had a clear and powerful voice, his style was always correct, he appeared to have an excellent memory for facts and for the arguments of an opponent, and it was possible sometimes, while listening to one of his more animated speeches, to be carried away so far as to believe him a genuine master of debate. But the impression did not long keep its hold on the mind of the listener, and most of those who had heard him often found themselves settling down into the conviction that Gathorne-Hardy could always make a good speech, and could never make a great speech.

I remember hearing John Bright once say that a man whose speeches were all equally good could never be a great orator, and I think the observation had much critical justice in it. Without imagination there cannot be eloquence of the higher order, and the gift of bold imagination brings with it as a matter of course the liability to make mistakes and the ambition which sometimes overleaps itself and falls on the other side. Gathorne-Hardy's speeches were always loud, clear, and fluent; their language was always correct, and their argument was direct and well sustained, but they maintained what may be called a dead level. When the debate was over the speech soon passed from the memory of the listeners. Still it must be owned that the faculty which enables a man to be safely relied upon for a good speech in any debate was one of much value to the conservative party when Gathorne-Hardy was in his prime. He held many high offices in conservative administrations, and his career in the House of Commons was brought to a close by his elevation to the peerage as Lord Cranbrook. Perhaps he will be best remembered by the fact that in 1865 he became a candidate for the representation of Oxford University, in opposition to Mr. Gladstone, and he succeeded in

GATHORNE GATHORNE-HARDY AND JOHN STEWART GATHORNE-HARDY, M.P'S.

defeating the greatest English statesman of his age. Gladstone was immediately elected as representative of South Lancashire, and with that event began a new era in England's political life. The most devoted among Gathorne-Hardy's friends and admirers did not go so far as to say that the defeat of Gladstone was a triumph won by the political genius of the successful candidate, for the majority of the voters at that election would most assuredly have given their support to any tory candidate whatever who came forward in opposition to Gladstone. Still, a victory is a victory, and the fact that he defeated such a man as Gladstone was undoubtedly, to adopt a phrase brought much into notice lately, "a feather in the cap" of Gathorne-Hardy. Lord Cranbrook must at least have had the gratifying conviction that no biographer could bring out a life of Gladstone which did not contain Gathorne-Hardy's name, and record the fact that he had "unmuzzled" Gladstone.

The portrait of John Stewart Gathorne-Hardy is that of the present Lord Medway, eldest son of Lord Cranbrook. Lord Medway when still only a Mr. Gathorne-Hardy sat as a member of the House of Commons during many years, but I must say did not do much, or so far as I can recollect, attempt much to make for himself a parliamentary reputation. I am inclined to believe that the historical fame of the family thus far must rest chiefly on the fact that its leading member accomplished, although unwittingly, the unmuzzling of Mr. Gladstone.

CHAPTER XI

FROM COMMONS TO LORDS

On August 30, 1861, the statesman who had been so long known in English political life as Lord John Russell took his seat in the House of Lords as Earl Russell of Kingston-Russell in Dorset and Viscount Amberley of Ardsalla in Meath. A few days earlier Lord John Russell delivered his farewell address to the electors of the City of London, which he had represented for some forty years. In this farewell address Lord John in a few sentences of melancholy humor likened himself to a celebrated emperor of three centuries before who had been engaged in all the great movements of his time, and, fancying that he would like to see what might happen after his death, had the pomps of his funeral prepared, and took part himself as chief mourner in the solemn rites. It is not difficult to understand that Lord John Russell might well have regarded his elevation to the House of Lords as the funeral ceremonial of his political life. His whole public career had been associated with the struggles and triumphs of his party in the House of Commons. He had known, as friends and companions, or as political opponents and rivals, many men whose names at the time of his leaving the representative chamber seemed to belong to the history of the far past. As Disraeli once said of him, he had sat at the feet of Fox and measured swords with Canning. He had been addressed in language of eloquent poetic panegyric by Thomas Moore, and he had had many conversations at Elba with the dethroned Emperor Napoleon. His work as a statesman did not, indeed, close with his removal from the House of Commons, and he was yet as prime-minister to introduce a measure of reform which was, like other measures of reform, defeated by a coalition between the conservative opposition and a number of seceding Liberals, but which led to the introduction of a still more advanced reform measure by a conservative government, whose leading members saw that such a change in the political system was inevitable, and made up their minds to have the honor and advantage of introducing it themselves. But it is nevertheless an unquestionable fact that when a man who has played for many years a leading part in the House of Commons becomes endowed with a title and is transferred to the House of Lords, his political activity seems to have sunk into something like a living grave. I heard many of Lord Russell's speeches in the House of Lords, and I never could suppress a feeling of melancholy when I recalled the effect which I had often seen him produce as leader of a government or a party in the House of Commons. When we think of the career of Lord John Russell we do not naturally associate it with the sixties, but his portrait is distinctly appropriate to this volume if it were but for the fact that the early part of the sixties heard his farewell to that great political assembly in which he had won his fame.

My first personal recollections of Lord John Russell belong to the year 1858, when he attended a meeting of the Social Science Association, held in Liverpool, where I was then working as a journalist. I had the good fortune to be presented to him and to have some talks with him, and I can well remember what a delight it was to me to hear him tell of his meetings with Napoleon and other remarkable experiences of his early years. It seemed to carry one back into a far-away time of thrilling historical movement and illustrious figures thus to have speech with a man who could tell from his own personal knowledge of such men and such days. After I had settled in London I had many opportunities in each session of hearing Lord John Russell in parliamentary debate. He was assuredly one of the most effective debaters to whom I have ever listened. It would not, perhaps, be possible to rank him with the greatest parliamentary orators, with men like Gladstone and Bright, or even with Disraeli and Disraeli's leader, Lord Derby. There was an almost indefinable something wanting in Lord John Russell's speaking which prevented him from taking a place among orators of the highest order. Perhaps he wanted imagination, although it is certain that at the opening of his public career he was regarded by most of those who knew him as a child of genius, as the apostle of a new political creed, as a young man of intrepid courage and adventurous spirit. Perhaps he wanted passion, although this, too, was a quality with which those who knew him in his earlier days of political life regarded him as eminently endowed. Perhaps his voice had not the power and musical thrill which lent strength and charm to the eloquence of Gladstone, Lord Derby, and Bright. It is certain that those who only knew Lord John Russell as a parliamentary debater in the sixties would hardly have recognized in him the qualities which his friends at the opening of his career appear to have considered especially his.

The predominant quality of Lord Russell's eloquence in these later days was its somewhat cold and clear reasonableness of argument. Russell analyzed or dissected the case of his parliamentary opponents with keen, firm, and merciless touch and exposed its weaknesses with unsparing skill. There was a fine vein of scorn in his eloquence and he had a keen and delicate sense of humor. Some of his happy, humorous retorts have become proverbial and are still often quoted in political debate and in newspaper criticism. Then, too, it must be said that when he had to deal with some question which made a direct appeal to the deeper emotions of men he could delight and uplift his hearers by passages of real eloquence. On these occasions I have felt more than once that Lord Russell had surely established his claim to be ranked among the orators, as I have thought that he might under other conditions have rivalled George Canning or Sydney Smith in wit and humor. But Russell was too earnestly devoted to the practical work of his parliamentary career to allow himself much time for the culture of his eloquence, or to go out of his direct line of argument in order to make his antagonist ridiculous by a jest. I do not remember any other example in my time of an English statesman who had so many gifts for great debate and yet who did not quite succeed in winning a place with the greatest orators.

I do not suppose that Lord John Russell was ever very popular among the members of the House of Commons, even on his own side. He was shy by nature; cold and reserved in manner, but in manner only, for the universal testimony of those who really knew him is that he had a feeling heart, a warm and generous temperament, and a most tender love for those who loved him. I feel quite sure that the seeming coldness and constraint of his manner was due altogether to that shyness which prevented him from showing his real self in the company of strangers. The ready means by which a statesman of a more expansive temperament can attain an easy popularity were denied to Lord John Russell, the formal presentation to whom of a newcomer was always a somewhat chilling ceremonial. I have sometimes felt disposed to believe that this same peculiarity of temperament may have been one reason why even the finest passages of his parliamentary eloquence showed a certain restraint and were not allowed their full and natural expression. There was one peculiarity in Lord John Russell's speeches which I have not noticed in those of other great parliamentary debaters. When even a real orator delivers an important speech the listener feels, as it comes to a close, that the orator has said all he wanted to say and has, so far as he is concerned, exhausted his subject. But when Lord John Russell concluded one of his finest and most convincing speeches the impression of most listeners was that he had yet a great deal to say which might have been said—that he had not nearly exhausted the treasury of his ideas, and that he could have added many other illustrations and arguments if he had not been unwilling to occupy too long the attention of the House. My judgment is that Russell never did complete justice to his own oratorical capacity, and that if he had been a little less fastidious and more daring he might have ranked among the most eloquent speakers of his time.

Lord Russell was a voluminous writer, and published several memoirs, some historical works, and actually two tragedies, neither of which is, I take it for granted, known to the play-goers of the present day. He was an intense lover of literature and of art, and throughout the whole of his life he welcomed in his home the companionship of men and women of genius and culture. He was one of the closest friends of Thomas Moore, and in later days had cultivated the friendship of Dickens and Thackeray. His second wife, the late Countess

LORD JOHN RUSSELL

LADY RUSSELL

Second wife of Lord John Russell

Russell, was the best companion and friend to him, and helped him with devotion and intellectual support in the accomplishment of every object he undertook. I had the honor of Lady Russell's friendship for more than twenty years, until her death in the beginning of 1898. I have never known a more perfect illustration of womanhood's highest order. She was endowed with a fine intellect, an exquisite taste, and a noble nature. She retained to the last her warm interest in every cause and movement that promised any increase of human happiness. She loved literature and art. She was the true, tender friend of the poor and lowly who came within the range of her influence. For many years before her death she had withdrawn altogether from London life and spent her days in Pembroke Lodge, Richmond Park, but she never allowed the quietude of her home to make it a hermitage. Her friends were always welcome at Pembroke Lodge, and she had crowds of friends who were only too glad to visit her. She maintained to the last the closest interest in all that was going on in the political and social life from which she had withdrawn. Lady Russell must have known during her time almost all the famous men and women who belonged to England, or who came there from any other part of the civilized world. She had the most delightful reminiscences of the acquaintanceships thus made, and she seemed to take a pleasure in entertaining her friends with them. I believe that the story of her life, with ample extracts from her correspondence, is to be told before long by her gifted and devoted daughter, Lady Agatha Russell. No other hand could fittingly accomplish such a work, and there need be little hesitation in predicting that the book will command the attention of the whole reading public.

Another distinguished member of the Russell family

is Mr. George W. E. Russell, whose *Collections and Recollections,* although published anonymously, have not been able to conceal their authorship, and have been accepted by most of us as confidently as if they bore their writer's name. I cannot help feeling much regret that George Russell has not resumed his career as a member of the House of Commons. He held office twice in liberal administrations, and during his later years in the House he gave brilliant evidence of a capacity for parliamentary debate. George Russell has undoubtedly many strings to his bow, if I may revive an almost forgotten phrase, and he never fails to make work enough for his intellect, his energies, and his kindly, sympathetic nature outside the domain of Parliament. Still, I must say that I cannot help regarding the House of Commons as the field in which he could give the most effective service to humanity and win the highest distinction. He could have no difficulty in finding a constituency at the next general election which would feel proud to secure him as a representative, and I can only hope that before long he may be seen again in his former place on the treasury bench.

No statesman in my time brought with him so many distinct recollections of great past days as did Lord John Russell. As from the gallery of the House of Commons while Russell was still a member, I listened to one of his speeches, I found myself carried back in imagination to the great days before the first Reform bill, to that tremendous parliamentary and national struggle which ended happily in a peaceful revolution, though at one time it seemed as if it were destined to be settled by a revolution costing a heavier price. But the listener to Lord John Russell in the House of Commons was carried back even farther than the days of the great national struggle for reform; he knew that he was listening to a man who, as a boy, had known Fox, and who came into the world only four years after the birth of Byron. Lord John Russell had lived through the great literary age of Scott and Wordsworth, Shelley and Keats; he had known the great painters and sculptors and men of science belonging to that immemorial time; and he had seen the up-coming and the growth of the age, not less wonderful, which produced Dickens and Thackeray, Tennyson and Browning, Darwin, Richard Owen and John Stuart Mill. He had seen in political life the rise of such men as Gladstone and Disraeli, Cobden and Bright, and it was an intellectual treat to hear him compare the great ones of the present with the great ones of the past. Unlike many men who have lived to a great age and studied successive changing generations, Earl Russell, even in his latest years, was quick to recognize rising merit in politics, literature, or art, and never entertained the idea that human greatness had come to an end with the days when his own activity and his own fame had reached their zenith. Nor was he ever governed in his estimate of a public man by the consideration that the public man was, or was not, on his own side of politics. I remember being much interested in Earl Russell's cordial appreciation of the eloquence of Lord Derby.

It need hardly be said that Lord Derby, during his official career, was utterly opposed to the political doctrines Lord Russell advocated, but Russell became animated and enthusiastic while describing in conversation the effect produced upon him by Lord Derby's eloquence. I must say that I thought Lord Russell somewhat overrated Lord Derby's capacity as an orator, and that I could not myself, much as I admired his eloquence, regard him as quite on a level with Gladstone and Bright. But what interested me most in the whole incident was the evidence it gave of Lord Russell's absolute impartiality in judging of political speakers, and also the evidence it gave that he was not one of those who believed that all true greatness ended with their own prime. Lord Russell's intellect was like his style of speaking, above all things clear and lucid. No cloud of prejudice ever obscured for him the real meaning of the question at issue. In his conversation as in his public speaking one was delighted now and then by those gleams of warm and almost impassioned emotion which showed that he had in him much of the spirit of the orator as well as the instinct of the artist. There have been greater speakers in the oratorical sense during our time than Lord Russell, and there have been greater statesmen, but I question whether the nineteenth century ever knew a political leader who had so many interesting experiences, so many delightful friendships, and who got so much out of life as was the happy lot of the statesman whom English history will always remember best by the name of Lord John Russell.

The sixties saw the removal of another remarkable figure from the House of Commons to the House of Lords. The word remarkable is one which applies with a special accuracy to the figure of Sir Edward Bulwer Lytton, who was raised to the peerage in 1866. Few men have ever competed in so many different fields and obtained so considerable a success in each of them as Lord Lytton. He wrote novels, plays, poems, essays, satires, and it must be admitted that everything he did was well done. In some of his novels and in some of his plays there was nothing wanting to complete success but that one divine spark of genius without which success is only a triumph of its own time. Some of Lord Lytton's novels divided popularity with the great

THE FIRST LORD LYTTON

After Maclise. Painted at Knebworth in 1850

creations of Scott and Dickens and Thackeray. Some of his plays held the stage for many years as no other contemporaneous dramatic works could do, and indeed some of them hold the stage still. It would be easy to point out the defects of Lord Lytton's work in prose and verse, the meretricious glare and glitter of the style, the unreality of the emotions, the sickly sentimentality which spoils so many romantic passages, the tendency to caricature which often interferes with the effect of the characters intended to be comic. But when a critic had said all that and much more which might be said with equal justice, the fact still remains that Bulwer Lytton made a success not possible to be achieved even for a lifetime without original artistic merit. Many of his best novels were written by their author under very trying conditions. He belonged to an old English county family; his mother was heiress of Knebworth, and he was brought up to a life of ease and luxury; but he made an unfortunate marriage which caused for a time his complete separation from his parents, and he had to work hard for a living like any other penniless young author. The family estates came to him in the end, but for some years he was dependent almost altogether on the work of his pen, and it was not unnatural that when he found he had struck upon a paying line of literature, he should strive to please his public in the style that had proved acceptable to it.

At a later period of Bulwer's life, when he was not in need either of money or popularity, he wrote and published one or two serial novels anonymously, and each of them won distinct and remarkable success, although in neither case did the public suppose the new book to be the work of its old favorite. The truth is that Bulwer could do well anything he earnestly endeavored to do. He never reached to the height to which only genius can rise, but he could accomplish all that can be accomplished by splendid talents, wide culture, high ambition, and untiring perseverance. His political career gives the most striking proof of this faculty. Nature, mere physical nature, would seem to have denied to Bulwer Lytton some of the essential qualities of an orator. He suffered, at least during his years of political life, from some trouble of the palate, which cruelly marred his articulation, and he was at the same time oppressed by a degree of deafness which rendered it very difficult for him to follow the course of a debate. Yet it cannot be denied that he succeeded on several occasions in commanding the attention and winning the enthusiastic applause of a House of Commons accustomed to the eloquence of Gladstone and Disraeli and Bright One other difficulty which might have stood in the way of his success as a parliamentary debater was the fact that he had in his earlier career obtained a seat in the House of Commons, had sat there for some sessions, and had proved a failure. The story went at the time that one of his bitterest quarrels with his wife arose out of the utter breakdown of his first effort to address the House and of the merciless scorn and jeers with which she greeted his humiliation. But he was not a man who could quietly put up with failure in any field where it was his ambition to win success. He had proved this again and again in his literary and dramatic work, in the resolute determination with which he had set himself to recover any temporary failure, and the keen, critical self-examination by which he had brought himself to see the reasons for the mishap and the possibility of retrieving it by a better attempt in a more congenial style.

Having accomplished as high a popularity as could well be his in literature and the dramá, Bulwer appears to have made up his mind that he would win success in the House of Commons also. He, therefore, returned to Parliament, and it was during this later part of his career that I had the good fortune to hear two of his successful speeches. When he began the first of these speeches the chief difficulty in the way of the crowded House, listening eagerly to his words, was the difficulty of understanding what the orator was trying to say. His articulation was so imperfect that in the opening sentences of the speech the House was thrown into something like consternation. Every one, on whatever side of politics, was sincerely anxious that he should do well, and no one was content to give up the task of trying to understand him. But as he went on he got over the nervous embarrassment which was adding to his natural defects of utterance, and he seemed to understand the absolute necessity of getting out each word distinctly and separately, and thus encouraging his audience to pay attention to the speech. He took care to speak in measured tones and not to allow the words to run into one another, and although the voice was still hollow and unmusical, he was able to impress every listener with the full meaning of each sentence and phrase. Then the House began to understand with universal gratification that it was listening to a speech full of exalted thought, splendid phraseology, ingenious argument, and brilliant sarcasm. I have never listened to any other speaker who had to contend with such physical difficulties and who succeeded in accomplishing so wonderful a success. No doubt the speech was carefully prepared in every sentence, but it did not seem to be a mere piece of studied declamation, a glowing essay committed to memory and got by heart; it had all the effect of a piece of spontaneous eloquence. There was one unanimous burst of applause when the speaker resumed his seat, and there was, I think, one common feeling of delight that the orator had succeeded, all the greater because of the knowledge that a triumph over such physical difficulties could be and actually had been achieved.

Many of the phrases employed by Lytton in that speech and in others stamped themselves on the memory of the House of Commons, were quoted again and again in subsequent debates and at meetings out-of-doors, and some of them are still preserved by quotation in the political utterances of our own day. So peculiar was the impression produced on my mind by the first of Lytton's speeches to which I listened that while at the present moment I hardly remember the subject of the debate, I have the most distinct recollection of the orator's glowing style, his happy illustration, and his superb skill in phrase-making. He never could have succeeded as a great parliamentary debater, for his defective hearing made it impossible that he could reply on the spur of the moment to a speech delivered in the course of the evening's debate, but when the opportunity was afforded him of opening the discussion he was able to prove himself a parliamentary orator of a very high order. The higher criticism would have found the same faults in his parliamentary style as it found in the style of his romances and his plays, but it was beyond all question that he had accomplished just the same sort of success in the House of Commons as in literature and the drama. If he was not such a novelist as Dickens or Thackeray, neither was he such an orator as Gladstone or Bright, but as it could not be denied that he had won a high position among story-tellers and playwrights, neither could it be denied that he had won a high position among parliamentary orators. When he became Colonial Secretary in Lord

Derby's government he did good work by calling into existence the colonies of British Columbia and Queensland, and it was he who had the honor of sending Mr. Gladstone out on that mission to inquire into the grievances of the Ionian Islands, which had such important and memorable results. Thus he added a new honor to those he had already won. The same kind of success attended his work as a colonial minister as that which he had achieved in his novels, his dramas, and his parliamentary speeches. There were others greater than he in every field he cultivated, but his name will be always remembered among England's novelists, playwrights, parliamentary orators, and colonial ministers.

I had the pleasure of knowing Bulwer Lytton's son, the second Earl of Lytton, who, like his father, had a remarkable versatility of talent. He won fame for himself by the poems he published under the fictitious name of Owen Meredith, poems which it must be owned showed a higher reach of poetic genius than any of those the elder Lytton had given to the world. The second Lord Lytton also wrote prose romances of unquestionable literary merit, although he never won anything like the popularity achieved by his father in the same path of literature. The second Lord Lytton had, as every one remembers, a distinguished and important career as a diplomatist in nearly all the great cities of Europe and in Washington, and in the yet more important position of Viceroy of India. I have never met a man more charming in manners, more rich in artistic and intellectual ideas, and more truly sympathetic. The memory of some conversations I had with this gifted man must always belong to my prized possessions.

Early in the sixties occurred a removal from Commons to Lords which may fittingly be commemorated in this chapter. In 1861 Sir Richard Bethell, then Attorney-General, was made Lord Chancellor with the title of Baron Westbury. Richard Bethell had been leader of the Chancery Bar, and was said to have earned a larger income than any other living member of that branch of the profession. He sat in the House of Commons for many years, and held the office of Solicitor-General and afterwards of Attorney-General in a liberal administration. Sir Richard Bethell was never much of a politician and was not very decided in his views as a party man. He began his political career as a mild Conservative, then joined the liberal party as what might be termed an unbigoted Liberal, and afterwards showed, on more than one occasion, a certain inclination towards conservative principles. But he made a very distinct mark on the House of Commons by his almost unrivalled skill in sarcasm and retort. I have never heard in the House more acrid, corrosive, and intensely amusing utterances of scorn and satire than those which used frequently to come from the lips of Sir Richard Bethell. The satire was all the more scorching because of the bland sweetness with which it was delivered. Bethell's way was to let his eyelids droop as if he were affected by a sudden access of shyness, just as he was about to pour out on some opponent in debate his most vitriolic sarcasm, and to deliver this sarcasm in tones of dulcet gentleness, as if he were paying a delicate compliment by which he hoped to endear himself further to its recipient. He had a clear, impressive voice, and could speak powerfully whenever he thought fit, but he was sure to adopt the cadences of bewitching blandness whenever he seized on the chance of making his opponent an object for the ridicule of the House. When he passed into the House of Lords he almost bewildered that grave assembly on the rare occasions which gave him an opportunity of taking part in a debate. The Lord Chancellor does not address the Peers from the Woolsack, the parliamentary throne which he occupies while he presides over the debates, but descends and takes his stand on the nearest available part of the floor, and thence delivers his speech.

Lord Westbury had an opportunity more than once of pouring scorn on some motion which had been made, or speech which had been delivered, and then he positively scandalized their lordships by the epigrammatic bitterness of his sarcasm and the mellifluous accent in which it dropped from his lips. I remember forming a mental comparison between the satirical style of Lord Westbury and that of Robert Lowe, who, during the sixties, was making himself a name in the House of Commons by the acuteness and brilliancy of his satirical replies to the arguments of his political opponents. I came to the conclusion that, effective as Robert Lowe undoubtedly was in all such parts of his speeches, he was not quite so effective as Richard Bethell, and for one especial reason. Lowe jibed and jeered at his opponents in rasping tones suited to the words. The listener was amused and delighted, but not surprised. Lowe was going in avowedly and obviously for making his antagonists feel uncomfortable and angry. The tone, the manner, the glances, and the gestures were all in keeping with that kindly purpose. There was no charm of surprise or contrast about it. But when Bethell, with half-closed eyes, head modestly bent, and mild and gentle tones, poured gently out his phrases of vitriolic scorn, the listener felt that a new and cruel charm came in to make the contempt all the more withering to its object and more intensely amusing to the audience.

Bethell's career in Parliament never quite equalled what might have been hoped from his intellect and his practical capacity. He was a great lawyer in every sense of the word and helped to carry many important legal reforms during his time. He had a keen and powerful intellect, and a marvellous faculty for seeing into the realities of things. He never allowed his mind to be clouded by mere conventionalities or time-honored prejudices. He was one of the ablest debaters of his day and he could hold his own against any opponent in the House of Commons. Yet he did not take as high a position in public life as he might have commanded by the mere force of his abilities. Perhaps one reason for his want of complete success may be found in the fact that even when he was contending for a great and just cause, he hardly ever thought it worth his while to address himself to the highest and the noblest qualities of man's reason and purpose. His effort always appeared to be to crumble away the case of his opponents bit by bit, and not to throw his soul into the wider issues which the question brought into the conflict. His appeal was to the intellect, rather to its destructive than its constructive faculty, and he seldom made any appeal to the emotions. It may be said that this was quite natural in the case of a great Chancery lawyer, but there have been other Chancery lawyers in the House who could appeal to the emotions and the higher law, and I believe that the want of this capacity, or of this inclination, was one reason why Bethell did not secure in the House of Commons the commanding position he might have been expected to obtain. He was a very high-minded man and endowed with a generous, unselfish nature, and it is quite certain that some of the official troubles in which he became involved arose from his too great willingness to lend a trusting ear to the representations of some members of his family who were dear to him and whom he believed he could trust implicitly.

Lord Westbury was accused of having allowed an official of the House of Lords to retire and receive a retiring pension at a time when it was known to him that a serious charge connected with the conduct of that official in another public office was hanging over him, and that Lord Westbury had appointed his own son to the place thus made vacant. The whole question was taken up by the House of Commons, and a leading member of the conservative party moved a vote of censure on the Lord Chancellor. The House did not agree to the proposed vote of censure, but it adopted an amendment which, although acquitting him of any corrupt motive, affirmed that the granting of the pension showed a laxity of practice and a want of caution with regard to the interest of the public. Lord Westbury had to resign his office on the passing of this resolution. The general impression of the public was conveyed fairly enough by the terms of the resolution. No one thought that Lord Westbury had been actuated by corrupt motives, but the general belief was that he had been led into error by the confidence he reposed in some members of his family, and by his carelessness in regard to the minor duties of his high official position. There were many, however, who thought that when every allowance had been made for the need of maintaining a high standard of duty in public office, Lord Westbury had been harshly used, and that an unexpected opportunity had eagerly been availed of by those whom he had made his enemies in his days of bitter controversy. Lord Westbury lived for some years after what must be described as his fall, and took part in more than one great parliamentary controversy. But his days of public influence were closed forever by the resolution of the House of Commons.

CHAPTER XII

"CROWNLESS SOVEREIGNTIES"

THIS volume has no claim to be adorned by the portraits of many imperial and royal personages. My political and social ways of life have not led me much into such august circles, and although I have seen at different times and in various places a goodly number of the wearers of crowns, I have preferred to present, in these pages, only the portraits of men and women about whom I had something to say more than might come within the range of every passing observer. The Emperor of Brazil was the only imperial sovereign with whom I had any personal acquaintance, and lest I should seem to make too much of my imperial associate, I think it right to inform my readers that the Emperor of Brazil was a dethroned sovereign at the time when I had the honor of meeting him. I met Dom Pedro, the dethroned Emperor of Brazil, some twelve years ago at Cannes. I had gone there in the winter to pay a visit to an invalid friend, and, of course, it was a matter of common talk throughout the place that the dethroned emperor was then staying there. I had, however, no expectation of meeting Dom Pedro, and certainly had no inclination to press myself on his notice. But the whole story of his reign and of its sudden close had always been to me a subject of deep interest, and I was, I hope not unpardonably, gratified when a Londoner of my acquaintance who was then on a visit to Cannes told me that he would present me to the imperial exile. He assured me that the emperor was always anxious to have an opportunity of conversing with any one who had taken a part in political movements or in literature, art, or science. Thus encouraged, I accepted the invitation, and I soon found that my London friend was well qualified to offer me such an introduction. Under his escort I went to see the emperor several times and had some conversations with him in which he showed himself most gracious and genial. The emperor impressed me by the dignity and the sweetness of his manner and by the seemingly unconscious ease with which he talked to put his visitors at their ease. He showed a quick and bright interest in all the subjects then occupying the mind of the English public, and conversed with much appreciation about political parties and statesmen. He offered frankly his own estimates about this or that conspicuous personage, and was anxious to supplement his knowledge by any information which could be had from one taking part in public affairs. He asked many keen, intelligent questions, and it need hardly be said that a man can never manifest more effectively his understanding of a subject than by the questions which he asks of those who have come fresh from the scene of recent movements. I was surprised as well as pleased to find how much Dom Pedro knew of English public affairs—surprised because he had lived so long removed from our merely local interests and never, so far as I knew, had had much opportunity of making himself personally acquainted with English public life and the figures which move across its fields. But the talk was for the most part about letters and art and the progress of popular education.

Dom Pedro had many questions to ask concerning the promising and prominent new-comers in literature and in art; about the latest novelist or poet who had made some mark; about any new school of painters which might be challenging attention; and about the manner in which education was spreading among the people of the British Islands. From much that he said to me, although it did not bear directly on any such subject, I could not help forming the fancy that the exiled emperor must have felt a certain relief in the freedom given to him by his exile, and must have found it a gratifying change to be released from the care of striving to maintain an exotic empire like that of Brazil. The longer I conversed with him the more I came to marvel at the curious decree of fate which had set that quiet, thoughtful, unassertive, and intellectual man to the rough, thankless, and hopeless task of holding that position against such odds and such difficulties. One who succeeds to the highest position in a long-established imperial state may well contrive, whatever his own personal inclinations, to carry on adequately and becomingly the task which has been entailed upon him by the successful labors of his predecessors. But the whole creation of the independent Brazilian empire went back only a few generations, and might well have been considered, even at its outset, a work without any natural foundation and hardly within the reach of human statecraft to make perpetual. The conditions of South America are not suited for the formation of empires.

As I spoke with Dom Pedro my mind went back to the melancholy history of another American empire not, indeed, belonging to the southern continent, but set up on a soil alike exotic and equally unsuited to such a growth—the Mexican empire, which may be described as the last stroke of the great political gamester Louis Napoleon, when he attempted to open a new and dazzling chapter of imperialism in order to recover his splendor in the eyes of the world. The brave and high-minded Maximilian of Austria, persuaded and beguiled by the imperial gamester, was the principal victim of that ill-fated enterprise, and I could not help thinking how much more fortunate was Dom Pedro in having been able to survive the ruin of his fallen empire and to have some years at least of a peaceful and honored life. Dom Pedro, of course, had incurred no personal responsibility for the foundation of the South American empire; the task had come down to him in the ordinary course of succession, and he did the best he could with it and merely failed to achieve, where it was beyond the art of man to accomplish, success. When the Brazilian revolution overthrew the empire and sent Dom Pedro into exile, Brazil established for herself a republican system modelled as nearly as possible after the exact pattern of the republic created by the United States, with its President elected at precise intervals, its Senate, its House of Representatives, and all the other arrangements. It has gone on thus far without giving much trouble to its neighbors or to the world in general, and without exciting any particular interest in western or eastern hemisphere.

I remember having heard Englishmen ask, at the time when the Brazilian empire was overthrown by popular revolution, why it was that the United States, having compelled Louis Napoleon to withdraw from his imperial enterprise in Mexico, should never have interfered with the progress of the empire in Brazil. If the Monroe doctrine, it was asked, applied to the empire started by Louis Napoleon in Mexico, why did it not also apply to the empire inherited by Dom Pedro in Brazil? The answer is very plain. One of the conditions of the Monroe doctrine is that no European sovereign shall set up an empire on American soil against the national wish of the population to be imperialized. At the time when Brazil was converted into an empire the country had long been an appanage of the Portuguese crown, and when Portuguese princes took refuge there from the invading enterprises of the first Napoleon the Brazilian population made no objection, and probably felt none, to the merely nominal change which converted the country into an empire. I am not able to form any estimate as to the rightfulness of the cause which was represented by the Brazilian revolution, but it is quite clear that the people of Brazil had by that time come to the conviction that they could get on better with a republic than with an empire, and nothing that has happened since shows that they yearn for a restoration of the imperial system. The Monroe doctrine, therefore, was in nowise affected by the setting up or the maintenance of the empire in Brazil any more than it is affected now by the fact that Canada is a dominion of the British empire. I need hardly say that I did not start this subject in any of the conversations which I had with the deposed Emperor of Brazil, and I only mention it now for the reason that it formed one of the thoughts then passing through my mind and made me contrast the happy relief given by fortune to Dom Pedro with the stroke of fate which had prematurely closed the career of the gallant Maximilian.

The emperor and empress were both fond of travel, and had gone about the world a good deal even while the empire of Brazil was still a flourishing institution. In the summer of 1871 the emperor and empress paid a visit to London during the course of their prolonged tour through Europe. The imperial visitors made it their pleasure to see everything in London which helped to illustrate the life of the people, and to become personally acquainted with every spot which had historic,

THE EMPEROR OF BRAZIL

[*See page* 158

THE EMPRESS OF BRAZIL

[*See page* 162

literary, or artistic interest. They lived quietly at Claridge's Hotel and did not go in much for court ceremonial, but there was one great occasion when the emperor expressed himself as gratified beyond measure by the action of the late Queen Victoria, who conferred upon him the Order of the Garter. Queen Victoria showed the emperor and empress great attention and kindness while they were in England, and every one who was brought into association with them seems to have been impressed by the intelligent interest they manifested in the historical monuments and memorials of English life. The emperor had during his reign proved himself to be a man of progressive mind, and had done much to forward every educational and philanthropic movement in the country which he was doing his best to govern. I can well remember that a certain sensation was created when the emperor and empress were in London by the fact that the emperor spent great part of a day in the Court of Common Pleas while the hearing of the famous Tichborne case was going on. The Tichborne case has long since that time vanished almost entirely out of public memory, but it was then and for long after an absorbing topic of interest. No trial which has gone on in this country in my recollection ever created anything like the amount of curiosity, excitement, controversy, and wonder aroused by the audacious claims of the self-styled Sir Roger Tichborne. There were some, I can well recollect, who thought it rather undignified on the part of a crowned emperor to manifest any interest in such a proceeding, but the general feeling was that he could not have better proved the comprehensive activity of his intelligence than by thus availing himself of the opportunity for a study of one of the most remarkable cases ever tried in an English court of law. The emperor had the good fortune to come in for a brilliant illustration of the processes of cross-examination applied to the Tichborne claimant by Sir John (afterwards Lord) Coleridge. Harun-al-Rashid himself might have thought his time well spent if he could have been present on such an occasion as that secured by the Emperor of Brazil.

I am wandering somewhat out of the range of the sixties, to which these pages are dedicated, but when one studies the portrait of an eminent personage he is not likely to keep his thoughts confined altogether to the precise period at which the picture was taken. I may say that the portrait of the emperor set out in this chapter does not, and of course could not, represent him as I saw him at Cannes nearly twenty years after. The emperor, when I first came into his presence, was looking rather older than even his years would have warranted, for his white hair and somewhat melancholy gravity of expression gave one the idea of a man whose life was drawing to a close by the accumulation of years. The emperor was almost exactly sixty-six years old when he died in Paris not much more than a year after I saw him at Cannes. We do not in our days regard such a life as one that has reached its natural length, but the Emperor of Brazil had lived much in his time, and when I saw him seemed to be already standing within the shadow of the approaching end. The task which had devolved upon him was probably beyond the strength of any statesman. Dom Pedro conducted his reign on high and liberal principles and won for himself the approval of the world in general, but there are countries in which an empire is not destined to hold sway for long, and the conditions surrounding and controlling Brazil could hardly have been favorable to the endurance of an imperial system transplanted from the old countries across the ocean.

The Emperor of Brazil succeeded to a crown, but when he had lost it gave up the game quietly and never made the slightest attempt to recover the precarious possession. Don Carlos of Spain, whose portrait also belongs to this chapter, represents the story of a struggle carried on through generations, of a claim never resigned or renounced, but asserted and maintained against the most overwhelming difficulties, sometimes carried to the verge of success, and still regarded with faith and hope by its acknowledged representatives and their devoted followers. The living Don Carlos, whose portrait here was taken during the early sixties, is still looked up to by many as the legitimate sovereign of Spain, and reckons for much more than a mere cipher when forces have to be counted in the event of political convulsions in the southwest of the European continent. During the troubles following the great war between France and Prussia in 1870 and the fall of the French empire, when the destinies of Spain seemed to flicker for a while between legitimacy and republicanism, Don Carlos appeared in the field as Charles the Seventh, and maintained himself for a considerable time in the northern part of the peninsula. We can all remember that there were intervals during that stormy time when the chances seemed great that the Carlist movement might hold its own and that the representative of legitimacy might come to be recognized as the reigning sovereign of Spain. The movement failed then as it had failed before, but even yet, if at any moment some political upheaval should be threatened in Spain, the first question in the mind of the observer is whether the crisis may not after all be fraught with the possibility of a restoration for Don Carlos. Many European countries have still shadowy claimants to royalty whom their followers would fain regard as substantial disputants for the crown, but whom the outer world looks upon as mere spectral curiosities. Many of us can remember how the streets of West End London were often visited by a singular and picturesque-looking personage who was supposed to insist upon his claims as the last of the legitimate Stuarts of the English succession. But the regions of Piccadilly and St. James's Street and the parks did not concern themselves much about the nature of his pretensions, and only regarded him with much the same kind of curiosity as might have been given to the leading figure in the recent Agapemone scandal. We all know that there is to this day a certain number of educated Englishmen and Englishwomen who do homage to a Bavarian princess as the genuine and legitimate sovereign of England. But Don Carlos has not even yet come to be considered as a mere shadow among the shadows of a past legitimacy. He still is an actual influence; his name might even yet become a name to conjure with if any unexpected crisis were to arise in the affairs of Spain, and even the most practical politicians cannot fail to take account of his possible influence. His son and heir, Don Jaime, now holds rank in the Russian army, and of him I have some distinct and interesting personal recollections. Many years ago, when he was still only a boy, I had the honor of spending some days in his company at an English country-house. The house was the home of an English nobleman highly esteemed by all who knew him, and who might have taken a conspicuous place in public affairs if he had made up his mind to devote himself to political life. Our host belonged to the Church of Rome, and was a strong believer in the principle of divine right and the cause of legitimate sovereignty. The guests at his country-house during my visit were but three in number. I think they made up a some-

DON CARLOS

what peculiar company. Don Jaime was one; a distinguished Jesuit was another; and I, who at that time held an official position among the Irish Home Rulers led by Mr. Parnell in the House of Commons, was the third. We had many delightful walks and drives together and interesting conversations at dinner under the inspiration of our intellectual and brilliant host, and that visit constituted an event in my life the memory of which is not likely to pass away. The fact that Don Jaime holds a commission in the Russian army is all the more remarkable because the nearest living representative of the great Napoleon's family is also in the military service of the Emperor of Russia. I have only seen Don Jaime once since that far-off meeting in the English country-house, and I do not suppose that if I were to see him now I should be able to trace much likeness to the boy whom I so well remember.

The living Don Carlos has had an active time of it since the days of the sixties. The struggle which he carried on in Spain, beginning during the life of the short-lived republic, is well described as the Four Years' War, and only came to an end in 1876. Then Don Carlos set out on a course of travel, passed through France to England, spent some time in London, where his tall and stately figure and handsome, dignified face were greatly admired, and made a tour in the United States and Mexico. Having no taste for a life of ease, he took service with the Russian army in Turkey during the war of 1877 and led a brilliant charge at Plevna, for which he was rewarded with a special decoration by the Russian Emperor. Since then he has visited India, and more lately still made a tour through South America. Don Carlos certainly must be admitted to have made the very most of his time and his opportunities in the active work of life. It used to be said during the sixties of the late Prince Napoleon, whose love of yachting and travel carried him through every accessible part of the world, that if everything else should fail him he could at all events set up as a teacher of geography. But although I do not by any means believe the common reports which long prevailed about Prince Napoleon's want of courage, it is certain that he did not seek for and obtain so many personal opportunities of studying the business of war as those which have come to the lot of Don Carlos.

It must not be forgotten that Don Carlos might, if he thought fit, claim to be regarded as the living representative of the House of Bourbon in France. Indeed, there is still an ever-reviving interest among those who study dynastic complications as to the possibility of some crisis arising in the affairs of France which might tempt the legitimists to make a new effort and put forward Don Carlos as the representative of their claims. It is quite certain that at more than one season of political commotion in France some of the devoted legitimists made approaches to Don Carlos with the hope of inducing him to put himself forward as a claimant for that relic of antiquity, the Bourbon crown of France. But it is also certain that Don Carlos has never given any encouragement to the proposals for such an enterprise. He has seen too much of the world; he has taken account too closely of the modern conditions which prevail over even legitimist dynasties; he has still, perhaps, too keen an eye to the changing fortunes of Spain to be easily led away by the fantasies of the French legitimists. There does not seem anything in the state of France now to show that the fortunes of the French republic are likely to bring about a crisis which might offer a tempting field for the intervention even of the most enterprising of the Spanish Bourbons. If Don

Carlos should still have any hopes of sovereignty, we may take it for granted that these hopes will be associated only with the possibilities of his own country.

We are apt to forget in the present day how deep an interest the struggles of rival dynasties in Spain had at a time not very long ago for many influential Englishmen. During the struggle between the Carlists and the supporters of Queen Isabella in Spain there were English volunteers of position and mark who took an active part on one side or the other, and sometimes found themselves confronted on the battle-field. I have a very distinct recollection of the gallant old soldier General Sir De Lacy Evans, who represented Westminster in the House of Commons for many years, and made it part of his parliamentary work to introduce every session a motion for the abolition of purchase in the army. The task was afterwards undertaken by Sir George Trevelyan, and, as we all remember, was finally carried to success by Mr. Gladstone. Sir De Lacy Evans, an Irishman by birth, had in the early part of his military career been engaged in the capture of Washington during England's second war with the United States, the war arising out of the controversy concerning the right of search. It used to be said that De Lacy Evans was strongly opposed to the destruction of the State Library in Washington, which aroused so much hostile criticism throughout the world. He took his share in the fighting at Waterloo; he commanded a division in the Crimean War, and received the thanks of Parliament for his services at the Alma and during the siege of Sebastopol, but that part of his career with which I am at present concerned is the episode created by his services as commander of the Spanish legion voluntarily raised to maintain the cause of Queen Isabella against the Carlists during the Spanish civil wars of 1835 and the following year or two. The story went that during his campaign as a volunteer supporter of Queen Isabella he had the singular fortune to capture a Carlist legion which was actually commanded by a British peer who had volunteered his support to the Carlist cause. It seems not easy to understand now how British soldiers could have felt themselves thus drawn into personal championship of either the one Spanish dynasty or the other, but it is beyond question that there were rival parties created in England as well as in Spain by the contending claimants for the Spanish crown, although England did not in our days, as in the days of William the Third and Queen Anne, engage her whole military resources in a war about the Spanish succession.

CHAPTER XIII

SIR RICHARD AND LADY BURTON

RICHARD BURTON was one of the celebrities of the early sixties. Indeed, he was surrounded by the glamour of an almost mythical fame as well as by the strong light of that fame which he had fairly kindled for himself. He had " lived a life of sturt and strife," to quote the words of the famous old Scottish ballad; he had been soldier, traveller, explorer, had passed from danger to danger, from new exploit to newer exploit, and had observed and turned to account everything he saw. But even the wonderful feats he had accomplished were not enough to satisfy his admirers, and he was credited with many adventures which had never belonged to his career, and had never been recorded, described, or acknowledged by him. He told me himself that certain episodes had been thus introduced into his personal history and continued to be narrated as part of its wonders, although he had not only never authorized the stories, but had even denied them publicly over and over again without being able to get rid of them. He had served under Sir Charles Napier in Scinde, had accomplished his famous pilgrimage to Mecca, had taken part in the Crimean campaign, and gone with Speke on the quest for the sources of the Nile before I came to know him. He had acquired a full knowledge of Hindustani, Persian, and Arabic. The leading passion of his life was his love for the East. He studied many other languages, as well as those of Asia, and was a master of many literatures.

I first made Burton's acquaintance during one of his occasional visits to London, where I had then settled down to a life of literature and journalism. I can well remember my first meeting with him. There was a sort of club made up of rising authors and journalists which used to hold its meetings at a small hotel in the Fleet Street region. It was like one of the clubs belonging to the classic days of Addison and Steele in the fact that it did not aspire to have any premises of its own and was content to have the shelter of a room in an ordinary hostelry on the evenings set out for its gatherings.

Among the men whom I remember in association with that club, and whose names still live in public recollection, were George Augustus Sala and William Black; and these two were of the company on the night when I first had the good fortune to meet Richard Burton. I met him several times during that visit of his to London; then an interval of several years took place, during which I saw nothing of him, and then in days which do not belong to the sixties I renewed my acquaintance with him and maintained it until his death. During the first period of our acquaintance, the period to which the portraits from the sixties belong, I knew in him a man very different from the Richard Burton I came to know in his later life. The Richard Burton whom I first met was exactly the type of man one might have expected to meet if one had read all the wonderful stories told, and truly told, of his travels and his adventures. If you had set to work to construct out of your moral consciousness a living picture of the hero of these experiences and exploits, you would probably have created an eidolon of the Richard Burton I came to know at the club in the Fleet Street region. Burton then seemed full of irrepressible energy and the power of domination. He was quick in his movements, rapid in his talk, never wanted for a word or an argument, was impatient of differing opinion, and seemingly could not help making himself the dictator of any assembly in which he found himself a centre figure. His powers of description were marvellous; he could dash off picturesque phrases as easily as another man could utter commonplaces; could tell any number of good stories without ever seeming to repeat himself; could recite a poem or rattle off a song, could flash out jest after jest, sometimes with bewildering meanings; he was always perfectly good-humored, and he was always indomitably dogmatic. If he thought you really worth arguing with on any question which especially concerned him, he would apply himself to the argument with as much earnestness as if some great issue depended on it, and with an air of sublime superiority which seemed to imply that he was keeping up the discussion, not because there could be any doubt as to the right side, but merely out of a kindly resolve to enlighten your ignorance whether you would or not. It was impossible not to be impressed by him, impossible not to admire him even if one had known nothing of his career and his fame—supposing such ignorance possible in a London literary club during the sixties. But it was impossible, also, not to be somewhat abashed by the supremacy of his domineering power, and I know that I should not have ventured to dispute with him even if he had asserted that in certain parts of Arabia three angles of a triangle were equal to five right angles. I was so deeply interested in all that he said and so delighted and dazzled by the flashlights which he shed upon us that I should not have had the inclination, even if I had the courage, to gainsay anything uttered by him, and was only too happy to acquire all the knowledge I could, and listen to all the stories he was willing to tell.

Then I lost sight of Burton altogether for many years, and time went on and soon left the sixties behind. Meanwhile the world was always hearing something about Burton and his travels and his doings. He had written and published many books and some translations, and had occupied himself much in the elaborate preparation of his own annotated version of the *Arabian Nights*. I renewed my acquaintance with him during the later years of his life, and met him often at the houses of friends in London. At that time I first had the good fortune to meet Lady Burton, the gifted, charming, and devoted wife whose influence had such a refining and ennobling effect on Burton's temper and manners. I have never observed a more remarkable change in the personality of any man than that which I saw in the manners and, so far as I could judge, in the very nature of the Richard Burton whom I knew in the sixties. The genius, the intellectual power, the unfailing variety of thought and expression, the quest for new ideas and new experiences—these were always the same. But the Burton of later days had grown kindly, considerate, patient of other men's opinions, ready to put the best construction on other men's motives, unwilling to wound, though certainly not afraid to strike, in defence of any cause that called for his help. I could not but ascribe this remarkable change in Burton's bearing to the sweet and gentle influence of that woman whose very eyes told the love and devotion which she felt for him, and the tenderness with which she applied herself to bring out all that was best in him. The favoring fates were never more kind to Burton than when they allowed that devoted woman to watch by him to the last. I have many bright recollections of the Burtons

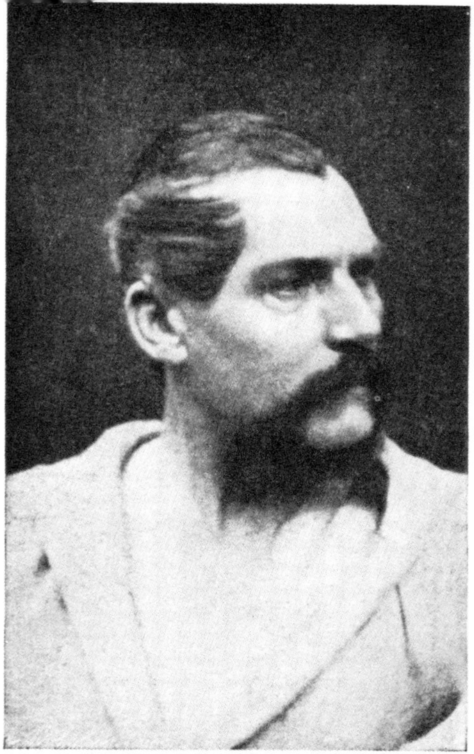

SIR RICHARD BURTON

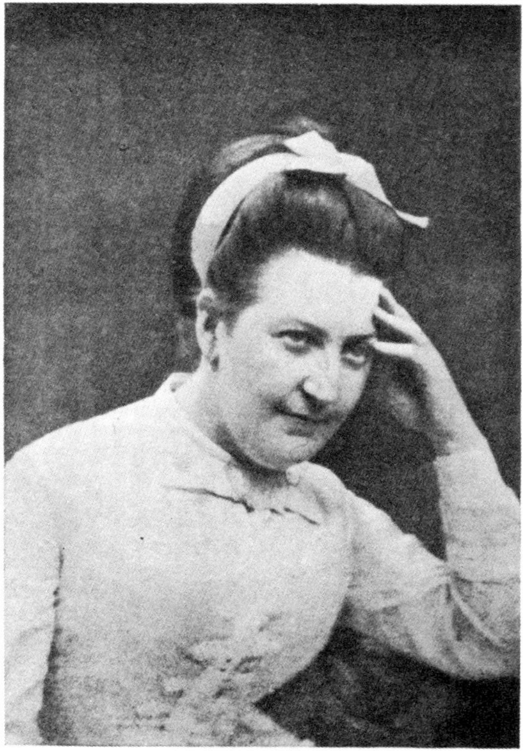

LADY BURTON

and their friendliness to me and mine. My son had a great love for the study of Oriental history, literature, and languages, and Sir Richard Burton lent him help, as kindly as it was precious, in all his efforts to gain something from the inexhaustible treasure-houses of Oriental letters. My son afterwards worked with Lady Burton in the preparation of a condensed edition of Burton's *Arabian Nights,* an edition adapted for the study and the enjoyment of the younger generation.

I cannot refrain from introducing here some mention of a curious incident which recalls with melancholy surroundings the memory of Lady Burton. My son and daughter and I were walking one day on the King's Road in Brighton when the figure of a lady passed silently by us. I did not see her face, and she passed very quickly, but my daughter suddenly stopped and surprised us with the news that Lady Burton had just gone by. Then she reminded herself and us that it could not be Lady Burton, for if she were at Brighton just then we must have known it from some friends of ours who were also intimate friends of the Burtons, and whom we had seen that very day. If Lady Burton were in Brighton, those friends would never have failed to tell us of the fact. These reasons prevented us from following the lady, who soon passed out of sight. My daughter declared that the woman who had passed us was so strikingly like Lady Burton that anybody might have been deceived by the resemblance. On our way home we bought an evening paper, and the first thing we saw on opening it was the sad news of Lady Burton's death. I do not want to attach to the story any of the peculiar significance which might have made it of special interest to the members of the society engaged in psychical research. I do not regard it as an illumination from the spiritual world. It was a strange coincidence, and nothing more but the coincidence was strange indeed, and as such is worth a record in these pages. We had not at the time heard anything of Lady Burton's illness, and our only feeling of wonder was that she should have been in Brighton just then without our having heard of it, and that she should have passed us without any sign of recognition. The reader will well understand our feelings when we opened the paper which told the story of her death.

I have not known in my experience any other illustration so impressive of the influence which a noble-hearted woman may exercise over a man of original and powerful mind as that which the love of Lady Burton wrought upon the life of her husband. Any one must have seen from the first that Burton had a true heart and a noble nature, but his was especially an impulsive spirit, and during his unmarried years he followed the sudden dictates of his impulses whither they led him. Nothing was ever said against him which, even if it were true, would have accused him of more than a certain reckless and eccentric energy, apt to lead him into all manner of wild enterprises from the sheer love of adventure. But it was clear enough that his overmastering love for movement and action, his temperament of self-assertion and antagonism, had made him responsible for some undertakings and many utterances which were not worthy of his genius and his better nature. He loved to assail the fond beliefs of other people and found a wild pleasure in the breaking of their idols and the disturbing of their beliefs. He loved to startle the timid and shock the precise. In the days when I first knew him I thought him possessed by the very genius of contradiction as well as by the genius of adventure, and those who admired him most must often have felt that he was throwing away his best faculties in the excitement of creating a sensation. Under the influence of Lady Burton the most complete change took place in these peculiarities of his, and he seemed to be inspired only by the desire to seek after the truth and the right in the work of life as well as in mere intellectual speculation. He was a stronger man in those quiet days when I knew him as the husband of Lady Burton, and his intellect appeared to do itself more justice than in the former time when he was still living for himself and his impulses alone.

Every one must have noticed now and then how by some strange process of mental grouping we come to associate in our minds two totally different personalities, unlike in nature and in no wise connected by fate, so that we can hardly think of the one without thinking of the other. In this way I find myself constantly associating the Richard Burton of my later meetings with a man of very different characteristics and a very different career, a man who was once famous, but whom the present generation has, I fear, wellnigh forgotten. The man I have in my mind is Richard Henry Horne, the author of the epic poem "Orion," which in the days of my early boyhood set the whole literary world aflame with controversy. One obvious explanation of my associating Richard Burton with "Orion" Horne might be found in the fact that during the later period of my acquaintance with Burton I had also frequent opportunities of meeting Horne. I met them both sometimes at the same house, the house of my dear old friend Dr. George Bird, of Welbeck Street, who died some years ago. But I met a great many other distinguished and some famous men at Dr. Bird's house and at other houses about the same time, and there is no one of these whom I feel compelled by some instinctive force to associate with Richard Burton. I never happened to hear Burton and Horne engaged in any manner of speculative or other controversy. Horne, to be sure, was a sort of adventurer in his own way as well as a poet, for in his early days he had taken service in the Mexican navy and had his share in many sea-fights, and in later years, not very long before I knew him, he had diversified his occupations as a poet and dramatist by going out to Australia to dig for gold. But in my mind, as in that of the ordinary world, the name of Horne was associated only with that epic poem of "Orion" which he published defiantly at the price of one farthing a copy in order thus to show his conviction that the British public would not rise to the payment of any decent price for poetry. That the light of genius was in the poem I feel well convinced, but that conviction does not do much to explain why I so often associate its author with another man of genius belonging to a different order. Horne did not show himself to my observation in any manner of contrast with Richard Burton, for his manner was as quiet, modest, and unasserting as that of Richard Burton himself in the days when I saw the two men together. If I have to all appearance gone out of my way in bringing the author of "Orion" into a chapter which professes to deal only with Sir Richard and Lady Burton, I can but plead in my excuse that the association once more came into my mind and that I followed it.

CHAPTER XIV

TWO PHILANTHROPISTS

LORD SHAFTESBURY during the sixties held a peculiar and distinct position. He was at once a memory of the past and a fresh, living influence. He was one of the most remarkable representatives of a school of practical and domestic philanthropy England has ever had. He had a heart and an enterprise for all questions of philanthropy, and had been, from his earliest days of public life, an active opponent of the slavery system in whatever region of the earth it was to be found. But it may be remembered that at one time a certain school of satirists had no easier or readier theme than the contrast between the zeal of the professed philanthropist for the emancipation of the remote negro and his total indifference to the utter servitude of some honest poor Briton at home. Lord Shaftesbury, or Lord Ashley, as he was during the earlier part of his public career, did not give the slightest excuse for any such display of satirical humor. He was sincerely concerned for the welfare of the negro, but he showed a yet more active interest in the condition of the British chimney-sweep. He was devoted to the propagation of the Gospel in foreign parts, but he made it at one time the main business of his life to obtain some opportunity of mental and moral education for the women and children employed in English factories. From the very beginning of his public career—and he entered the House of Commons in 1826—down to the close of his long and honored life in 1885, he labored untiringly for the benefit of every movement which had for its object the improvement of the condition of the working classes.

I never saw Lord Shaftesbury while he was a member of the House of Commons, and only came into any manner of personal acquaintance with him during those sixties to which the portrait in this volume belongs. I first met him in 1864, and on a remarkable occasion, to which I have already made reference in this volume. It was during the visit of Garibaldi to England, when the famous Italian spent some days in the Isle of Wight as the guest of Mr. Seeley, then a member of the House of Commons. Lord Shaftesbury was one of the many guests invited to meet Garibaldi. I had the honor to be one of the number, not because I was supposed to have any political association with the former Dictator of Sicily, but because I was a writer for a radical newspaper, and I was glad to have the opportunity of becoming personally acquainted with a man about whom the whole world was talking at that time.

Lord Shaftesbury's manners were always serious and even grave, but there was much geniality and sweetness in them, and it was impossible not to be impressed by the modesty and unvarying courtesy of his demeanor. I had heard him speak in the House of Lords and on public platforms before that time, and had formed the opinion of his capacity and his unselfish public purposes which I have retained ever since. He was narrow-minded in a certain sense; that is to say, he held to his own objects and his own ideas, and was not easily to be drawn into sympathy with purposes not coming directly within his sphere. It used to be said by light-minded critics that he never made a joke or saw the point of one, and comical stories used to be told about his frequent misinterpretation of the jocularities of Lord Palmerston, with whom he had a family connection by marriage. My acquaintance with Lord Shaftesbury was not close enough to enable me to form an accurate judgment as to his capacity for making or understanding a joke, but I can certainly say that neither in public nor in private did I ever hear him indulge at any attempt at pleasantry. I have never met a man in any station of life who was more thoroughly courteous in his manner or who seemed to recognize more fully in ordinary intercourse that equality of human beings which Rousseau would have made part of the social code. He had his political principles and he held to them, but he could never be counted on as an absolute partisan when any question arose which was not to be settled by the recognized articles of the party creed. He would not support some particular measure merely because it was brought in by the government of which he was a regular adherent. He must see for himself whether the measure was one deserving his support on its own merits, and only when he had satisfied himself on that point could he be induced to give it his countenance and his vote.

In one sense Lord Shaftesbury must be regarded as a very advanced reformer. There was a time in English public life when the more progressive section of Liberals who were also philanthropists and humanitarians differed widely from him as to the best manner of promoting the interests of the working classes and the poor generally. Men like Cobden and Bright, thoroughly devoted to the welfare of these lowlier classes and to every humane cause, were yet strongly opposed to some of Lord Shaftesbury's theories for the improvement of their condition. Lord Shaftesbury was an advocate for the intervention of the state in every possible way by which the burdens of the poor and the heavily laden could be lightened. The leaders of the Manchester School, as it used to be called, were opposed to state intervention where it could possibly be avoided, and were accustomed to maintain that the interference of the state, even when inspired by the most benevolent intentions, would be likely to do much more harm than good. The general belief of the Manchester School was that through freedom of action, so far as industrial problems were concerned, men were most likely to achieve in the end their own social improvement and their own happiness. That principle of freedom which the Manchester School applied to trade its disciples were inclined to apply also to the whole social organization. I think it must be admitted now that the principles of Lord Shaftesbury have, on the whole, justified themselves more fully by the teaching of experience than those advocated by the equally sincere and disinterested men who dreaded the effects of state intervention.

In our days we seem to have almost forgotten the theory at one time so earnestly set up that great social reforms can be best accomplished without the direct intervention of the state. Lord Shaftesbury gave up the whole of his career as a social and industrial reformer to the advocacy and enforcement of the principle which we may now regard as thoroughly established and recognized. He and his leading opponents had exactly the same objects in view, but he believed that many of these objects could be only attained, or could best be attained, through the intervention of the state and the application of state machinery, while his opponents were at that time convinced that the true and final remedy for industrial and social disorders and failures was to be found in the development of private organization and private competition. Many of the disputed questions have long been settled, so far as we can now see, on the lines laid down by Lord Shaftesbury, and I do not suppose there is now any British theorist who believes in the possibility of securing proper protection for working-men, and more especially for working women and children, without intervention and regulation by the state. I know well that Lord Shaftesbury was not intellectually the equal of some great Englishmen who differed from him on this subject, but he made out a complete case for his own policy, he carried the public completely with him, and there is as yet no evidence of any reaction against the principles he helped so effectively to establish in our social system.

Lord Shaftesbury's style as a public speaker was well suited to the objects he had in view. He had none of the orator's gifts or graces; he did not seem to have a gleam of poetic imagination; and he had no sense of humor. Fortunately for himself and his cause, the subjects he had to deal with did not call for much appeal to the imaginative faculties, and could be brought home to the ordinary mind without the special illumination of eloquence. His style was clear, his voice was strong, he used no superfluous words, when he was speaking on one of his own special subjects he knew precisely what he wanted to say, he never wandered from his direct line of argument, and he could hold the attention of his audience to the last. His tall form and expressive face were familiar to the public of London, at least to that part of the public which attended great meetings on philanthropic or religious questions, and he was as ready to take part in the business of an assembly in one of the poorest and lowest quarters of London as in Exeter Hall or St. James's Hall, or any other of the great centres of English public life. Indeed, I am ready to believe that Lord Shaftesbury found a greater pleasure in giving his services to one of the lowlier parts of the metropolis, where the whole success of the meeting might depend upon his personal presence, than in standing on the platform of some great hall which was recognized as the natural home of every commanding demonstration.

Lord Shaftesbury was by temperament and thought an advanced reformer in all fields of public life where reform was needed in the existing systems. He had supported Peel in his measure for the introduction of free-trade, and had lent his best help to many another work in the cause of political, industrial, and social progress. But he sometimes concerned himself with side issues, with some incidental controversy arising indirectly out of a great public event, and then he was apt to get astray in his arguments and to make it evident that he was not quite at home in these by-ways or unexpected emergencies of living history. The truth is that he was not a politician in the ordinary sense of the word, but was, above all things else, a devoted humanitarian. With the ordinary contests and controversies of parliamentary and political life he was really as little at home as a preacher or a professional exponent of science might have been. This was, according to my judgment, only another illustration of the noblest part of his character. It merely proved that he had his own work to do, which he thoroughly understood and to which he was absolutely devoted, and that if he allowed himself to be drawn suddenly into any other kind of work he was almost certain to find himself out of his element and to make the fact plain. No doubt it would have been better still if he had never allowed himself to be tempted thus out of his own self-chosen course, but I

LORD SHAFTESBURY

GEORGE PEABODY

could not help thinking that the occasional mistakes he made—and they were not many—were of interest and of value to impartial observers of his career because they showed how entirely he had absorbed his intellect and his energies in that wide-spreading, homogeneous order of philanthropic work with which his name must ever be associated. His fame is to be found in his well-earned title to have his name written, like the hero of Leigh Hunt's poem, as that of " one who loved his fellow-men."

I have heard and read many anecdotes of Lord Shaftesbury's ready and unvarying kindness and courtesy of manner. I remember one little incident within my own personal experience which has never been published before, and is so characteristic of the man as to deserve a place in this tribute to his memory. Only a year or two before Lord Shaftesbury's death I was walking with a relative—a little girl—in Bond Street one day. She was holding in her hand a letter from a young school friend of hers and was reading it as she went along. Some acquaintance met me and I stopped to exchange a few words with him, while she walked slowly on, still reading her letter as she made her way through the crowded street. Suddenly a gust of wind blew the letter out of her hand and tossed it into the road. The child was about to rush after it, heedless of passing carriages and cabs, when a gentleman with tall, commanding figure and gray hair stopped her in her rash course, went himself into the middle of the road, captured the flying letter, and brought it back to her with a sweet smile and a gracious bow. I came up at the moment, recognized Lord Shaftesbury, and offered my tribute of thanks to him; we exchanged some words of greeting, and my niece received his kindly notice. She has ever since felt pardonably proud of this voluntary service rendered to her with such characteristic kindness by the great philanthropic peer.

The name of George Peabody, whose portrait appears in this chapter, is fairly entitled to be associated with that of Lord Shaftesbury. It may perhaps be necessary to tell some of my readers that George Peabody was an American by birth and bringing-up, who made a fortune after years of hard and varied struggle and then came to settle in London. He devoted himself to a life of good works, and especially to improving the condition of the working-classes, and providing them with habitations where the decencies as well as some of the comforts of life could be maintained and the hideous moral and physical evils of squalor and overcrowding could be mitigated. It did not enter into Peabody's hopes that any complete reformation in the system of overcrowding could be accomplished by the efforts of an individual, however humane, generous, and rich, or even by the efforts of one generation. His object was to set up a substantial and, if I may thus put it, a monumental example for the work of other philanthropists, other millionaires, and coming generations.

In the early sixties Peabody began his operations for improving the condition of the London poor and especially the hard-working population. For this purpose he contributed altogether about half a million sterling. The millionaires of that time had not yet reached to anything like the mass of wealth owned by their successors of the present day, and Mr. Peabody's contributions were regarded as gifts of unexampled munificence. The principal purpose Peabody had in view was to provide better dwellings for the working classes and the poor generally, and the first block of these buildings, known then and now as the "Peabody Dwellings," was opened in Spitalfields in February, 1864. Other blocks of

"Peabody Dwellings" were built and opened soon after in Bermondsey, Islington, Chelsea, and other populous regions of London. In these great structures, which were all properly ventilated and made in every way suitable for human habitation, sets of rooms were allotted at very moderate prices to poor families who could bring recommendations as to their good character, and every set of rooms was a complete home in itself. I cannot compel myself to say that these huge, barrack-like erections were positively ornamental to the quarters of the metropolis in which they were set up, but Mr. Peabody did not claim to be the pioneer of a new artistic or æsthetic movement, and I do not know that the "Peabody Dwellings" were in any way less attractive to the eyes of the artist than most of the vast and magnificent piles of building erected in New York City for the accommodation of the rich. Many objections, reasonable enough in themselves, were made to the whole principle of the "Peabody Dwellings" on the ground that it is not desirable to have a great mass of human beings pent up within the four walls of one immense structure, no matter how carefully and with what regard to sanitation the interior of the structure may be divided into separate homes. Some, it was urged, of the evils, moral and physical, of overcrowding must be brought about by the mere fact that so many human creatures are thus domiciled within one vast barrack.

Undoubtedly there is a good deal to be said for this point of view, and no one will deny that it would be much better and happier for the working-classes if each family could have a separate cottage surrounded by a neat garden in a healthy suburb outside the range of London smoke and fog. But at that time no practical efforts had been made to provide ready means of access to and from the country, for working-men who had to perform their daily toil in London. The system of working-men's trains had not yet come into operation. Mr. Balfour expressed a hope not long since that the motor might soon be the common means of conveying the London working-man to and from his home in the rural suburbs, and would thus settle one great question about the housing of the poor. But in the days when the "Peabody Dwellings" began to be occupied the motor had not come into existence, or the bicycle as we now know it. Its precursor was the velocipede, a ponderous and costly machine which as yet was only the luxury of men who had money to spend, and was regarded with favor by very few of these. Somewhere about the time with which I am now dealing I have a distinct recollection that the late Lord Sherbrooke (then Robert Lowe) was regarded as a very eccentric person because he sometimes rode to the House of Commons on his velocipede. Therefore the prospect which Mr. Balfour looks forward to hopefully had not dawned upon Mr. Peabody when he began his scheme for the erection of working-men's habitations, and it was for the most part only a question whether the decent working-man should with his family occupy a well-ventilated and well-provided set of rooms in a "Peabody Dwelling" or stow himself, his wife and children, in some filthy, overcrowded tenement-house in one of the worst quarters of London. The idea of "garden cities" had not yet entered the mind of even the most far-seeing philanthropist, and Mr. Peabody's beneficent enterprise was thought by many an heroic innovation. Peabody only regarded his dwellings as the first effort made in the new direction, and was well satisfied to have set a movement going which would be sure to have imitators, and to bring about a new condition of things for the poor of London and other great cities. He may be safely credited with having thus opened a fresh chapter in the great history of the work undertaken with the object of providing decent homes for those of our population and of all other populations who live by the labor of their hands. Since his time we have had the dwellings called into existence by Lord Rowton and bearing his name, and many other benevolent enterprises of the same order. The whole movement which now sets us thinking of "garden cities"—a movement aiming at the benefit of all classes—may be said to have had its origin in the appeal made to public feeling when George Peabody began to put his humane, benevolent, and enlightened ideas into practice. Queen Victoria took a deep interest in Peabody's projects, and sent him an autograph letter with her portrait in miniature and an inscription saying it was sent by the queen "to the benefactor of the poor of London." The Prince of Wales (now King Edward the Seventh) unveiled a statue of Peabody at the Royal Exchange, and when Peabody died in 1869 there was a funeral service for him at Westminster Abbey. I ought to say that during his life Peabody was offered a baronetcy, but declined to accept any title. I have dwelt altogether thus far on his efforts to provide decent homes for the poor, but he was also a liberal giver to every public object, including arctic expeditions, which belonged to the domain of education and practical philanthropy. We have had so much splendid work done by millionaires, native and foreign, during later years that I am afraid the beneficent enterprises of George Peabody have been fading out of public recollection. I think this is exactly what George Peabody would himself have desired, for it would have much gratified his generous and unselfish nature to know that other men had followed his example with such splendid effect as to outshine the lustre of his charitable deeds.

I had a curious illustration not long ago of the manner in which the benefactor of one generation may be forgotten even by men who take an active part in the business of the generation that comes later. I was talking with a Londoner who is well acquainted with the public life and the public men of the present day, and to whom I should naturally turn for information if I wanted to know what subjects were now occupying the attention of metropolitan circles. The talk turned on some of the lofty piles of flats which are rising in London, and I asked him whether one of the newest of these, a building I had not seen, did not bear some resemblance to the "Peabody Dwellings." The name did not seem to carry any clear idea to his mind, and I explained that I was speaking of the houses erected by George Peabody the millionaire. Then he said, as if some light were coming on him, "No, not in the least like that—you mean that great big house erected long ago in Kensington—but I don't think the name was Peabody." Some further talk showed that he had forgotten all about George Peabody, and thought I was referring to the great house built by the once famous Baron Grant, whose career did not in the least resemble that of the American philanthropist. My friend, to be sure, was not of the elder generation, but it was none the less strange to me that he had forgotten George Peabody, and remembered Baron Grant.

CHAPTER XV

RUSKIN AND THE PRE-RAPHAELITES

JOHN RUSKIN was one of the great intellectual forces of the sixties. His influence was in its way as strong, far-reaching, and penetrating as that of Carlyle, Dickens, or Tennyson. But there always seemed to be this peculiarity about Ruskin's dominion over his public—it was the power of an intellectual influence merely, and not of a man. The general public never saw anything of the living Ruskin. He seldom, if ever, attended a public meeting, or was a guest at public banquets; he never unveiled any memorial statue and delivered a discourse thereon; he was never, so far as I can remember, seen in the boxes or the stalls on the first night of some great theatrical performance. I can remember one time, when the British Association or the Social Science Association—I am not certain now which it was of these two learned bodies—was holding its annual session, and we were all delighted by the announcement that a paper was to be read by Mr. Ruskin. I was among the eagerly expectant audience, but I was doomed like all the rest to disappointment, for Mr. Ruskin did not present himself to the meeting, and his paper was read for him in his absence. Of course the paper was well worth hearing, and well worth going a long distance to hear. But we could all read it in the newspapers, and what we especially wanted was to hear it read by Mr. Ruskin himself. That was, I think, the only occasion when I was promised an opportunity of hearing Ruskin speak in public, and even at that time I was much more in the way of listening to great men in distinguished assemblies than many or most of my fellow-subjects.

The Londoner had many a chance of seeing Carlyle or Tennyson, Dickens or Thackeray, and he had only to walk to Palace Yard on any day when Parliament was sitting if he wanted to get a sight of Palmerston or Gladstone or Disraeli. But Ruskin's was not a familiar figure in the streets or parks of London. He did not spend much of his time in the metropolis, and even when he spent any time there, the ordinary world knew nothing of his presence, and his photograph was not familiar in the windows of the picture-shops. One could hardly enter any company in those days of the early sixties without meeting somebody who announced with pride that he had just seen Carlyle in Chelsea, or Dickens in the Strand, or Tennyson in St. James's Park, but nobody ever asserted that he had just encountered Ruskin on Piccadilly. In later years of his life, when Ruskin had been elected, and was again and again re-elected, to the Slade Professorship of Fine Art, he did, indeed, deliver lectures on artistic subjects to crowded audiences. On some occasions he had to deliver the same lecture twice over, as it was impossible to accommodate, at the one hearing, all those who were entitled to attend, and he had long before this delivered discourses at Oxford and other places. During the early sixties he was not known as a lecturer in London, and the vast body of his devoted admirers could not reckon on any opportunity of looking up to him in person. But among all the eminent men of the time there was none who commanded a greater body of admirers and followers. He created whole schools of artistic thinkers,

JOHN RUSKIN

and gave occasion to incessant controversies on subjects belonging to literature and art.

Sometimes Ruskin ventured outside his own spheres of thought and opinion, and set much indignation going by undertaking to lay down the law on subjects concerning which he had no claim to be recognized as an authority. In 1862 he wrote four essays for the *Cornhill Magazine,* which were entitled "Unto this Last," and were afterwards republished in a volume. These essays dealt with subjects some of which were beyond the range of Ruskin's familiar studies, and they provoked much criticism from writers who refused to acknowledge his right of dictatorship outside the realms of art. One irreverent critic ventured to be facetious, and declared that the very title of the work embodied a motto which ought to have been a warning to Ruskin, inasmuch as the proper work of his life was to mend art, and that "Unto this Last" he had better stick. Ruskin was a born controversialist, and wherever and on whatever topic a discussion was going on he was apt to feel that he had a mission to take part in it. This was but a trivial and pardonable weakness on the part of a man who had rendered, and was throughout all his life to render, splendid service to literature and art, and the world thought none the less of him because he now and then led a forlorn hope in some struggle which was not his own. As a controversialist there was much in his temperament which reminded one of Carlyle, the same spirit of magnificent dictatorship made him utterly indifferent to any temporary repulse, and left him just as ready as ever to engage in another battle.

It is no part of my task to attempt an exposition of the triumphs Ruskin accomplished in his own especial fields and of the new era he opened in the world's appreciation of English art. A more thoroughly disinterested man never worked in the cause of artistic education. The generosity of his endowments to institutions which were helping to promote that cause was only limited by the extent of his personal resources. His brilliant, imaginative, poetic style called up hosts of imitators among literary men and women who professed no craftsmanship in pictorial art, and for a time there was a style of Ruskinese just as there was a style of Carlylese, and a style fashioned after that of Dickens or of Thackeray. No imitation proved to be more than a mere imitation, and Ruskin stands, and is ever likely to stand, alone. We have now completely passed through the era of controversy; we judge of Ruskin by his greatest triumphs and accept him as one of the best literary exponents of true art whom the world has ever known. But one should have lived during the sixties and many of the years following in order to understand what a battle-call to controversy was always sounded when Ruskin sent forth any proclamation of his creed on this or that subject of possible debate. I know whole sets of men and women whose most eager and animated conversation was founded on some doctrine laid down by Ruskin, and who debated each question with as much earnestness and vehemence as men commonly display when they are fighting over again in private life the battles of party politics. There was something thoroughly healthy in the animation of literary and artistic controversy thus created in a public which up to that time had not concerned itself overmuch with the principles and doctrines of high art. In other countries more especially consecrated to artistic culture such a condition of public feeling would not have been new, but it was new to the England of Ruskin's early fame, and the breath of that artistic awakening has suffused our atmosphere down to the present day. I think it is not too much to say that the English public in general had never taken art seriously and earnestly until Ruskin began to write, and that his influence has never faded since and shows no signs of fading.

But I am again brought back to the fact that all this time Ruskin was to the great mass of the public only an influence and not a living personality. Among a large circle of friends in those far-off days I knew very few who had any close personal acquaintance with the great teacher and could tell me what he had been saying or doing last week, when he was likely to come up to London from his home in the Lake country, and where there might be a chance of seeing him when he did come within the range of our streets. The influence exercised by Ruskin was, in my opinion, even more distinctly original than that of Carlyle. I am not suggesting a comparison of the value of the two influences, but merely considering the relative independence of either inspiration. It cannot be questioned that Carlyle's way of thinking was much guided by German thought. There are passages in *Sartor Resartus* which may almost be called translations from Jean Paul Richter. We can easily understand that this was not a conscious adoption by Carlyle of ideas from the German writer, but merely came from the fact that Richter's ideas had settled into his mind and become part of it. The influence of Goethe and of Schiller may be recognized through most of Carlyle's writings at one period of his literary career. But Ruskin's ideas are all his own, as his style is, and the shadow of no other thinker seems to have come between him and the page on which he wrote. When he avowedly adopts and expounds the theories of other men he always does this in his own way, and manifests his own individuality even in his interpretation. His influence, so long as he kept it within the range of subjects he had made his own, was always of the healthiest and purest order. The keen, artistic controversies which he set going had something inspiriting and elevating in them. We, the commonplace mortals, were ever so much the better for being taken now and then out of the ordinary controversies, political and social, the Stock Exchange, the income-tax, and the odds at the Derby, and drawn into partisanship with one side or the other in some dispute on the true principles and the best methods of the painter's art. So far as the truest lessons and the highest practice of art are concerned, it may be said without hesitation that Ruskin left England much better than he found it, and that his best influence, to adopt Grattan's words, "shall not die with the prophet, but survive him."

It would be hardly possible to write of Ruskin without recalling memories of that famous pre-Raphaelite school which was already becoming powerful in the early sixties. That school did not spring into existence directly out of the precepts of Ruskin, and was in some ways independent of his teaching and even opposed to it. But its origin and growth were part of that great artistic awakening belonging to his time. I do not intend to discuss the creed and practice of the pre-Raphaelite school, but my earliest recollections of its leaders and its influence belong to the period with which this volume is associated. Some of these leaders were poets as well as painters, and all of them were filled with poetic feeling and reverence for beauty of landscape, or thought, or of the human form. There is much rather needless dispute even still as to whether Dante Gabriel Rossetti was greater as a painter or as a poet. It may be taken as settled that his poetry and his painting were alike genuine art, and that they both belonged to the same order. I never had the good fortune to meet Dante Rossetti, but I met his gifted sister Christina, a true poetess, and in later years I had the privilege of close and enduring friendship with his brother, William Michael Rossetti. For the last few years I have been living not far from that churchyard at Birchington in Kent which encloses the tomb of Dante Rossetti designed by his companion in art, my late friend Ford Madox Brown. I often visit that grave, and am always the better for the associations which it calls up.

Ford Madox Brown was generally regarded as the founder of the pre-Raphaelite school, and although he never wrote poems, so far as I know, or published books, he had a thorough appreciation of the artistic in every form, and was a man of remarkably varied culture and keen original observation. His house in Fitzroy Square was for many years a centre of artistic and intellectual companionship for all who had proved or seemed likely to prove themselves worthy of a place in such society. I have been a good deal among authors and painters in my time, and I never met anywhere more brilliant gatherings of men and women belonging to these arts than those which used to assemble in Madox Brown's home. During the years I am now surveying Dante Rossetti's broken and sinking health never allowed him to take part in these assemblies, but almost every other man distinguished in art, to whatever school he belonged, was sure to be met at one time or another in that delightful company. William Michael Rossetti has published many charming recollections of his friends and companions in those days, and every page that he has written I have read again and again with ever-renewing although melancholy enjoyment. The peculiar influence of the pre-Raphaelites suffused all intellectual society throughout England in those days and spread itself over continental Europe and across the Atlantic. A whole host of young poets and poetesses came up whose song-notes were instinctively attuned to the melody of Dante Rossetti, just as a whole school of young painters came into being whose peculiar form of art was the birth of his inspiration. *Punch* and the other comic journals made much fun of these aspiring and imitative young pre-Raphaelites, and it must be owned that some at least of them reproduced the contortions of the sibyl without her inspiration. The stage lent itself to many a burlesque of pre-Raphaelitism, and more than one comic actor made a decided hit by his presentation of a self-inspired typical worshipper at the Rossetti shrine. Households were divided, once happy homes were disturbed by the unceasing controversies between the new school and the old. The result of my general observation was that the elders of the family set their faces against the new worship and the younger were prepared, if necessary, to go into the fiery furnace, metaphorically at least, on its behalf. It had, of course, a phraseology of its own as distinct as that of the "precious" school immortalized by Molière, and the most familiar and ordinary phenomena of life were commonly described by devotees of the pre-Raphaelite cult in terms which failed to convey any idea to the mind of the ordinary listener. I think the influence was even more marked and more haunting in literature than in painting. Perhaps the obvious explanation of this may be that it is easier to prove one's devotion to an artistic creed in print than in painting. To write an essay or a poem, supposing one has any capacity for writing, calls only for the sacrifice of a few pages of paper, while one who would paint a picture must have devoted considerable time to the mere mechanical work of the craft before he can exhibit the public testimony of his devotion.

The age of pre-Raphaelitism was decidedly full of interesting sensations even to the unpledged and impartial observer who studied it merely as a passing intellectual pastime. If it did nothing better it at least gave us a fresh subject of conversation in social life and lifted us now and then out of the barren commonplaces of talk. I am convinced that with all its affectations, extravagances, and absurdities it did much real and enduring good by inspiring the public of these countries with a new interest in the life and lessons of art. I must ask my readers to understand that in this somewhat qualified praise I am not speaking of the great pre-Raphaelite leaders and teachers in painting or literature. Such men as Ford Madox Brown, Dante Gabriel Rossetti, and Burne-Jones rank with the great painters of all time. Poets like Swinburne and William Morris created a new chapter in literature. But even the schools which they unconsciously founded, of imitators who reproduced more often the mannerisms than the artistic qualities, exercised an influence on the whole beneficial to the intellect of the country and deserve to be remembered with approval and gratitude.

Something has to be said about that æsthetic movement, as it was called, which was a curious offshoot of pre-Raphaelitism and manifested itself in mannerisms and tricks rather than in efforts of artistic achievement with pen or pencil. The æsthetic movement obtruded itself into social life everywhere and affected a style of speech, manners, and costume peculiarly its own. The ambition of the æsthete was to be regarded as a pre-Raphaelite, and he generally thought that the easiest and best way of passing off as a pre-Raphaelite was to show himself as unlike as possible to the ordinary

Briton. He talked a jargon quite his own, he clothed himself with affectation as with a garment, and in his material garments he adopted a style which presented to social life an imitation of the semi-Bohemian garb—the velvet coats, turned-down collars, and soft felt hats which may be described as the sort of uniform adopted for comfort and convenience in the working-studio of the painter or sculptor. I have said that "he" did all this, but the women who were anxious to parade themselves as disciples of the æsthetic school, and whose name at one time was truly legion, outrivalled their masculine comrades in peculiarities of dress and manner. The lady who appeared at all manner of social gatherings in long, lank, clinging draperies of faded, melancholy hue, and bearing a bunch of lilies in her hand, was a figure as familiar as it was characteristic of the movement.

The æsthetes created much amusement in their day, and it must be owned that they also aroused much admiration and not less imitation; but their day was comparatively short and they have almost passed out of the memory of the living world. The present generation can study them and their ways if so inclined by turning back to the pages of *Punch* and gazing on the typical figures of Maudle and Postlethwaite and the charming creatures of the other sex who competed with them in vagaries of dress and manner. Perhaps the zenith of their career was reached when they were set before the public in the delightful dramatic presentations which we owe to the combined genius of Gilbert and Sullivan. I hope I shall not be thought wanting in respect to the noble character and the exalted intellect of Ruskin because I have introduced some mention of the æsthetic movement into the chapter adorned with his portrait and dedicated to his name. The plain truth is that the great awakening of England's artistic life which was accomplished by Ruskin could not have been brought about without its accompaniment of blundering misinterpretation and its servile crowd of perversely mistaken imitators. Every great original movement in letters or art or political life is doomed to be thus parodied and burlesqued by inane admirers who fancy that by aping a mannerism they are reproducing a style. Sincerity is at the core of all true art, but to imitate sincerity is to be insincere and to be doomed to failure and oblivion.

CHAPTER XVI

JOHN ARTHUR ROEBUCK

John Arthur Roebuck was one of the most striking and, in a certain sense, one of the most picturesque figures of the sixties. He was especially what Americans would call a "live" member of the House of Commons. The observer did not always know where to have him, and no matter how clearly marked the dividing lines might be on any question, it was not easy to tell beforehand what views John Arthur Roebuck might take upon himself to advocate. But it was always certain that whatever opinions he held he would express them with decisiveness and emphasis, and would throw his whole soul into the support of his cause. Roebuck was a man short of stature and of seemingly delicate and fragile frame. He had a very expressive face, which gave full meaning to every argument and sentence, and he often added point to his utterances by emphatic though never extravagant gesture. His voice was clear, strong, and penetrating, and he always appeared to be addressing himself directly to his hearers, not merely talking at them or speechifying over their heads. His manner seemed from first to last as if he intended to drive into the mind of his listeners the conviction that whatever they might think about what he was saying they must listen to it and not lose a word. Now this peculiarity of manner might have had a very poor effect, and might soon cease to have any effect at all, if Roebuck were merely a man who had the art of saying nothing in penetrating tone and with emphatic gesture. But Roebuck never talked nothings, never uttered platitudes, never descended to commonplaces, and never took a merely conventional view of any subject, no matter how often it might have been discussed before.

Roebuck was not an orator in the greatest sense of the word: he wanted the imagination, the enthusiasm, the passion which are needed to create eloquence of the highest order. No flashes of the poetic illumined his penetrating and destructive argument, and we may take it for granted that no passages from his speeches will be preserved for the study and delight of readers in coming generations. But he was one of the most impressive and captivating parliamentary debaters of his time. The stranger in the House of Commons who had been fortunate enough to hear a debate in which Gladstone, Bright, Disraeli, and Roebuck had spoken might be trusted to carry away with him a distinct and abiding memory of Roebuck's speech, however he may have been impressed and influenced by the eloquence of the greater orators. Roebuck's style showed itself most effectively in sarcastic analysis of the arguments to which he found himself opposed. His natural work in debate was destructive and not constructive. He did not often plead any cause of his own, but was most thoroughly himself when showing up, in satirical exposition, the weaknesses of the cause of his opponents. Even when he encountered Disraeli, as he often did at one period of his career, he proved himself able to hold his own against that master of flouts and jeers, if I may employ towards Disraeli himself the words he applied on a famous occasion to the late Lord Salisbury. It must be remembered also that Roebuck's mind was full of ideas, that his education had been helped by unusual experiences, and that no matter how often or how unexpectedly he changed his opinions he always spoke in the tone and with the effect of one whose whole previous lifetime had gone to form the convictions he was expressing with such earnestness at that moment.

I have just said that Roebuck's experiences were somewhat unusual. He was born at Madras, and derived the impressions of his earliest years from Indian atmosphere and ways of life. While yet a boy he was taken to Canada, and lived there until he had grown to full manhood. Then he came to England for the purpose of studying law, and was admitted a barrister of the Inner Temple. At this time he was not quite thirty years old, but he had already made a distinct mark for himself as an advocate of reform and a masterly exponent of the views entertained by the progressive party of those days. He was sent to the House of Commons as representative of Bath during the first election after the great Reform bill. The reformers of Canada regarded Roebuck as one of themselves, seeing that the whole of his early manhood had been passed among them, and when the disputes broke out between the Canadian populations and the home government—disputes which were followed by the rebellion in Canada and were brought to a happy ending by the enlightened statesmanship of Lord Durham—Roebuck was appointed agent for the House of Assembly of Lower Canada, and pleaded their cause at the bar of the House of Commons.

It will be seen that Roebuck had in addition to his natural gifts an experience and training very different from those of the ordinary legislator. During that period of his political career to which this chapter has especial reference he was member for Sheffield, and long after he had been elected to another constituency

JOHN ARTHUR ROEBUCK, M.P.

From an Engraving by D. J. Pound, after a Photograph by Mayall

he was still regarded by the British public in general as the member for Sheffield and nothing else. Few men were more often alluded to in debate, and during the greater part of the sixties it would hardly have been possible for a stranger to sit out a whole evening in the House of Commons without hearing pointed reference made to something which had been said by the honorable member for Sheffield. Roebuck was always involving himself in controversy of some kind, was unsparing in ridicule and bitter of speech. He seemed to take a pleasure in rubbing people up the wrong way. Not that he was an unkindly man by nature. Those who knew him could always tell of kindly actions he had done, and despite his occasional outbursts of quarrelsomeness he kept many friendships unbroken to the last. So far as I had any means of judging, his spirit of sarcastic and acrimonious controversy became aroused only when he was engaged in public dispute, and did not possess him in the ordinary intercourse of life. At least I can offer the testimony of my own observation that when I had frequent opportunities of meeting him in private I cannot remember that he ever displayed an acrimonious or domineering temper in conversation. He was especially interesting when led on to describe some of his past experiences, and he was very happy in spontaneous and vivid descriptions of great parliamentary scenes in which he had taken part. I do not know that I ever got a better idea of the eloquence of Daniel O'Connell than was conveyed to me in a short talk with Roebuck, who had always fully recognized the powers of the great Irish orator. Roebuck liked to hear of all that was going on in the world around him, even of social developments which might appear to have little or nothing in common with his own ways of life. He was a frequent visitor to the annual exhibitions of the Royal Academy and other picture-galleries, and he could keep his place in a long talk over painting and sculpture with a sincerity of interest which would never have suggested to the listening stranger that the greater part of Roebuck's life had been absorbed in political warfare.

At the time when I came to know Roebuck personally his life was already drawing to its close. I do not mean to convey the idea that Roebuck was becoming an old man and that he must soon pass out of this world. That would only be to say of him what must be said of every man who had numbered so many years. But there was at that time something in Roebuck's whole manner and way of looking at things which impressed one with the conviction that he regarded his political career as over, that he had laid it in its grave and was composing its epitaph. It was not that his years or his physical infirmities shut off all possibility of his still doing work in the political field. At the time of his death he had only attained an age when Gladstone was still actively directing the fortunes of a great party and was looking forward with hope to fresh triumphs of legislation. Many men are able to keep up their active concern in public affairs until the moment when a complete break-down compels them to absolute quietude. But Roebuck appeared to have made up his mind that his political career belonged to the past, and to have sat in the House of Commons just as an outworn veteran sits in his fireside chair and talks of the events of passing life as matters in which he has no personal concern. But he was not one of the men who settle down contentedly to old age and find it something of a relief to be counted out of all struggle. Roebuck chafed at the advance of years, and was sometimes quite pathetic in his complaints against the process of growing old.

JOHN ARTHUR ROEBUCK

Many men who were members of the House of Commons during the last session or two of Roebuck's life must remember the struggles which some of his friends used to make in order to have his usual place on the benches always reserved for him. The rules of the House are strict as regards the occupation of seats. The front bench on the government side is always reserved for members of the administration. The front opposition bench is reserved by the same sort of understanding for the leading members of the party out of power who once had seats on the treasury bench and might come, after any parliamentary crisis, to have seats there again. But there is no rule of the House, written or unwritten, which secures a privilege of this kind for an independent member, even if he be a man of the highest political influence and distinction. One of the established usages of the House is that a member to whom for any great public services, civil or military, the thanks of the House have been voted, is regarded as entitled to keep the place he occupied when this distinction was conferred upon him. The ordinary members of the House can only retain their seats by right of priority. Each man comes to Westminster Palace as early as he can, selects the best seat he finds available on the benches open to his choice, and later on, after prayers have been said, by putting his card into a little frame at the back of the bench, secures the right of the place for that one sitting. It is, perhaps, hardly necessary to remind my readers that the House of Commons—that is, the debating chamber—does not hold nearly a sufficient number of seats to accommodate all the members. When a great debate is expected members come down to the House at the moment when its doors are first opened in the morning—sometimes they plant themselves outside the doors long before they are opened—and then struggle as best they can to secure a place by a competition that is not uncommonly rather fierce and turbulent. When a member has thus secured his seat he can spend his hours in the library or the newspaper-room, or any other part of the House, but he must not leave the precincts of the House, and his hat must be left behind him on the seat which he proposes to occupy, or else he will forfeit his right to assume his seat there when the Speaker takes the chair and the House opens its business with prayer.

It was not to be expected that a man of Roebuck's age and physical infirmities should come down to Westminster Palace early in the morning on some day when a great debate was expected and hang about the building for all the early hours in order to secure a place during the sitting. But the rules of the House are clear, and there was no other way by which Roebuck, who had not been a member of a government, and had never been publicly thanked by a vote of the Commons, could hold himself free from the ordinary competition. The courtesy of members could always allow his favorite seat to remain free for his occupancy, and this was just the privilege which some of his friends were of late strenuous to obtain for him. But the trouble was that the House is always having an accession of new members, and that the men latest returned to Parliament might not know anything about Roebuck's wishes or the privilege his friends were endeavoring to secure for him. A man who had come down to Westminster Palace at seven o'clock in the morning to secure a seat, and had hung about the library and reading-rooms, corridors and lobbies, until three o'clock, when the House met for the despatch of business, might show himself somewhat dissatisfied if, an hour or two later, Mr. Roebuck entered the chamber and made confidently for the occupied seat. Moreover, Roebuck was always setting men against him by the bitterness of his comments on something which they or their party had done, and so they were not inclined to be chivalric in self-sacrificing politeness. Therefore, there was for a long time a constant struggle made by the watchfulness and activity of some of Roebuck's friends to secure for him his favorite seat at any time when it suited him to enter the House. I can remember many odd and amusing little episodes arising out of this peculiar source of dispute which enlivened the ordinary business of the House, and were a subject of wonder to uninformed strangers in the galleries.

My personal knowledge of the House does not go back so far as the days when Roebuck won his highest reputation there as an independent fighter and debater of the highest mark. My close observation of the House only began with the sixties, and at that time the career of Roebuck as a real parliamentary influence was already on the decline. Perhaps his most remarkable achievement in the House of Commons was accomplished when, during the Crimean War, he succeeded in carrying his famous motion for the appointment of a committee of inquiry into the conduct of the campaign, and thus brought about the fall of the Aberdeen ministry and the creation of a new government under Lord Palmerston. He was always saying and doing unexpected things, and no session was likely to pass without his creating a sensation by some motion or some speech which set the public talking and wondering. His way, apparently, was to yield himself absolutely up to promptings of the moment and to express his mood in some thrilling sentence, some audacious paradox, or some rasping sarcasm without any reference to general principles or to personal consistency. He had passed much of his life in association with men who devoted themselves to the advancement of human freedom and the teaching of an exalted political morality. Yet no one could ever count on Roebuck's applying these principles to any subject which happened to be the occasion of a stirring political debate. He became an impassioned advocate of the Southern Confederation during the American civil war, and went so far as to bring forward a motion in the House of Commons calling on the government to recognize the Southern States as an independent power. There were many men on Roebuck's side of the House who held the same views with regard to the American civil war, and who were ready to call for the recognition of the South, but they were not men of Roebuck's culture or up to the level of his intellect. It was very disheartening, at the time, to find that the early and close associate of John Stuart Mill and George Grote should thus go utterly astray both as to the principles and the possibilities of the great American struggle.

When difficulties arose between the settlers and the natives in one of our Australasian colonies, Roebuck astonished most of his friends, who still regarded him as an advocate of equal human rights, by delivering a speech in the House of Commons the purport of which was to lay down as a law of nature that wherever the white man and "the brown man" were brought together the brown man was destined to disappear off the face of the earth. This might have been a very harmless proposition if it were enunciated to some scientific society, but when it was put forth in a parliamentary debate with a view to discouraging the House of Commons from adopting measures for the protection of native populations in the colonies, it could not fail to startle and grieve many of Roebuck's sincere admirers and friends. Probably Roebuck had no theory on the subject when the debate began, but as he listened to the discussion and felt the impulse to take part in it, it may have flashed upon his mind that such a maxim would be an epigrammatic and taking form for the settlement of the whole question. Roebuck was especially happy as a phrase-maker, if we only estimate the phrases on their own merits as phrases and without any troublesome inquiry into their meaning and application. He was familiarly known for a long time as the "dog Tear'em," an epithet adopted from one of his own speeches. His exaggerations of style gave great offence now and then to whole classes of the population.

At one time while Roebuck was engaged in an impassioned controversy on the subject of trades-unions and strikes he made a speech, not in the House of Commons, if I remember rightly, in which he described the working-man of a certain order as one who, when he returns from his work in the evening, first caresses his dog and then kicks his wife. Working-men in general resented very naturally this way of depicting them as a calumny and an insult to the whole laboring population. Roebuck was well justified in his vehement condemnation of much that was done at one time by the organizers of some of the great strikes, but he never distinguished carefully between those who committed or authorized some act of wrong and those who were maintaining by fair means their side of the controversy, which the wrong-doing, through no fault of theirs, endangered and disgraced. I have often seen it stated during recent years that when Roebuck lost his seat for Sheffield in 1868 his defeat was entirely due to the manner in which he had condemned the strikes. But this is not a fair description of the facts. Roebuck had aroused among a large number of his constituents a strong feeling of hostility because of the reckless support he gave to the side of the South in the American civil war, and that hostility was one of the principal causes of his defeat. Six years after, when the heat of the controversy about the American struggle had cooled down, he was once again elected for Sheffield and continued to represent the constituency until his death.

When John Stuart Mill was elected member for Westminster in the House of Commons, Roebuck declared that he would have gone upon his knees to Mill and begged of him not to accept a seat in Parliament if by such prostration he could have prevailed upon his friend not to waste any part of his life in the House. Many quiet observers felt at the time that this declaration of Roebuck's, although set forth with characteristic extravagance, represented a reasonable and rightful feeling. Mill acted, as he always did, with a purely unselfish desire to do all he could for the public service. He had been prevailed upon to enter Parliament by the earnest representations of friends, on whose judgment he could rely, that just at that time he could do no work in his study so important for the service of more than one great cause as to ally himself with the small section of advanced and enlightened Liberals in the House, and give them the support of his personal advocacy and influence. But there could be no doubt that Roebuck's friendship and admiration for Mill were genuine, and that it was entirely because of such friendship and admiration that he shuddered at the thought of seeing Mill involved in the wrangles and the political intrigues of the House of Commons. There was a strong dash of sentiment in Roebuck, although he went in especially for intellectual strength and practical judgment as the essential characteristics of a public man. Nothing, I should think, would have pleased Roebuck less than to be told that there was something of feminine sentiment in his composition, but the truth was that he often gave way to what seemed to be the capricious and almost hysterical impulses we associate with the temperament of woman. His nature was made up of contradictions to a degree which often bewildered those who had known him longest and best. One noble quality I have never heard denied to him, even by those most often brought into antagonism with him, and that was the quality of sincerity.

If Roebuck's ambition had been to make for himself a high place in a liberal or tory government he could have found no difficulty in satisfying his desire. Men without a tithe of his intellectual capacity, men who could not have compared with him as debaters, were obtaining well-paid offices in one or other administration, and were securing the certainty of reappointment whenever their party should come into power. But that was not Roebuck's way, and when he got some new idea into his head, right or wrong, he was sure to follow it without the slightest regard for his own parliamentary prospects. He was known to be a poor man, but he was never suspected of venality. The severest criticism that could be brought against him is that he was sometimes inspired by a perverse desire to make the worse seem the better cause for the mere sake of displaying argumentative ingenuity. Those who think most highly of him will always be glad to remember that the finest speeches he ever delivered were made in the support of some cause which had the approval of such among his early associates as Grote and Mill. I have not taken account in this chapter of Roebuck's written works, some of which, like his *History of the Whig*

Ministry in 1830, made a considerable mark in their time. I have been thinking only of the man himself as I knew him, the man who did not always do justice to his own highest capacities, but who must ever have an honored place in the history of English political life.

CHAPTER XVII

ITALY'S ENGLISH SYMPATHIZERS

Those who can remember England in the sixties must remember well the outpouring of English sympathy with the Italian struggle for release from the rule of Austria and the Bourbons. I have already made passing allusion to the enthusiasm aroused by Garibaldi's visit to England, and the demonstrations of welcome, private and public, made in his honor. One of Italy's most ardent advocates in those days was the late James Stansfeld, and his devotion to the Italian cause brought him into some unmerited trouble at the time. James Stansfeld was a man of great ability, and, even in the early sixties, of known distinction. He was educated at University College, London, and took his degree there. He was called to the Bar at the Inner Temple, but never did much work in the courts of law, and gave himself up to that political career for which he had unquestionably very high qualifications. He was elected to the House of Commons in April, 1859, as one of the representatives of Halifax, and entered Parliament as an advanced Liberal—very advanced, indeed, for those days. He soon proved that he possessed remarkable capacity as a debater and even orator, and one of his first speeches received a tribute of praise from Disraeli, who, to do him justice, was always ready to give a word of encouragement to rising talent.

There were undoubtedly in Stansfeld qualities

which promised to win for him a higher position than that of a mere debater, however ready and capable. He had a gift of genuine eloquence, a thrilling voice, and a most impressive delivery. He was one of the men who seemed to me to have all the promise of great oratory, but who somehow never succeeded in achieving a place among orators of the highest rank. He had the imaginative power which is usually understood to be the one quality needed to make a man an orator, and not merely an effective parliamentary debater. Yet when we think of the orators of those days we think of Gladstone and Bright, of Lord Derby and Disraeli; we do not think of Stansfeld. This kind of negative judgment must, I suppose, be taken as decisive, but I have listened to many speeches of Stansfeld's which filled me with the conviction that I was listening to a real orator. Stansfeld had always been devoted to the cause of liberty everywhere, and he was especially devoted to the cause of Italian freedom. He was a man who threw his whole soul into every movement which won his support, and he had been a champion of Italy's freedom long before the time when Louis Napoleon, as Emperor of the French, struck the first blow for the emancipation of northern Italy from Austrian rule.

Stansfeld was a close personal friend of Mazzini, and it was this friendship which brought on him the trouble I have already mentioned. In 1863 Lord Palmerston, who recognized his distinct political capacity and had some sympathy with his views on Continental politics, gave him a place in the administration as one of the Lords of the Admiralty. Soon after Stansfeld's acceptance of office the French government discovered a plot against the life of the Emperor Louis Napoleon, and professed to have discovered also that

Alla gentile Miss Cobden
G. Garibaldi

Mazzini was one of the conspirators engaged in the plot. There can be no possible doubt that Mazzini was concerned in many conspiracies, as they would have been called, against the despotism of foreign rulers in his native country, but I have never seen any reason to believe that he was engaged in a conspiracy against the life of a man, even though that man might happen to be a despotic ruler. It is perfectly certain that there were Italians, of otherwise good repute, who lent themselves to such enterprises, and the common opinion of the despotic courts of Europe was that Mazzini's influence was the inspiring force of all these schemes. The French government discovered, what was already well known to every one in England who took any interest in the subject, that Mazzini was one of Stansfeld's close friends, and that at Stansfeld's London house he was allowed to receive letters addressed to him under a feigned name.

The English public in general has long since forgotten the scandal created before the early sixties by the discovery that letters addressed to Mazzini had been opened in their passage through English post-offices, a practice which called forth many strong expressions of indignation in the House of Commons, and received the stern condemnation of Thomas Carlyle. I only refer to this old story now for the purpose of showing that it was not unreasonable for Mazzini to use a fictitious address when letters were to reach him through an English post-office, or for his English friends to help him in carrying out these measures of precaution. When an English postmaster-general, a man of the political position and importance of Sir James Graham, could have defended and justified the official opening of letters addressed to exiles from foreign states, it was but natural that James Stansfeld should do his best to protect his friend Mazzini against a renewal of the practice under another postmaster-general. It is, however, certain that the French government's professed discovery of Mazzini's complicity in the plots against the emperor's life created much excitement and alarm in England. There were two schools of public opinion in England at that time with regard to Mazzini and the Italian national cause. The men of the old school made it part of their creed to regard all Italian patriots as wild revolutionaries and assassins; the men of the new school were prepared to acclaim every Italian conspirator as an ideal patriot and hero. Under these conditions it was natural that the politicians of the old school should seize with delight the opportunity of assailing Lord Palmerston's government on the ground that one of its members was actually engaged in helping that apostle of anarchy, Mazzini, to carry out his plots for the assassination of sovereigns. Lord Palmerston was not a man to feel much alarm by such indications of trouble, but Stansfeld made up his mind that he had no right to subject the administration to any disturbance or annoyance because of his personal association with the leaders of the great Italian movement for national independence. He resigned his office in the government, acting in this instance on the same principles which always guided his political and private career. He made it clear to all reasonable listeners in the House of Commons, and all reasonable observers outside it, that he had nothing whatever to do with movements abroad or at home of which a high-minded Englishman could have cause to feel ashamed, and he vindicated with full effect the character of his friend Mazzini from the imputations the French government had endeavored to cast upon it. The whole incident only left on the public mind of England a higher

GIUSEPPE MAZZINI

estimate than ever of Stansfeld's sincerity, his honor, and his readiness to make personal sacrifice for any cause which commanded his sympathy.

The debate in the House of Commons was marked by a curious episode which created much amusement and some bewilderment at the time, and will always have interest for the students of political biography. Disraeli became quite unexpectedly the principal figure in this new chapter of the story. Disraeli spoke in the debate and condemned Stansfeld for the avowal of his personal friendship with Mazzini and his defence of Mazzini's character. He was not even content with that condemnation, but took the pains to remind the House of evidence which had been given long before in support of the belief that Mazzini had encouraged and personally advocated the doctrine of tyrannicide. The sole evidence of this was that of an Italian journalist and politician, then well known but now quite forgotten, who had published a statement to the effect that when he was a very young man of wild revolutionary ideas Mazzini had approved of some suggestion for a plan to take the life of Charles Albert, King of Sardinia, who was regarded as an obstacle in the way of Italy's liberation. The House was not greatly impressed by the value of this evidence, and the whole affair might soon have passed into forgetfulness but for the intervention of John Bright. Bright's object was to call the attention of the House to the vagueness and insubstantiality of the charge made against Mazzini, and more especially to the fact that Stansfeld could well be excused if he had not been much impressed by a story told on such authority and constructed from the memories of so distant a time. This came with a better effect from a man like Bright, whose profound, conscientious convictions were recognized and admitted by his most extreme political opponents, who was well known to have no sympathy with revolutionary plottings and but little interest in the struggle for Italian independence. But Bright had something more to say which gave an unexpected piquancy to the debate and freshened it with a new personal element. He went on to tell the House in his most placid tones of good-humor that nothing was more common with a certain class of rhapsodical young writers than a glorification of the doctrine of tyrannicide. Then, to the amusement of his listeners, Bright asked whether the right honorable gentleman, Mr. Disraeli, had not in his earlier days been the exponent of that doctrine. Disraeli shook his head in angry and scornful denial, and his friends cheered him lustily and called upon Bright to withdraw his accusation. Bright then asked whether honorable members had ever read or heard of a poem written by Disraeli nearly thirty years before, called "The Revolutionary Epick," in which occurred some impassioned lines vindicating man's right to slay an oppressive tyrant. This brought Disraeli to his feet, and in tones of some excitement he denied that those lines or any lines which could possibly be interpreted into the expression of such a sentiment could be found in that youthful poem which the world had willingly allowed to die. The moment Disraeli had resumed his seat Bright arose and assured the House that he readily accepted Disraeli's disavowal. He explained that he had never read or seen the poem himself, but that it had been positively affirmed, on what he believed to be good authority, that "The Revolutionary Epick" did contain such a passage. He offered Disraeli the fullest apology for the charge he had been led to make.

There the matter ended so far as the debate in the House of Commons was concerned, but the public had not heard the last of the story. Who brought it up again to the attention of the world? Only Mr. Disraeli himself. The author of "The Revolutionary Epick" appears to have felt so deeply the injustice of the charge that he determined to republish the forgotten poem in order that its text might prove that no words of his had ever vindicated tyrannicide. The new edition was dedicated to the author's friend, Lord Stanley. So far Disraeli would appear to have vindicated himself completely and to have rendered an additional service to the public by supplying it with a new edition of a poem which had now for the first time become the subject of public discussion and of which the earlier edition had passed out of print. It then turned out, to the further amazement of the public, that the new edition of "The Revolutionary Epick" was not a complete reproduction of the first edition and that the first edition did contain certain words amply justifying Mr. Bright's statement. In the first edition there was a somewhat magniloquent passage about the glory and freedom of classic Rome, and in this passage two lines declared that:

> "The bold Brutus but propelled the blow
> Her own and nature's laws alike approved."

Here was, beyond all question, something distinctly resembling a justification of tyrannicide. But no such lines appeared in the new edition, published by its author with the proclaimed purpose of proving that he had never deserved the accusation. How was this? Disraeli said in his preface to the new edition that it was printed from the only copy in his possession, "which with slight exceptions was corrected in 1837, when after three years' reflection I had resolved not only to correct but to complete the work." He added, "the corrections are purely literary." It would be impossible, when we consider that the sole occasion for the new edition was the controversy about tyrannicide, to believe that Mr. Disraeli regarded the omission of the lines about the bold Brutus as a purely literary correction. We can all understand that these lines were left out when the amended edition appeared in 1837, and that as Disraeli had only that version in his library when he started the final edition he may have forgotten all about the bold Brutus and the blow which nature's law approved. But it seems rather surprising that he should not have taken the pains to refresh his memory by looking up the first edition and satisfying himself that it contained no objectionable passage. The original edition had disappeared altogether from book-shops and even book-stalls. Some few copies remained in the hands of private possessors, one of whom, I believe, had supplied Bright with the information on which he based his speech, and there were also, according to regulation, one or two copies in the British Museum which were eagerly sought after during many days by curious inquirers. No doubt Disraeli had forgotten the lines in the first edition, but the whole world fell to wondering why, before issuing a new edition to prove that he had not uttered certain sentiments, he did not visit the British Museum, get hold of the original version, and see whether it did or did not contain the lines which made the subject of the controversy. Such an unlucky piece of forgetfulness might have injured the reputation of another public man, but no one ever seemed to take Disraeli quite seriously or to hold him responsible for freaks of memory or casual inaccuracies of narrative.

During the debate on Stansfeld's connection with Mazzini, Gladstone uttered a sentence which I remember impressed me deeply at the time. Gladstone was repudiating earnestly the imputations made against Stansfeld and against Mazzini, and in the course of his speech he said with emphasis, "Mr. Speaker, I never saw Signor Mazzini." Gladstone's purpose in making this statement was merely to show that he was not influenced by any feeling of personal friendship to Mazzini, but the statement impressed me in a different way. I knew that Mazzini had spent a large part of his exiled life in London. I knew that he had lived there as a poor man and had all the time endeavored to render whatever assistance he could to his yet poorer countrymen in the lowliest parts of the English metropolis. During all that time Gladstone had been one of the most conspicuous among the English friends and champions of Italian liberty, and yet it was plain that Mazzini had not tried to win Gladstone's favor or even to make his acquaintance, had never put himself in Gladstone's way, nor sought any benefit at his hands. This was a new evidence added to many other evidences I had already received of Mazzini's modest and retiring ways where his own personality was concerned, and of the unselfish devotion with which he gave himself absolutely up to the cause of his country. There were many passages of Mazzini's public career which one could not but regret and condemn, and one was sometimes forced into a sort of hostile mood by the extravagance of enthusiasm with which many of Mazzini's English worshippers followed his sayings and doings at that time, but everything I knew or heard concerning Mazzini only bore additional testimony to the unselfishness, the purity, and the truthfulness of his character.

At the time of the Stansfeld controversy it was openly asserted by some speakers and writers that Mazzini was concerned with Orsini in the attempt made to assassinate the Emperor of the French in the Rue Lepelletier, Paris, in January, 1858. Apart from my personal conviction that Mazzini was utterly incapable of sanctioning such a scheme, I had reasons of a more particular kind for disbelieving the assertion. Not long before the attempt made on the life of Louis Napoleon, Orsini, a political convict who had escaped from an Austrian prison, came over to Liverpool, where I was living, and delivered lectures there. He was then known only as an Italian patriot who had been sentenced to imprisonment because he strove for his country's independence; he had always borne a high personal character, and nobody in England could have supposed him likely to take a part in schemes for assassination. He met with a cordial reception in Liverpool and made many personal friends there among all political parties, and I had several opportunities of meeting and talking with him. We spoke more than once of Mazzini, and I was surprised to find that Orsini expressed himself in terms of dislike and almost of disdain concerning the man whom we all then regarded as the leader of the movement for Italian independence. So far as I could understand Orsini's objection to Mazzini it was that Mazzini was too scrupulous and too timid in his policy, that he shrank from bold attempts, and was more likely to mar than to make any fresh and original scheme for the accomplishment of the national purpose. I could not help thinking at the time, and ever since, that the reason Orsini felt that dislike for Mazzini was just because Mazzini would have nothing to do with plans of tyrannicide, such as the murderous attempt in the Rue Lepelletier to which his enemies professed to believe he gave his sanction and co-operation.

The reputation of James Stansfeld suffered in no sense from the absurd attempt made to associate him with the evil doings of Italian conspirators. He held many high offices under liberal administrations, and I believe that towards the close of his political career he was offered a peerage, which he decisively refused. Stansfeld had no ambition in that way. I do not believe that he was during the course of his life ever influenced by personal ambition. The noble disinterestedness of his nature and his absolute devotion to great principles made him, in a certain sense, an unsatisfactory member of an administration. A man who wants to get on in political life and to rise from step to step in an administrative career must be prepared to make a sacrifice, at least a temporary sacrifice, now and then of some cause to which he has pledged himself. There is a particular movement he has long been devoted to, but which it may not suit the purposes of the government he holds a place in to satisfy by some legislative measure. If he wants to get on he must wait for the convenience of his leader and his other powerful colleagues and must be content to see the measures he specially desires to promote set aside for session after session, and left perhaps without any hope of an early introduction.

Stansfeld was not a man who could enter into the spirit of compromise so completely as to accept such conditions of office. There were three or four great public questions he was especially interested in, and the promotion of these was of far greater importance to him than the success of any government, or than any advantage to his own political career. I know that on one occasion when Stansfeld was offered a high position in a new liberal government he made it a condition, before accepting the offer, that he should be held quite free to advocate in the House of Commons, and from his place on the treasury bench a cause not then regarded with much favor by the leading men on either side of the House. His position was clear. He would support every measure introduced by a liberal or a conservative government if he believed it to be for the public welfare, but he would not consent, for the convenience of an administration, to withhold his public support from any such measure. He was not a pliable man, and when he had set his heart on the promotion of a movement he could not be prevailed upon to wait in silence for an indefinite time until its advocacy might find an opportunity acceptable to his political chief. Therefore he began to be less anxious, as the years went on, to hold office, and more inclined to devote himself freely and unreservedly to the advocacy of the measures with which his deepest convictions were associated. Men who could not be compared with him for political ability, for wide and varied reading and information, or for eloquence, rose to higher political positions than he, and he looked on with perfect serenity and never started any opposition to a government because it had not given him one of its highest places. Yet in every department which had been put in his charge he had proved himself endowed with genuine administrative capacity, and he was beyond question one of the most eloquent speakers in the House of Commons. Every one who knew him found his society delightful, and all who were his friends must have felt proud of his friendship. He was modest and unassuming in manners, a lover of literature and art, yet his house was always a centre of intellectual companionship, and his zeal for any one cause never made him forget that other men had other causes also worthy of his interest. In one sense at least James Stansfeld realized his highest ambition—he had been able to render invaluable service to every cause on which he had set his heart.

The portrait of Peter Alfred Taylor comes in the

natural sequence of companionship immediately after that of James Stansfeld. Peter Taylor was Stansfeld's brother-in-law, was, like him, a member of the House of Commons, and was associated with him in all or almost all great public questions. He was not endowed with the brilliant qualities of Stansfeld, but he was a thoughtful and a capable man who might have won a distinguished position in parliamentary debate if he had devoted himself to the steady cultivation of such gifts as he had for public speaking. But I do not think that Taylor ever quite put his heart into the business of parliamentary life, that he enjoyed the debates merely as debates, or that he would have cared to spend his days and nights in the House of Commons if it were not that he had some measures of legislation especially at heart to which he felt compelled to devote his whole attention. He was a good speaker, with a good manner, and when he addressed the House he was always able to command the attention of his more thoughtful listeners. But he never made success the object of his ambition, and he never made a speech unless he had something to say which he feared might be left unsaid, or not fully expressed, if he did not make himself its exponent. Without any disparagement to the House of Commons it may be said that this is not exactly the spirit which must actuate a man who is ambitious to become a successful debater. A member who wishes to become a leading debater must make use of the House as his training-ground, and must be prepared to cultivate very often his own faculties for debate at the expense of his audience. Of course a man endowed with a gift of real eloquence can always assert his position no matter at what rare intervals he chooses to address the House, and no matter how little interest he may take in its ordinary proceedings. But Peter Taylor was not a man of this order, and he had not the ambition or the inclination to regard the House as the training-ground for a rising debater. He devoted himself especially to the advocacy of two or three reforms, one of which was the abolition of flogging in the army and navy. He brought forward every session a motion on these subjects. He was an advanced Liberal, an advocate of the cause of liberty at home and abroad, and although he never really enjoyed the life of the House, he never absented himself from the division lobby when a vote had to be taken which concerned a question belonging to such spheres of politics. But he was not a man upon whom the whips of any party could always safely reckon; he would vote against a liberal government just as readily as against a tory government if the liberal leaders brought in a measure, large or small, of which he conscientiously disapproved.

Fortunately for himself Peter Taylor had no particular reason for desiring to be of service to any administration. He had no ambition to obtain office in a ministry, and he was endowed with ample private means. He had during the earlier years of my friendship with him a delightful abode not far north of the park, but which might have been miles away from London so far as its appearance and its immediate surroundings were concerned. It was a fine old mansion, which looked as if it might have been in ancient days a monastic building of some kind, and it was surrounded by an extent of garden and shrubbery like manorial grounds. Peter Taylor and his wife, who was a woman of intellect and culture, loved above all things to gather around them the society of interesting people from all parts of the world. They used to have frequent gatherings in this delightful old home during each London season, and there any one who had the good fortune to be a regular visitor was sure to meet with distinguished authors, artists, politicians, teachers of science, and philanthropists from every civilized land. I am not likely ever to forget some of the evenings I passed in that house. In later years the house itself and the grounds had to yield to the advances of what I suppose we are bound to regard as civilization. Probably some railway company obtained legislative authority to run a line through that part of the metropolis. I do not know what actually happened, because the change took place during a prolonged stay of mine in the United States, but the result was that the house and the grounds underwent a process of transformation, and when I next became a visitor to the Taylors they were settled in a fine and spacious flat in the Victoria region of London. The hospitality of the Taylors had, however, suffered no change, and the same interesting and delightful gatherings were to be found in the up-to-date flat as we had been accustomed to find in the old-fashioned and picturesque abode. If Peter Taylor and his wife had any personal ambition, it was the ambition which certainly could not be regarded as in any sense mean or ignoble, to be surrounded by brilliant and eminent or at all events rising and promising men and women. It was always their kind and generous way to look out for merit before it had yet won general recognition, and I can call to mind the names of many men and women who have since risen to fame in letters or art or politics who were wholly unknown to the public at large when I first met them under the hospitable roof of the Taylors. But I feel bound to say that the strongest ambition of Peter Taylor and his wife was the ambition to render substantial service to every public movement which commanded their devotion, and to help all fellow-creatures who deserved and could benefit by their judicious and generous assistance. Peter Taylor made for himself no lasting name in parliamentary or public life, but I think I may fairly say of him as I have said of his brother-in-law, James Stansfeld, that he realized his highest ambition by rendering service to many a great cause.

Another name I associate with James Stansfeld is that of Emilie Ashurst Venturi, a lady who was connected with his family by marriage. Madame Venturi was an Englishwoman by birth, daughter of Mr. W. H. Ashurst, who belonged to an eminent firm of London solicitors. She married an Italian, Carlo Venturi, a Venetian who had left Italy because he could not endure the severity with which the Austrian government, then in dominion over his part of Italy, was endeavoring to suppress every patriotic effort for Italian unity and independence. Madame Venturi and her husband settled in London after having lived for some years in Italy, working as well as they could for every patriotic movement. I only knew her in later years after the death of her husband. She then had her home in Carlyle Square, Chelsea, and she loved to gather around her all who were in sympathy with her cause or with any cause in which she took a deep interest. It was a pleasure to her also to welcome in her house men and women who had distinguished themselves, or who seemed worthy of acquiring distinction in art or letters or science, for she did not limit her circle of friendships to those who worked in the political field.

I had the good fortune to be numbered among her acquaintances, and thus I met many men and women who had won for themselves eminent names. I remember that it was at her house I first had the honor of meeting M. Yves Guyot, the famous French journalist, author, and statesman, who held a high place in several

French administrations. Madame Venturi was a charming woman in every sense, and the sincerity of her nature showed itself transparently in her conversation as well as in her actions and her life. I felt a peculiar sympathy with her because of the deep and earnest interest she always took in the efforts of Irishmen to obtain for their country a system of government which should recognize their national claims for self-rule in all that related to the domestic affairs of Ireland. She felt a strong admiration for Charles Stewart Parnell, and expressed it frankly at a time when such a sentiment was least likely to secure for her the favor or even the toleration of that vague class which we are accustomed in England to call "society." There were even then a great many advanced English Liberals who could enter as cordially into her feelings towards Ireland as towards Italy or Poland. I have heard her say more than once that she regarded Parnell as a second Mazzini. After her death M. Yves Guyot paid an eloquent tribute to her disinterested and noble life. "Her death," he said in a published letter, "carries away something of myself; it is a diminution of my being." Then he goes on to say: "In my moments of melancholy and incertitude I will reread the marvellous letters which she wrote to me so often, and in which she treated with the independence which gave them their confidential character all contemporary questions and the great problems of the past and the future. They reveal a logical grasp, a play of fancy, an animation, a thrilling charm which make them masterpieces without models in the past. Her thought had the solidity, keenness, and brilliancy of the diamond."

Madame Venturi was a devoted friend and admirer of Mazzini, many of whose writings she translated into English. She had come to know him in the days of her girlhood, when Mazzini used to be a constant guest at her father's house—a house which I have heard Mazzini was in the habit of calling his English home. An intimate friend of Madame Venturi has lately been kind enough to place at my disposal a reminiscence which brings together the names of Mazzini and Madame Venturi, and contributes what I believe will be a new idea to most English students of Dante, and even to many of Dante's own compatriots. Mazzini was a most enthusiastic and appreciative admirer of Dante, about whom he had written much, and Emilie Ashurst had followed him in his studies of Italy's supreme poet. One evening a discussion arose in Mr. Ashurst's house as to the meaning of the passage in canto iii. of the *Inferno,* which describes Dante and Virgil passing through the regions where abode the souls of those who had taken part neither with God nor with Satan, but had lived for themselves alone. Dante tells that among these he saw and recognized "the shadow of him who from cowardice made the great refusal." Many theories have been maintained by Italian and other scholars as to the identity of this unhappy man. The theory most generally accepted is that he was Pope Celestine the Fifth, who abdicated within a year of his election in 1294, and whom the poet was supposed to have regarded with great disfavor because of his withdrawal from the responsibilities of his position at a period of great stress and danger. I need not enter into any consideration of the other theories which have been raised and ingeniously defended. The friend who has supplied me with some interesting facts in Madame Venturi's life tells me that Mazzini regarded none of the explanations as quite satisfactory, and that he had sought in vain for a character in history whom the passage fitted. Emilie Ashurst at last ventured on a suggestion of her own. "I believe," she said, "that Dante means Pontius Pilate, and there is no mention of him elsewhere in the poem." Thereupon Mazzini exclaimed: "You are right—without a doubt you are right! I am surprised that this has not been made clear before." Mazzini became intensely interested by this suggestion, and the more he thought over it the more he became convinced that Emilie Ashurst had rightly divined the meaning of the passage. The friend to whose kindness I am indebted for this anecdote describes the personal appearance of Madame Venturi in her younger days. "Not one of her features, except the forehead, could be called beautiful, but their harmony irradiated them with a subtle beauty that never waned. A wealth of hair, black in youth and silvery white in later years, was drawn back from a forehead that noted great intellectual powers, and well-marked eyebrows lent additional character to eyes whose direct, honest, fearless gaze made a lasting impression upon almost all with whom she came in contact. Few persons wholly forgot Madame Venturi even after a casual meeting, for some one of her many gifts was sure to show itself and cause the stranger to feel that he had encountered an unusual mind." I can well endorse the words of this last sentence. From my first meeting with Madame Venturi I formed an impression of her which I knew could not well be effaced, and the more often I saw her the more distinctly I became impressed by her artistic capabilities, her noble nature, her wide sympathies, and her force of character.

There were many questions in which Madame Venturi showed a warm and active interest concerning which I was not in full sympathy with her views, but I could none the less recognize the force of her arguments and admire her resolute purpose. She was one of the earliest advocates of woman's emancipation—in this she had my fullest concurrence—and she advocated with consistency and indomitable perseverance the opening up, as far as possible, of every career to women. She maintained, in fact, just the same principles regarding woman's emancipation which were expressed with such convincing force and eloquence by John Stuart Mill. Not even the authoress of certain once famous articles could seriously have contended that the sweet and modest Madame Venturi belonged to the order of "the shrieking sisterhood," or that her ambition was to induce women to unsex themselves, as the phrase went, or to attempt any work incompatible with the first and most sacred duties of womanhood. It might well be argued that Madame Venturi was herself a perfect type of noblest womanhood. It was a high privilege to know such a woman, and her memory is sure to be a lasting and an elevating influence for all who had the good fortune to come within the sphere of her guidance and her inspiration.

Another portrait properly belongs to this group. It is that of Jessie White Mario, an Englishwoman who married an Italian and devoted herself with enthusiasm to the advocacy of the Italian cause. She had a remarkable eloquence and became a regular lecturer on behalf of the cause. At one time she used to draw large audiences in London and in many cities and towns of Great Britain. I have a distinct recollection of some lectures I heard her deliver, and I was greatly impressed by her power of expression and her admirable elocution. She had the gift of making the tones of her voice correspond in every word and note with the feelings she desired to express, and she threw a certain poetic charm into passages which, if spoken by another, might have seemed but commonplace declamation. I had only a slight and passing acquaintance with her, but she impressed me as I have seldom been impressed by any of the women lecturers, many, indeed, in number, to whom I have listened in this country and the United States. Her career was especially characteristic of the epoch I am now endeavoring to illustrate, and she is well worthy of any tribute which can be paid to her by the presentation of her portrait in this chapter.

CHAPTER XVIII

STARS THAT ROSE IN THE SIXTIES

THESE portraits from the sixties illustrate hardly any career more interesting and more peculiar than that of James Abbott McNeill Whistler, the artist and art-controversialist who first began to exhibit his pictures at the Royal Academy in 1859 and settled in London in 1863. The merits of Whistler's pictures are too well known, the controversies to which they gave rise are too familiar, and the school he may be said to have founded is still too much of a living influence to require any description from me. I feel inclined rather to speak of the man himself as I knew him than to discuss the peculiar qualities of his art. I first made his acquaintance at the house of George Henry Boughton, the distinguished painter and academician, and I had the good fortune to be often in his society until he ceased to be a resident of London. Whistler was an American by birth; he was born at Lowell, Massachusetts, but he soon made himself a citizen of the world, and was as well known personally in Paris and London as in his native land. While studying art in Paris he was a companion of George du Maurier, who long afterwards gave some highly amusing pictures or caricatures of him in *Trilby*.

Whistler was a controversialist by nature both in public and in private, and he never got hold of a new idea in art or letters which he did not succeed in turning into a subject of keen controversy. He was a humorist and a wit, and had the readiest and happiest gift of artistic phrase-making. He was not content to paint a picture according to his own principle of art, but he must also endeavor to found a school for the propagation of that principle which he believed to be initiated and illustrated by his style of painting. I have said that he was a humorist, but I cannot help remembering that Thackeray defined humor as the union of love and wit, and Whistler was certainly somewhat too acrid to be a master of humor in that genial sense. Nevertheless I believe that many even of his sharpest sayings had in them much of the quality of humor as well as of mere wit. Some of them became almost proverbial, and passed into the ordinary conversation of society, where they were often quoted by men and women who had no clear recollection as to the source from which they came. He soon formed around him in London a whole school of artistic admirers, men and women, the essential article of whose faith was not merely that Whistler was a true artist, not merely that he was a great artist, but that he was the first and only true and great artist who had ever condescended to teach poor humanity how to reproduce atmosphere and color, light and shadow, form and substance on canvas or paper. I think Whistler himself was often amused by their extravagance of praise, but he certainly encouraged it, perhaps for the fun of the thing.

Whistler's "Ten o'Clock Lecture" was at one time a recognized institution in all that part of society which professed to make art one of its cherished fashions. The "Ten o'Clock Lecture" was a discourse given by Whistler on some subject which just then happened to command his attention, and he appointed the ten o'clock hour as a time suitable to the dining arrangements of the fashionable public. Each lecture was an exposition by Whistler of his own theories, creeds, or paradoxes, spoken in his crisp and sparkling style, and gave the listener the impression sometimes that Whistler was merely thinking aloud for the relief of his own mind, and sometimes that he was propounding puzzles for the bewilderment of his audience. But all of them had the peculiarity that they held with absolute command the attention of the listener, whether he knew what the lecturer was talking about or was trying to discover what the lecturer believed himself to be talking about. One never knew what stroke of brilliant audacity might be coming next, what bewildering paradox was to be so set forth as to pass for some profound and eternal doctrine in art. Whistler's manner was admirably suited to his purpose; every sentence of the lecture seemed as if it were spoken on the spur of the moment, and at the same time the quaint originality of many phrases and the fantasy of the startling conceits set one wondering how long it must have taken any man to arrange, in seeming sequence, such oddities of conception. The London lecture was delivered publicly at Princes Hall, but was also given in some private houses whose owners were fortunate enough to prevail upon Whistler to become for the occasion the instructor of a limited audience. I remember that I had the good fortune to listen to Whistler more than once under the roof of a genial hostess. He was always getting into some controversy or other, and there were even occasions when these controversies had to engage the attention of a court of civil law. His book, *The Gentle Art of Making Enemies,* was one of the London sensations of a season, was remembered, quoted from, and discussed for many a succeeding season, and is not likely to pass into oblivion for a long time yet to come. He used to have frequent breakfast-parties at his own home, and to have a standing invitation to them was in itself enough to confer a certain distinction on the favored mortal whom Whistler thus recognized as belonging to his select circle of friends. One thing the favored guest might safely count upon—he was sure not to meet a nonentity or even an uninteresting personage at any of these gatherings. Despite his *Gentle Art of Making Enemies,* Whistler always seemed to me a man of kindly disposition and a good friend to his friend, although it must be owned that he was rather a bitter enemy to one who made himself his enemy.

Whistler had some years ago a personal quarrel with a rising painter, a man younger than he, who had been at one period of his artistic career a devotee of his and one of his recognized followers. I never made thorough investigation into the merits of the quarrel, but I had a very friendly feeling for the younger artist, as well as for the elder, and when an opportunity arose I endeavored to bring about an amicable settlement of the quarrel. I tried to arrange for a meeting between the two separated friends, but without success. To explain what followed I must say that the world was then profoundly interested in the fate of Father Damien, who had lost his life in endeavoring to mitigate the sufferings of the victims in one of the southern islands where leprosy was doing deadly work. Some time after I happened to meet Whistler, and expressed a hope that he cherished no unfriendly feeling to me because of my attempt at pacific intervention. He smiled a cordial smile and shook my hand, assuring me that he had not misunderstood me in the least, and then he added, "I know you meant it well and I am sure you have courage enough, but remember that

Damien died of it." I need not explain this fiercely ironical comparison between the labors of Father Damien and my efforts to help my absent friend. I shall only say that there was a look of quiet benignity on Whistler's face as he spoke the words which lent an additional drollery to their application.

I have heard Whistler say many bright ill-natured things which were not so ill-natured as this. One day I met him at luncheon at a private house where among the guests was a rising literary celebrity who went in for saying clever things, and was believed by some of his critics to be not always quite original in his quips and cranks and paradoxes. This man sat at the other end of the table from Whistler, and Whistler let off some brilliant saying which was only heard by those in his immediate neighborhood. The rising celebrity at the other end of the table was attracted by our laughter, and expressed a wish to know what good thing Whistler had said. The jest was repeated for his benefit, and then in the enthusiasm of his admiration he called out to Whistler, "Oh, Jimmy"—it was thus that Whistler's admirers and friends commonly addressed him—"I wish I had said that." "Never mind, my dear fellow," Whistler blandly replied, "you will." I have no doubt that his prediction was fully verified.

It would be impossible to regard Whistler merely as the comet of a season or of many seasons, because he was undoubtedly an artist of great and original power who did work that in its way is never likely to be surpassed. But he flashed upon London society, if not upon English art, with a comet-like suddenness which seemed to foretell an equally sudden disappearance. He aroused, too, very much of the feeling of surprise and bewilderment occasioned by the unexpected flashing of a comet on the horizon. Moreover, he had a way of withdrawing from London and betaking himself to Paris or New York or some other foreign capital with a suddenness which set his London admirers wondering whether they were ever to see him again. During my latest visit to New York, now a good many years ago, I was once in a company where a young literary man from London made himself the hero of the hour by announcing that he had seen Whistler that very day on Broadway. I knew that he must be mistaken, for I had just heard from London that Whistler was still there, and all his friends knew him to be engaged in work which must keep him there for a long time. I expressed my conviction and explained my reasons for entertaining it, but one of the company promptly said, "I dare say our friend here is quite right, for the very fact that Whistler had made up his mind to remain much longer in London is the best possible reason for our expecting to see him now in New York." As it turned out my London friend was mistaken, and Whistler was certainly then in London, but the comment made on the odd promptitude of his unexpected movements was an appropriate tribute to the reputation for eccentric goings and comings which the "master" had acquired.

My last meeting with Whistler was in Paris some years ago. He had settled at that time once again in the French capital, and I believe that he stayed there for the most part until shortly before his death. I have always thought it a fitting and appropriate fact in our friendship that I should have met him for the first time in London, and have seen him for the last time in Paris. In London and in Paris were to be found his most admiring and devoted followers; in London and in Paris the best of his work was done.

In his own native country the light of his fame burns as brightly as in any other land, but somehow we do not associate his paintings and writings, his artistic theories and controversies, his humors and paradoxes, his social successes and newspaper popularity with any city of the United States as we do with London and Paris. It seems to me that if I were again to settle down to literary and artistic society in London, I should think the life there not quite the same now that it wants the fascinating, fantastic presence of James Whistler.

The portrait of Edward Sothern appears to have its appropriate place in this chapter. Sothern was an Englishman by birth. He was born in Liverpool, and in his early years his gifts as a comedian began to show, and he played for some two or three years in English provincial theatres. He then went to the United States, where he began to acquire a reputation, and made a full success when he acted the part of Lord Dundreary in Tom Taylor's comedy "Our American Cousin." When he came to England in 1861 and the play was brought out at the Haymarket Theatre, Sothern's renown was entirely that of a great success accomplished in the United States. From his first performance at the Haymarket he was recognized at once as a really great comedian. "Our American Cousin" became the talk of the metropolis; ran for more than four hundred nights at the Haymarket, and its success depended altogether on his performance of Lord Dundreary. Sothern seemed to Londoners almost as much of a foreigner as Whistler, and I think, therefore, that his portrait finds a fitting place in its present association. The play itself has no essential value as a comedy, but the extraordinary performance of Lord Dundreary by Sothern held us all willing captives. The character of Lord Dundreary would have been in the hands of any other actor an absurd burlesque of the English "milor," as he was at that time commonly pictured in French comedies and French newspapers. Sothern succeeded in making him seem a living possibility, and the London world went wild with delight over the grotesque absurdities of Dundreary. In fact, we thought nothing of the absurdities and the impossibilities; we did not stop to ask ourselves how any Englishman, noble or plebeian, could have talked and behaved after the fashion of Dundreary. We only felt that we had before us an actor who could make us believe in anything he said and did, and who, by the mere force of his genius, converted Dundreary into a living and fascinating reality.

The story went at the time, and I believe there was truth in it, that Sothern had first appeared in the part while he belonged to an American company of which Joseph Jefferson, the creator of Rip Van Winkle, was the chief actor, and that it was Jefferson who first discovered Sothern's genius and gave him the opportunity of turning it to immediate account. In the play as originally produced the part of Lord Dundreary was very small and quite insignificant, but Jefferson, who was playing what was then a much more important part, encouraged Sothern to amplify it by new speeches and fresh humors, and under his inspiration Sothern made it the great figure of the play and won a complete success. When Sothern presented the play at the Haymarket in 1861 nobody thought of anything in the piece but the part of Lord Dundreary. The wonder to those who knew anything of its previous history was how an actor, even endowed with the originality and genius of Jefferson, could have made anything out of another character in the comedy. Sothern was the great success of that season and of many seasons following. He played the part of David Garrick in Robertson's comedy with equal or almost equal success. His own part might be described as perfection; but other English actors have won success as David Garrick, while there never was more than one Dundreary and that Dundreary was Edward Sothern.

I had the good fortune to make Sothern's acquaintance, and I found him, as all did who knew him, a charming companion, a courteous gentleman, and a keen observer of the humorous side of life. It happens not seldom that the brilliant comedian of the stage is grave and quiet, not to say uninteresting, in private life, and that some of those whom he has kept in constant laughter while he appeared before them on the stage find him but poor company when they meet him in the "dreary intercourse of daily life." But any one who met Sothern for the first time, and, if such a thing were possible, had never heard of his success as a comedian, must have been immediately impressed and captivated by his winning manners and his wonderful gift of humor. Sothern was very fond of practical jokes, but only of practical jokes which were purely good-natured, unless when he employed his powers in the detection of impostures. He was engaged more than once in investigating and exposing attempts made to delude the London public by persons professing to have mysterious means of communicating with the other world, and of calling spirits from the vasty deep and other resting-places to enlighten credulous inquirers as to the secrets of the unseen. There were many amusing stories told of his achievements in the detection of such impostors in association with my dear old friend John L. Toole, who still lives to tell the tale, if he feels so inclined.

Sothern was a very social man, and enjoyed the company of all who had anything to say worth listening to whatever their rank or degree. His society was much sought after in London, but he allowed himself to be sought after, and never went out of his way to obtain admission into the houses of the great, as the conventional phrase goes. The great sought after him very much, but Sothern did not become in any sense the spoiled child of fashion. One never heard him telling about his invitations to the duke's or the compliments paid to him the other day at dinner by that delightful duchess. He was above all things an artist in heart and soul, and the one regret of many of his friends was that he never had an opportunity of proving his capacity for the performance of greater and nobler comedy than could be found in the character of Lord Dundreary. I never saw him in any part but that of Lord Dundreary or David Garrick, and I suppose the same might be said by the vast majority of those who remember him as an actor. But there was quite enough of difference, artistic and realistic, between Dundreary and David Garrick to make it clear that Sothern was not intended by nature to be merely a one-part actor. I always felt that what I saw of Sothern was but one side of a many-sided capacity, and my admiration for his dramatic gift was blended with a keen regret that I never had a chance of estimating the full range and variety of his powers. It was as if some great musician were compelled by despotic edict to play nothing but one or at most two pieces of music, and to go through the whole of his life without allowing his audiences the chance of enjoying any other display of his art.

We must all have observed instances, in many an artistic career, of a man who has struck out a new line for himself which captures the public admiration, and although he knows he is capable of better things, finds that his patron the public will have nothing from him but a repetition of this one kind of work. I was talking quite lately to a very promising and rising young artist with the pencil who suddenly attracted great attention by his humorous pictures of cats in all manner of fantastic illustrations. He told me that he felt sure he could do other and better work, but that the publishers and the public would insist on keeping him to that one line of humorous art and would not allow him to escape from his self-assumed task of picturing cats. My mind went back at once to the case of Sothern and Lord Dundreary, and to many other instances of men and women thus chained to the oar in one artistic galley. The story of Joseph Jefferson, the creator of Rip Van Winkle, is perhaps the most striking illustration of this tyranny enforced by the public. Jefferson had the best reason for believing that he could play some of Shakespeare's parts—Mercutio, for instance—in a manner which might have added to his great reputation, but the theatrical managers and the theatre-going public would insist on Rip Van Winkle and nothing else, and thus he went through life, and is still going through life, as the illustrator of one sole dramatic character. Sothern remained in England for many years and then went back to America. He died in 1881, and his fame still lives as that of the actor who created out of nothing and immortalized the part of Lord Dundreary.

I include in this chapter the portrait of Fechter, for the reason that he, too, came upon England with the suddenness of a comet. He was not, however, limited by fate to the performance of one part alone. Fechter, like Sothern, was born in England, but he was a foreigner by parentage and extraction, and was brought up in France. He began his education there, but took to the stage when he was only sixteen years old and soon made his reputation as an actor of the highest order.

EDWARD SOTHERN

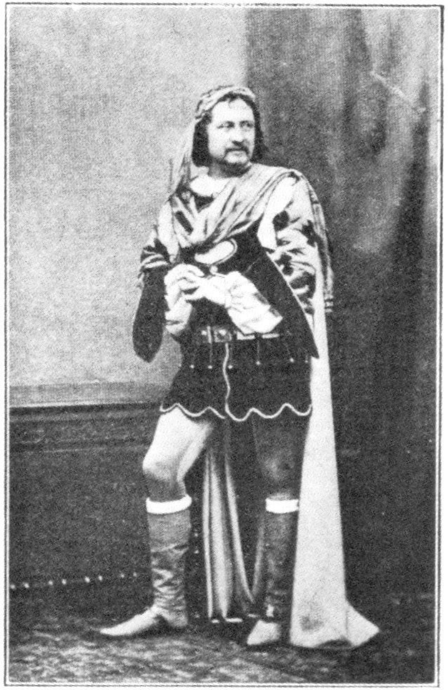

CHARLES ALBERT FECHTER

His first appearance at a London theatre was in 1860, and at that time he was almost unknown to the general public of England. The first part he played in London was in an English version of "Ruy Blas," and the public realized in a moment that a new tragedian had come upon the English stage, well qualified to defy competition in his own field of dramatic art. But his Ruy Blas was soon cast into the shade when in the following season he ventured on playing the part of Hamlet. There was much credulity among theatre-goers when the announcement was made that he was about to play Hamlet, and the general opinion was that only sheer audacity and extravagant confidence in his own powers could have led a foreigner to venture on such an undertaking in London. Fechter spoke English perfectly, so far as fluency and grammatical accuracy could make him perfect, but he had a most marked foreign accent even for a foreigner, and never could pronounce a single sentence in such a manner as to pass off for an Englishman. We did not heed that defect when he was playing the part of Ruy Blas. It seemed only natural and in keeping that the hero of a French play should not speak in the accents of a Briton. But how will it be, some people asked, when he attempts to pass off on us the Hamlet of Kemble and Edmund Kean and Macready with the accents and the manner of an immutable foreigner? The first audience, therefore, which crowded the theatre to see his Hamlet was already prepared for a complete and even ludicrous failure. There was a certain feeling of resentment, too, mingled in the emotions of the English men and women who attended that first performance. Yet the play had not gone far before every one in the theatre felt satisfied that, despite all his natural and national disadvantages, he had accomplished a great and thrilling success. Fechter's Hamlet was not the Hamlet of English tradition, the Hamlet to which generations of Englishmen had grown to be accustomed. It was not merely that his accent and manners were impressively foreign, but the Hamlet itself was something quite new to the British stage. Fechter's idea was above all things to make his Hamlet a living and natural creature, a man who, despite his tragic fate and the gloomy part he had to play, was yet a man like others, and was accustomed to speak and move after the manner of ordinary human beings. He discarded all the old theatrical traditions of measured stride and measured pause, the dramatic tones of unbroken gloom, the statuesque attitudes, the portentous, awe-pervading melancholy. His manner brought out for the first time to many Englishmen the unmistakable fact that Shakespeare had given to his great creation many moods of kindly or scornful levity, and that the Prince of Denmark often concealed his deepest feelings by a flash of sarcasm or by mere jocularity. I do not know whether Fechter had studied Goethe on the character of Hamlet, but he certainly seemed as if he were endeavoring to embody Goethe's ideas in a living form. This seemed especially evident in the immortal scene with the grave-diggers before the newly opened grave. Other actors were accustomed to stand in picturesque attitude at the very front of the stage, and to deliver Shakespeare's words with the manner of a popular preacher addressing a hushed and reverent congregation on some of the great lessons of mortality. Fechter sat for the most part on an old and decaying tombstone, had one of his legs carelessly crossed over the other, and talked to the grave-diggers in a tone of easy levity, which sometimes gave the idea that he was amusing himself by drawing them out and chaffing them for the benefit of the listening Horatio.

His attitude was that which a great French painter has embodied in his picture of Hamlet and grave-diggers. Soon we began to see that this manner of ease and assumed levity only added in reality a new depth of meaning to the whole tragic import of the scene. Here was a Hamlet drawn from nature and not from stage tradition; a Hamlet of varied mood; a man of genius and of fate, whose humor it was to clothe his profoundest thoughts sometimes in a disguise of careless indifference utterly impenetrable to such dull and commonplace observers as the homely grave-digger and his men. Fechter was also the first to introduce to the English stage a Hamlet with the fair complexion and the bright yellow hair which is characteristic of the northern peoples. This was Goethe's theory as to the outward presentment of the Danish prince. There was some ingenious controversy raised on this, and people were reminded that Hamlet's father is described in the play as having in his later days hair and beard of a sable silvered. It was urged that Hamlet could not be supposed to have differed utterly in appearance from his own parent. The controversy created some lively discussion at the time, and I leave it for the consideration of my readers. It is certain, however, that Fechter's Hamlet was a complete success with the English public, and that, for the time at least, the yellow-haired Hamlet held the stage.

Fechter played many other great Shakespearian parts and in every instance with the same result. He created a controversy which was, indeed, a part of his success, and it was impossible to look upon any of his impersonations without being captivated by its originality, its thrilling power, and its quality of fascination. Fechter became the lessee of the Lyceum Theatre, and for many seasons he was able to draw crowded audiences whenever he appeared. Then he went to the United States, where also he achieved a complete success. I had the pleasure of seeing him in New York and in Boston. In Boston he was made welcome to the great literary society for which the city was then distinguished. There was a famous club still flourishing at that time of which Emerson, Longfellow, Oliver Wendell Holmes, James Russell Lowell, and others of the Boston group were leading members. This club used to give weekly dinners, to which each member was allowed to bring a guest, and there I had the good fortune to meet Fechter and to observe the honor with which he was received by those gifted authors who were not in the habit of regarding the ordinary actor as one belonging to their circle. Fechter was a man who had read and studied much, and was able to hold his own in conversation, even in the companionship of men like those I have named.

It was in Boston that I saw Fechter for the last time, for he did not return to the scenes of his early successes, but died in a home which he had made for himself with a considerable extent of ground attached to it in Pennsylvania. His name will always live in the history and traditions of the English stage, and his management of the Lyceum Theatre did but add to the lustre which so long, before and since, illumined that home of the drama. His fame was entirely his own. He had no predecessor in his peculiar style of acting and he left no successor. Other men made for themselves in our times a fame not less great than his, but he will always be remembered for his own gifts and for the originality and the independence of his creations. If I were to define his dramatic principle I should say that it consisted in his endeavor always to reconcile the natural with the dramatic and to make the hero of tragedy seem, after all, but an ordinary human being like one of ourselves. It was a revolt against the traditional school of Kemble and some of the great French actors of the past. It has left at least its impression and its memory on the drama of more recent days, although no other Fechter has yet appeared, so far as I know, upon any stage. Up to the time of his appearance in London our tragic actors had been giving themselves up more and more to mere tradition and stage conventionality. A literary friend of mine once told me an amusing story of a tragedian then very successful in London and in the English provinces who got into an argument about Fechter's style after Fechter had made his first appearance as Hamlet and won his great success. Our British actor —I shall not mention his name, and it is now almost entirely forgotten—eagerly contended that Fechter's natural style of acting had nothing in it new to this country or from which English performers could learn any lesson. He declared that his own effort had always been to make tragic acting seem natural and human. He said that if you have only to move a chair across the stage you should do it just as any ordinary man in real life would do it, and he jumped up and illustrated his meaning by suiting the word to the action. "This is how it should be done," he said. Then seizing a chair he moved it across the floor after a fashion in which no human being in real life ever set about to accomplish so simple an act. I do not think that readers of the present day whose memory does not carry them back to the time when this discussion took place can have any idea of the utterly unnatural and ultra-dramatic style in which the popular tragedians of that time were wont to enact the most ordinary movements of human life. Our leading tragedians have now shaken off these antiquated methods, and Hamlet is no longer understood to be a creature who must follow implicitly the stage traditions of the old school even when moving a chair from one part of the stage to another. I believe that we owe much of this happy change in our theatric ways to the genius and the courage of Fechter.

CHAPTER XIX

LORD CLARENCE PAGET—THOROLD ROGERS

I NOW come upon a number of portraits which I may form into a group, as they illustrate some figures which were very familiar to all observers of parliamentary life during the sixties, and have somewhat faded from the memory of the public. Each man had in his time the impress of a distinct individuality, and those who often observed them in those days and have almost forgotten them since will find their memory come back clearly and freshly when they look upon the portraits in this chapter. Lord Clarence Paget was for a long time one of the most conspicuous among the number. During the sixties, long before I obtained a seat in the House of Commons, I observed closely the members of that assembly from the watch-tower of the press-gallery, where for one session I used to report the speeches, and for many sessions after used to comment on the doings of the House, as I then contributed leading articles to a London daily newspaper. Lord Clarence Paget was made Secretary to the Admiralty in 1859, and was from that time always closely occupied with the debates on the condition of the navy. The navy, then as now, was a frequent subject of animated discussion in the House of Commons. Lord Clarence began his life as a seaman under conditions which give him a fair title to historical fame. When a midshipman on board the *Asia* he took part in the memorable battle of Navarino, that famous and decisive struggle described by one great British authority as " an untoward event." King William the Fourth, then Duke of Clarence, was popularly believed to have stimulated it by a few words addressed to the admiral in command, scrawled at the end of a long, official despatch from the Admiralty, formally recommending care and caution, the avoidance of all rash movements, and a due regard for the non-committal of England to any unnecessary responsibility at a great international crisis. The admiral in command of the British fleet was believed to have interpreted the wishes of his superiors from the hastily scribbled words and not from the formal, official despatch. He acted upon this interpretation and thus brought about, consciously or unconsciously, the final emancipation of Greece from the rule of the Ottoman power. It is something to remember that one has seen and known a man who bore a part in that immortal sea-fight, as Lord Clarence Paget did in his early youth. If King William the Fourth really wrote the words which led to Navarino, we must set down to his credit that breach of official discipline which redounds more to his honor than any other action of his life.

In the later days, to which my own observation belongs, Lord Clarence was always a popular figure in the House of Commons. He was a good debater on his own subjects; he was never overbearing, always had a kindly demeanor towards his political opponents as well as his political friends, and after the hottest controversy was ready to exchange social courtesies with all members of the House. I have often seen him when the debate was done, engaged in the most genial conversation with men who an hour before had been denouncing the Admiralty and himself, and laboring hard to prove that the doings of his department were destined to destroy the position of England as a great naval power. Then, as now, the majority of the House of Commons always agreed that England's greatness depended mainly on the strength of her navy. Even those who were scornfully described as the advocates of peace at any price were ready to join in every effort to maintain the efficiency of the navy, because they regarded it as England's weapon of defence and not of aggression. This was the avowed principle of so great a lover of peace as Richard Cobden, who again and again declared that he was willing to approve of any reasonable expenditure to keep up the navy as the cheap defence—cheap at almost any pecuniary cost—of England's national security. No one now believes, and not many believed then, that Cobden and Bright were advocates of peace at any price. Bright, as a matter of fact, was never a member of the Peace Association which existed in those days, and was now and then rather aggressive in its insistence on a pacific policy. On one occasion, after a very animated debate in the House of Commons, during which the advocates of peace vehemently denounced the ministry on the ground that they were pushing too far their naval preparations for some possible war, an interchange of letters took place between Bright and Lord Clarence Paget, in which each cordially recognized the good purposes and the reasonable policy of the other.

Lord Clarence was a Liberal in politics, but he was an official Liberal, as the phrase went, and it would not be easy to distinguish an official Liberal of that time from the ordinary Conservative of the present day. I am now talking of the period when Palmerston was supreme, the closing years of his life, when, although still almost a revolutionary in foreign politics, he opposed a steady resistance to the movements of the advanced

English Liberals, before the influence of Gladstone had been given to the liberal cause. I remember being much impressed by the tone of the letters interchanged between John Bright and Lord Clarence, and the evidence it gave that these two sincere men were able to recognize that each was engaged, according to his lights, in the promotion of England's welfare. Lord Clarence was always a busy, even a bustling personage in the House of Commons, and he showed nothing in his demeanor or in his official conduct of the red-tapeism which used to be regarded by satirists as the essential quality of an official of any state department. There was a distinct impression of individuality about Lord Clarence; you never mistook him for anybody else even if you had only the slightest acquaintance with him. I have often noticed that there are men in the House of Commons, as indeed everywhere, whom you may see often and yet whose identity you easily forget if you remain for a considerable time without seeing them. I can recall one instance in which I committed myself to a mistake of this kind. There was at a later period a member of the House who had held a subordinate office in an administration, whom I was in the habit of seeing very often and with whom I was on speaking terms. After a general election I came back to the House, and failed to observe that the honorable member did not make his appearance there. A long time passed before I saw him again, and then I met him at a dinner-party. I remembered his appearance and his name at once and we got into conversation. I remarked that I had not seen him in the House for some time, and that I was afraid he had been rather neglecting his official duties. I saw a look of surprise and of something like dissatisfaction come over his face, and he then said he had not been a member of the House for more than two years,

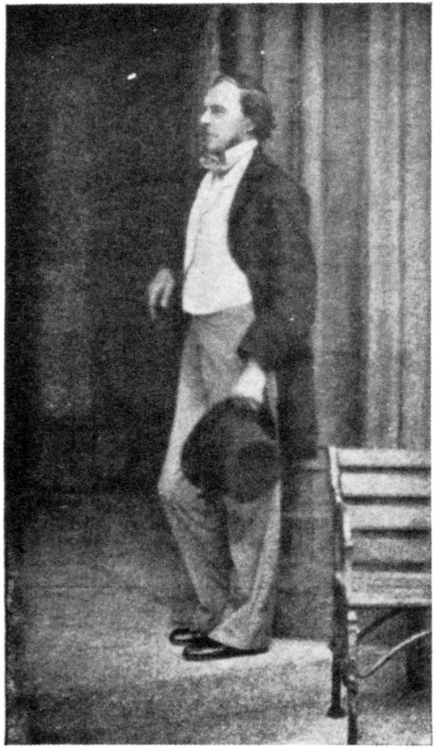

LORD CLARENCE PAGET, M.P.

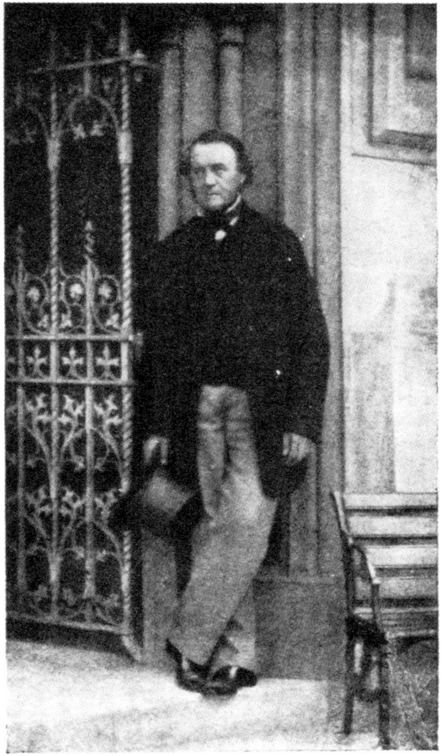

GEORGE CLIVE, M.P.

having lost his seat at the last general election. I tried to make some explanation, but I am afraid the explanation was not quite satisfactory. Out of concern for my own credit I forbear to tell his name, because to do so would only render my mistake the more ridiculous. The fact is that he was one of the men who do not impress one with a sense of individuality. My acquaintance with him had always been slight; I had associated him only with a certain administrative office and with the occasional answering of questions addressed to his department, and as I had seldom put any of these questions I ceased to think about him when he no longer held his place on the treasury bench. Lord Clarence Paget never belonged to that order of official humanity. When you had seen and heard him once you always remembered his presence, his voice, and his bearing. He could not pass from your memory. He was engaged in the command of a vessel during the expedition to the Baltic in 1854, but that enterprise was not one to give opportunity for the display of great naval capacity, even in a Dundonald, and it must have seemed a strange anti-climax to him who in his youth had borne a part in the history-making battle of Navarino.

George Clive is the subject of another portrait in this chapter. I remember him well in the House of Commons in the early sixties. He was Under-Secretary for the Home Department for some three years, and a familiar figure in parliamentary life, although it cannot be said that he made a profound impression even on the passing history of the House of Commons. He was regarded as an advanced Liberal in those days, although he was only a Liberal of the official order; but he entertained the political principles which were then considered decidedly radical. He was described in Dod's *Parliamentary Companion* as an advocate of franchise reform vote by ballot, and the abolition of church rates. It must be remembered that most of the leaders of his party regarded such doctrines as the tenets of downright radicalism, tending directly towards the government of the empire by a lawless democracy and the complete overthrow of the British Constitution. The recognized official opinion of a liberal administration in those days was that enough had been done in the way of extended franchise, that secret voting could only lead to the upsetting of all legitimate authority, and that any interference with the rights of the state church was but opening the way to irreligion and anarchy. The introduction of the ballot was then the subject of a motion introduced every session by some eccentric and uncontrollable private member whom the leaders on both sides of the House treated with tolerance or indifference, and whose annual motion they looked upon as an inevitable incident to be disposed of on each successive presentation by a merciful ministerial reply. The maxim that constant dropping of water wears away a stone had not yet come to be applied as a fact in politics by most of the leading men of either party. We must, therefore, give George Clive the credit for his views as an advanced reformer, and admit that he saw a good deal further into the progress of our constitutional development than most of those who were at the time his superiors in office. He is well entitled to a place in this collection of portraits, and his memory deserves to be rescued from parliamentary oblivion.

I do not know whether the description of a man as a Liberal-Conservative would convey any clear idea to a reader of the present day. Undoubtedly we have now Liberal-Conservatives as we had then and at all other times. Of late years we have seen in the Commons, and even in the Lords, many Conservatives whose opinions on some important question are more liberal than those of official Liberals in general. But it must have been somewhat peculiar in the early sixties to meet with an Irish landlord who boldly proclaimed himself a Liberal-Conservative. Such a man was Colonel Dunne, the Irish landlord who at that time represented Portarlington in the House of Commons, and he was thus described in the accurate record of Dod, which sets out the political opinions of a member according to the member's own definition.

I remember hearing an amusing speech, made before the sixties but brought back to my mind by this description of an Irish landlord with the political opinions of Colonel Dunne, by a man who had a parliamentary, literary, and social position in his day, who was a friend of Thackeray, and has been mentioned by him more than once. This man was Sergeant Murphy, a distinguished advocate, and the speech was delivered at an election in Cork city. Sergeant Murphy was being "heckled" by an Irish tory landlord because of his liberal opinions. A lively discussion took place, during which Sergeant Murphy made some allusion to the Encumbered States Act, which the Irish landlord seemed not quite to understand. The learned sergeant seized the opportunity, and went on to say that he might have thought, before the reply he had just heard, that there was a task opened to him more difficult than that which Diogenes undertook when he searched with a lantern through the streets of Athens to find an honest man—the task of seeking with a lantern through the streets of Cork for an Irish landlord who knew nothing of the Encumbered States Act. The delighted laughter which followed this hit prevented the perplexed landlord from making any prompt and audible explanation of his awkward position. But for the record of Colonel Dunne's opinions I should have thought it would be as trying an ordeal to find in the House of Commons, in the early sixties, an Irish landlord of Colonel Dunne's class with his political principles.

Of course there were liberal Irish landlords in the early sixties, although not belonging to the same set as that which would have claimed Colonel Dunne. There was, for instance, Richard Montesquieu Bellew, whose portrait we give, and who was for some years a lord of the treasury in a liberal administration before the date to which this volume belongs.

Bellew was an advocate of short Parliaments, vote by ballot, the removal of all religious disabilities at universities, and the establishment of tenant right in Ireland—a declaration of opinion which would sound liberal even in our own days. I have a distinct recollection of him as a parliamentary figure, although his political career made no great impression on the House of Commons or on the history of his day. He deserves a record in these pages if only for the fact that he could see so far in advance the reforms destined to come in their own good time, and in the establishment of which conservative as well as liberal governments may claim to have had a share.

I come now to a man who made a much greater impression on political and on intellectual life than any of those already mentioned in this chapter. This man was the late Professor James E. Thorold Rogers, who taught political economy in the University of Oxford and economic science in King's College, London. Many of my readers will have a very distinct recollection of Thorold Rogers, for he sat in the House of Commons from 1880 to 1886, and died so lately as October, 1890. I had the honor of knowing him dur-

COLONEL DUNNE, M.P.

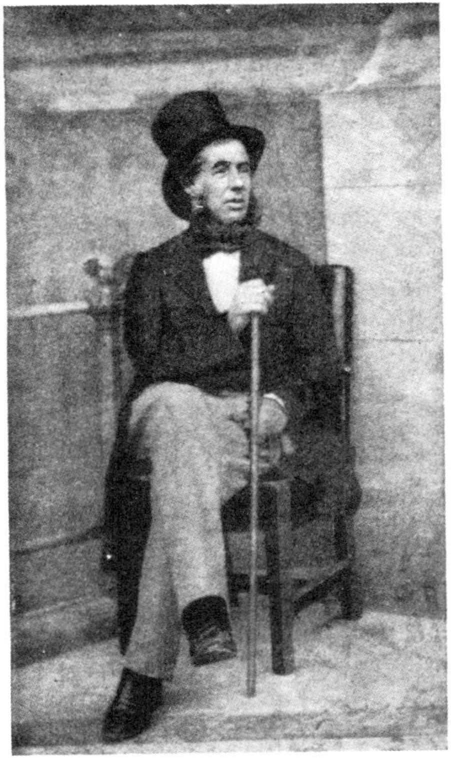

RICHARD MONTESQUIEU BELLEW, M.P.

ing the years when he was in Parliament and when I, too, had a seat there, but his fame does not belong to his years of parliamentary service. His seat in the House was only the recognition of the great services he had rendered at an earlier date to political reform and the advancement of economic science. Thorold Rogers was associated with many of the movements in which Cobden and Bright took a leading part. He was a man of the most marked individuality, and had, in every sense, the courage of his opinions. Some of his opponents thought, and said in their different ways, that he had rather more than the courage needed to sustain his personal opinions, for he was a very aggressive controversialist and a decidedly hard hitter. He was often engaged in acrimonious discussion, and generally gave his opponents much better than they brought. His education was broad and deep, his culture was refined, and he had a most intimate acquaintance with all the problems of economic science.

Bright, who was commonly accused of nourishing a contempt for university education, once declared in a public speech that even if he did entertain such a contempt he must have to make an exception in favor of men like Thorold Rogers and Goldwin Smith, who always turned their university education to the best account by making themselves the advocates of every great reform in the interest of the working-classes and the poor. At that time many of us were in the habit of associating Thorold Rogers and Goldwin Smith as fellow-laborers in every great cause of political advancement, and we seldom heard the one name without thinking of the other. Thorold Rogers—and here again he resembled Goldwin Smith—was a man of thoroughly independent opinions, and his resolve to think for himself brought him more than once into direct antagonism with the leaders whom on ordinary questions he always followed. He could not be called eccentric in his ideas even by his extreme opponents, but he could not absolutely give himself up to any school of political or economic opinions. The friends and allies who sometimes believed him to be going wrong were quite ready to admit that he was only following the light of his own convictions even when, according to their judgment, his views were distinctly wrong. He rendered most valuable service, during that period of the sixties when the American civil war was going on, by his efforts to keep English public opinion on the right side of that memorable struggle.

The great bulk of what was known as society took up the cause of the Southern States, and had made up its mind that the South had not only the right of the controversy but was certain to get the best of it in the war. There was an extraordinary idea pervading that class, and receiving encouragement from English statesmen who ought to have known better, that the Americans of the Northern States could not fight, and were destined to make but the poorest show in a contest with Southern chivalry. Lord Palmerston in more than one of his public speeches made great fun of the Northern armies and of the Northern defeat at the battle of Bull Run, and there was an inclination among those whom he especially addressed to believe that the Northerners were merely a crowd of traders and shopkeepers who did not know how to fight and who were sure, whenever they came into contact with a Southern force, to make what Palmerston called " certain rapid strategic movements to the rear." Men like Cobden and Bright and John Stuart Mill took a different view of the Northern cause and of the Northern fighting-men, and Thorold Rogers maintained their views with admirable force of argument and expression. For a time it seemed as if Thorold Rogers and those with whom he associated himself were fighting a hopeless battle out of sheer perverseness. For some inexplicable reason they were regarded by their opponents as un-English and unpatriotic because they advocated the claims of the Northern cause and encouraged the men who maintained it on the battle-field. I saw a good deal of Thorold Rogers at that time, and of the statesmen with whom he allied himself, and I could not but admire the unflinching courage and devotion with which they held their course, undeterred and undismayed by the social forces brought to bear against them. The great mass of Englishmen outside what are called the privileged classes, and including almost without exception the working-men and the democracy everywhere in the country, were with them even at the time when the prospects of the North and of the antislavery advocates seemed darkest. The progress of the war soon made it clear that the Northern States were certain to carry the day, and then there began to be more and more evident a gradual change in the views of society. I heard Thorold Rogers often make contemptuous and sarcastic allusion to this fresh evidence of the familiar proposition that nothing succeeds like success.

One of the most valuable productions of Thorold Rogers's pen is *The Industrial and Commercial History of England,* edited by his son, Arthur G. L. Rogers, and published by Fisher Unwin not very many years ago. There is a remarkable passage in the preface, by the younger Rogers, in which he describes the labors of his father in endeavoring to teach his great economic doctrines through the medium of lectures to university classes. "Let the professor of political economy teach what he will, even the undergraduates who seek honors in the history school soon drop away. In this way it came about that these lectures were attended by an extremely small audience. Had the professor of political economy given these lectures in some industrial centre, hundreds of workmen would, I believe, have paid to listen to them. But, in the home of learning, some dozen men of education attended lectures thrown open, free, to every member of the university." Mr. Rogers concludes his preface by saying that "if any apology were needed for the publication of this book, this alone would suffice." The comments are full of interest, and it is well for the world that they should be made and published even though the collection of the lectures into a volume needs no manner of apology. The book is a most valuable addition to the literature of economic science, and would of itself secure for Professor Thorold Rogers an abiding-place among the world's political economists.

The book is a characteristic illustration of Thorold Rogers's style as a controversialist. No man could be more fair and liberal in the meed of praise he gives to all who preceded him in such work, and from whom he professes to have derived most valuable instruction. But it is the work above all things of a fighting-man, and the learned professor seems never so much himself as when he is assailing and ridiculing the doctrines of his opponents, and denouncing the systems of administration which gave practical force to this teaching in the form of taxes and systems of economic law unfairly raised and recklessly misapplied. There is something highly refreshing to the ordinary reader, who is apt to regard political economy as a study without heart and without enthusiasm, in the ardor, the vehemence, and even the bitterness with which Rogers shows up the absurdity and the social wrong of many processes of taxation then regarded by too many British statesmen as a sacred embodiment of the wisdom of our ancestors. Thorold Rogers could be as enthusiastic in denouncing a badly conceived and misapplied impost as if he were showing up deeds of despotic oppression or of individual cruelty. A false action in economic science he condemned with as much severity of censure as if he were dealing with a blasphemous doctrine of faith. The emphasis of his convictions in this domain of thought had its effect upon his career as teacher of economic science. He was elected professor of political economy at Oxford in 1862, but, as one of his biographers tells, he "made so many enemies by his outspoken zeal for reform" that when his occupancy of the position came to its due term in 1867 he was not re-elected to the office until 1888. He had taken orders in the Established Church and was for a time a devoted follower of the Puseyite doctrines, but he had no calling for the Church, and finally renounced the religious profession in 1870, and devoted himself entirely to his own cherished studies in history, biography, and political economy. He could not, according to the laws of this country, have obtained a seat in the House of Commons without this complete withdrawal from his functions in the Church, but no one who knew anything of Rogers supposed that ambition to obtain a place in Parliament or any personal advantage could have had aught to do with his change of profession. I never knew a man with whom personal ambition or the desire for advancement had less influence in directing the course of his life than Thorold Rogers. The sincerity of his belief alone guided him through the whole of his career. There was nothing of the sentimentalist in him; he did not allow himself to be governed by emotions or instincts, but merely examined every question by the dry light of what seemed to him practical reason, and he would have renounced his most cherished convictions on any subject, without a moment's hesitation, if he found good reason to believe that his previous study and examination were leading him the wrong way. He was in this sense, but in this only, a thoroughly self-absorbed man. He only asked to be shown the right path, and that path he firmly trod without more regard to a reputation for consistency than he showed for his own individual interests. If he had to stand alone he would have stood alone quite undismayed, and probably with a firm belief that the best of those from whom he had turned away would some time be converted to his latest opinions and come up with him in the end. If there was in such a course any blending element of so poor a quality as self-conceit, that certainly was the only self-conceit which the closest observer could have found in the unselfish nature of Thorold Rogers.

CHAPTER XX

GOLDWIN SMITH

Goldwin Smith well deserves a chapter to himself in a volume given up to portraits from the sixties. All that part of his active and thoughtful career which was most conspicuous and influential in England belongs to the sixties. Before the epoch had actually closed he withdrew altogether from English life. To the younger generation of Englishmen the name of Goldwin Smith seems probably a part of the history of the past. Every youth who has had anything like a fair education is well aware that Goldwin Smith was a man of high intellect and great argumentative power who rendered splendid services to political, economical, and intellectual progress during his day, but I can well believe that many such a youth might be a little uncertain whether Goldwin Smith belonged to the period of Adam Smith or had come as far down in our times as John Stuart Mill. The explanation of this possible vagueness in the minds of the younger generation is easily given. More than thirty-five years have passed since Goldwin Smith found a home across the Atlantic, and he has since only been heard of at intervals in his native country. During the years when he was a moving figure in English life he was a very influential and prominent figure indeed, and we read in every day's newspapers the account of the part he had taken in some great controversy then occupying public attention.

Goldwin Smith was educated at Eton and Oxford, took first honors in classics, gained prizes for the Latin essay, for Latin verse, and for the English essay. He was appointed by the government assistant-secretary of the royal commission on the state of Oxford University. He was afterwards appointed to the Regius Professorship of Modern History, and held that position until 1866. Before this later period all the great questions had come up which were raised by the antagonism between the Northern and Southern States of the American republic ending in the outbreak of the civil war. Goldwin Smith threw himself heart and soul into that momentous controversy. He took his side because of his objection on every ground to the existence of slavery, which he justly regarded as the foundation of the whole dispute, and he published several pamphlets enforcing his opinion in eloquent language, addressed to the hearts and consciences of all intelligent readers.

In writing of Thorold Rogers I have already given a short account of the effect produced on English public opinion by that great dispute and of the manner in which the majority of that class which we describe as society took the side of the South, while the best intellects of England in politics, literature, and science, and the whole mass of the English working population adhered to and advocated the cause of the North. Never within my time has there occurred an epoch more full of absorbing interest in English public controversy. Men like John Stuart Mill and Herbert Spencer, who had never taken any public part in political life before, were to be seen and heard at meetings as champions of that cause of human freedom which they believed to be at issue in the American civil war. It was probably then for the first time that Goldwin Smith came into close and constant association with Cobden and Bright. As a rule the followers of Cobden and Bright had not until that epoch found themselves much in companionship with leading representatives of university culture in these countries. The university don kept himself for the most part away from popular organizations, and there was a sort of vague impression permeating society that culture and scholarship could not give much countenance to the popular doctrines about the equality of classes, the civic rights of man, and the rights of labor which were advocated from what was called the Manchester platform. I can well remember the delight, not unmingled with surprise, felt by Cobden and Bright when they found university scholars and magnates like Goldwin Smith presenting themselves at great public meetings as champions of these popular but not socially recognized doctrines. Goldwin Smith was able to encounter the higher culture on its own field, and to show that science and scholarship, political economy and university education, were on the side of those who maintained the right of the negro to be free, and of the British working-man to have some voice in the government of his country. The advocates of those principles were proud to be able to tell their opponents of the higher culture order that the very best men of their own most honored class were against them in this vital dispute. "You may be very learned persons, but you can hardly think that you are endowed with quite as many intellectual gifts and quite as much mental instruction as Herbert Spencer and Stuart Mill, Goldwin Smith and Thorold Rogers."

Goldwin Smith was especially fitted to be a champion in such a cause and at such a time. He was imbued with the very spirit of controversy. He loved an argument, and as he had fully thought out every question before giving his judgment on it, he was prepared to follow his convictions whither they might lead. Everybody who knew Mill and Herbert Spencer knew that their natural inclination would always be to keep themselves from platform or parliamentary debate as long as possible, to think out every subject in the calm seclusion of the study, and to give forth their opinions only through the form of printed essays and volumes. The platform was only ventured on by these men when they saw that a crisis had arisen calling on them to sacrifice their own personal predilections and ways of life to the duty of lending every possible assistance to the support of the opinions they believed to be just. But Goldwin Smith, when once he had come forth from the seclusion of university life, appeared to feel a positive delight in the conflict and to be ready at a moment's notice for an encounter with any opponent worthy of his steel. Never was a cause better served and by a more capable and self-sacrificing advocate than was the cause of human freedom, during that momentous struggle, by Goldwin Smith. The effect of his advocacy was all the more impressive because it was well known that he was a thoroughly independent thinker, and that no merely dogmatic school could count upon him as one of its pledged and obedient followers. At the very hour when he was helping Cobden and Bright to fight out their great battle there were many of their views on other political and economic questions with which he could not agree, and he never hesitated to proclaim a difference of opinion when he felt it.

Goldwin Smith cared nothing about the names of parties, and although his convictions made him a Radical, so far as the questions then mainly under dispute were concerned, he would have gone to the help of a tory party on any subject concerning which he believed the tory party to be in the right. If he had been a member of the House of Commons he would assuredly have been from first to last what is known as an independent member. He would have sat on one of the benches below the gangway, and if the party with whom he had voted nine times out of ten happened according to his judgment to go wrong on the tenth question, he would have done his best to show its leaders that they did not understand what they were talking about, and he would have gone resolutely into the lobby against them. He could never have consented to be an independent member of that more docile order who is content when he cannot quite agree with his leaders to go quietly out of the House without speaking or voting and thus save them from the discomfort and discredit of a seeming act of mutiny within their own ranks. He would have felt it his duty to argue against them and vote against them on that one particular question, just as if he had never agreed with them on any subject during the course of his life. This resolute and thorough independence was of immense value in lending influence to Goldwin Smith's advocacy of those great questions wherein as a controversialist out of Parliament he found himself drawn to take the side of that section of the liberal party then regarded as radical. I had many opportunities of knowing that for this very reason men were sometimes deeply influenced by the arguments of Goldwin Smith who might have paid but little attention to the pleadings of recognized radical orators. "We know what Cobden and Bright would naturally say on such subjects," these men would urge; "we know what their doctrine is about liberty and the rights of humanity and all that sort of thing, but when a man like Goldwin Smith comes out from his college retirement to stand up for a cause, then we begin to feel that there must really be something in it." I have heard such utterances over and over again, and they helped me to understand the inestimable advantages given by Goldwin Smith's adhesion and arguments to the great cause then represented by the radical party in England.

Goldwin Smith's championship of the Northern cause made him, as was to be expected, immensely popular in the Northern States, and while the civil war was still going on he was prevailed upon to undertake a lecturing tour in America, where he met with a splendid success. Then it began to be said in England by those who had felt the force of his arguments only too keenly for their political satisfaction, that the Oxford professor was becoming thoroughly denationalized, and that he could no longer be regarded as a genuine Englishman. His political opponents said that he had gone over to republicanism and that he could no longer endure the ways of a country which acknowledged a sovereign and the principle of hereditary succession. Those who knew Goldwin Smith somewhat better were satisfied that he would never give himself up body and soul to any mere formality or convention where the welfare of communities was concerned, and that if he did not thoroughly approve of the way in which things were managed under a republican government, he would be just as ready to express his opinions as he had proved himself to be under a monarchical system. Goldwin Smith returned to his native country and published his valuable books on *England and America* and *The Civil War in America.* But he remained in England only four years. In 1868 he resigned his position at Oxford and went out again to the United States. There he accepted the position of Professor of English and Constitutional History in the Cornell University at Ithaca in the State of New York.

This Cornell University was then a novelty in American institutions. It was founded by Ezra Cornell, a man who had made a great fortune as a contractor for telegraphic systems, and who showed an honorable desire to associate his name with educational institutions. I had many opportunities at one time of meeting Ezra Cornell in New York, and he always seemed to one exactly the sort of man whom an English caricaturist with pen or pencil would have selected as a type of a modern American capitalist. He was a lean man, tall and wiry, with a dry, curt, and somewhat chilling manner, sententious, and given to laying down the law on his own subjects. There did not seem to be in him one gleam of the emotional, and one's utmost imagination could not picture him yielding for an instant to an impulse of the sentimental or romantic order. One who only met him occasionally might well have thought that the last thing in life he would be likely to concern himself about was the spread of education. Yet it was quite certain that Cornell was sincerely devoted to that cause, and he founded his university in the State of New York as a means of making the higher education attainable to the poorer classes of American students. In this institution Goldwin Smith, as I said, held a high position, and many others of its professors were men of distinction. When Goldwin Smith accepted a chair at the Cornell University all his disparaging critics in England at once proclaimed that he had now become completely denationalized, and that in fact he might be regarded in future as the most American among Americans and the most anti-English among the anti-English.

I can quite understand that imperial institutions of whatever kind had certain elements in them not suited to the temperament and the philosophy of Goldwin

Smith. He appears to have had always a profound and inherent objection to all wars of aggression and of conquest, to the passion for acquisition of territory and the extension of empire which passes for patriotism in the minds of so many otherwise peaceful citizens. At that time the phrase "imperialism" had not yet come into vogue, but if it had then been used to represent a prevailing sentiment we may be sure that Goldwin Smith would have been regarded as an inveterate anti-imperialist. It is none the less certain that Goldwin Smith found much of which he could not approve in the policy prevailing among leading American statesmen during his settlement under the banner of the republic. He remained in the United States for but a comparatively short space of time, and in 1871 he transferred his home to Toronto, in the Dominion of Canada. Thus he proved that he had not become denationalized, as ill-natured critics had declared, and that he could find good work to do under the protection of the British empire. From that time to the present he has remained a resident of Canada, has occupied a high position in the University of Toronto, edited and founded Canadian magazines, and maintained in every sense his characteristic literary activity. He has, indeed, visited England since his settlement in Canada, and he has always acted as one whose intellect and heart alike go with the best interests of the English people. But so far as one can know he may be looked upon now as one who has made his home in Canada and expects to find his last resting-place there. He has published many books and treatises since he lived in Canada, and he has never lost his keen, quick interest in the movements of England's intellectual and political life. Whenever any great dispute is going on concerning a legislative reform brought forward in England, we are sure to read letters from

Goldwin Smith, expressing his views, in some English newspaper or periodical. No man writes a more lucid and, in the truest sense, eloquent English style, and there is a positive fascination in his way of arguing out his case whatever it may be. You may agree with him or disagree with him; you may think him a prophet, or you may try to set him down as a mere crank, but one thing is certain—that if you are a person of any intelligence you are not likely to put aside any of his writings until you have read it to the end.

I should think that in ordinary private life many men must have found Goldwin Smith too intensely in earnest for the easy-going ripple of social conversation. I may even say that I doubt whether any of Goldwin Smith's warmest admirers, and I count myself as one of them, can have been able to keep always in agreement with him on important questions. We are most of us inclined to make our judgment upon one subject rather too comprehensive, and in our zeal for the reform to which we are at present devoting ourselves to assert some general principle which is meant to be an all-including law of life. Then Goldwin Smith, whom we believed ourselves to have been faithfully following up to that moment, suddenly comes down upon us with an argument designed to show that we had, according to the familiar phrase, run away with the story, and that we must not be allowed to impel our heads against the proverbial post. I can easily understand that Goldwin Smith may have disappointed many of his republican admirers in the United States by the frankness and keenness with which he criticised some chapters of American policy. I believe that in Canada he has engaged in more than one controversy when it appeared to him that the tendencies of the influential classes were moving in opposition to the principles of that liberal creed which he has made the guide of his political life. It has never been his way to believe that patriotism consists merely in supporting every policy and every measure which happens at the time to arouse the enthusiasm of the prevailing majority. Indeed, I find it hard to associate Goldwin Smith with any dominant majority, and I think of him always as of one whose work in life is to advocate the principles of an enlightened minority and to lend a never-tiring hand to the support of some cause which has not yet won its full success. Perhaps that gallant, combative spirit would find itself out of place in a period of rest and contentment after an accomplished victory, and might yearn instinctively for the brave days when it was yet doing battle against heavy odds. There are some political questions on which Goldwin Smith and I have never been in full agreement, but even when I cannot accept his conclusions I can still thoroughly understand and appreciate the absolute sincerity of his purposes and the method of his reasoning. Many years have passed since I became acquainted with this gifted and true-hearted Englishman. I knew him first during the early sixties, and I hope that I have been accounted among his friends from that time to the present. Of late years we have only met at very rare intervals, but we still exchange letters, and I have the advantage, highly valued by me, of learning his views on questions of great public interest as they arise from time to time. I always regard him as a man of that rare order whom Robert Browning delighted to picture—a man who must be ever a fighter for some cause he has set his heart on, who could never under any conditions sink into that inactivity of personal contentment which could withdraw him from interest in the movements of the world around him, or who could rest satisfied to let the world go its way without disturbing his peace of mind by any question as to whether it was going right or wrong. Those who know Goldwin Smith know that he will never think the less of them because they maintain sincerely their own views, although he may find himself compelled to maintain the other side of the controversy. I know that he rendered splendid service to his own country by the part he took in its political questions at a time when such a voice as his was an inspiring force in its highest interests. I know that the enlightened opinion of the best minds in America bears willing tribute still to his intellectual work for university education in the republic, and I am equally certain that the Dominion of Canada will ever hold in grateful recognition and memory the value of his teachings to that colony now growing into greatness. He may even yet have many years before him, for the activity of manhood seems to grow in its duration, and I feel sure that whatever time and physical energy may still be allowed to him will be spent to the last in work for the good of the human race.

CHAPTER XXI

THE KEELEYS, ROBSON, AND WEBSTER

ROBERT KEELEY, the famous comedian, died in London in the closing year of the sixties. London was his birthplace as it was the scene of his death. He was one of the most successful comic actors of his time, and it was a time which saw some of the greatest comedians of our modern days. Keeley might be said to belong to the order of low comedy, but it must be owned that he was able to convert low comedy into a genuine art. He soon found his own peculiar line and he kept to it. His field was limited, but within its limits he had, so far as my judgment goes, no equal. His especial gift was in the dramatic realization of honest, prosaic stupidity. If I had known or heard nothing of Keeley beyond what I knew from seeing his performances, I should have felt sure that he was a man of high intelligence because of the very skill with which he had taught himself to represent the workings of a stupid person trying his best to make out the meaning of some problem or some situation that puzzled him. I have seen him in parts which an actor of less intelligence might have rendered well enough for the purposes of the play, but none save Keeley could fascinate the spectator by the lifelike presentation of bewildered dulness resolutely and patiently trying to work out a meaning which still baffles it. Keeley's face at such a moment in the part he was playing became positively an artistic study of intense interest. One saw first the look of utter and seemingly hopeless non-intelligence, then there came into the forehead and eyes some faint suggestion of an idea, some evidence that the character was beginning to comprehend that there really was a meaning in certain spoken words which at first had not roused any gleam of understanding in him. Then one saw that the problem was becoming too much for his mental grasp, and that he was about to renounce the whole struggle for its mastery; then there came another sudden gleam of light into the eyes, and after a moment of what appeared to be an intense inward struggle the full significance of the matter broke in upon him, and his whole face lighted up with a look of triumph which might have passed as a caricature of the expression on the face of a philosopher who has at last solved the problem to which he had been devoting his intellect and his life. Many of the broadest and, at the same time, simplest comedies in which Keeley played a leading part became artistic triumphs by the mere skill in facial expression and facial non-expression which he was able to accomplish without an explanatory word or gesture. It might seem to a reader who has not been long enough in the world to remember Keeley, that the actor whose chief excellence consisted in the representation of struggling stupidity had but a very limited range for his dramatic effects and must soon have become wearisome to his audiences by his monotony. But this younger reader who does not remember Keeley would be rash if he were to come to such a conclusion. One who never saw Keeley might well have no adequate idea of the various forms, degrees, and moods, the positives and the negatives of expression by which human stupidity is capable of showing its straining after light. Keeley as a stupid man in one piece could be totally unlike Keeley as a stupid man in another piece. More than that, Keeley in one mood of stupidity could be quite unlike the same Keeley when depicting a different mood of that same character's stupidity.

We all accept the fact, even in our most untutored days, that genius has its different modes of expression, and we take this as one of the elementary conditions of human nature; but I at least never quite understood, until I saw Keeley in one of his favorite parts, the infinite variety of facial expression by which a stupid man can make known at once his stupidity and his struggle to get the better of it. I often saw Keeley in the popular farce "Box and Cox," which delighted for season after season the pit and galleries in so many London and provincial theatres. It was a piece with only three characters, the two whose names I have just mentioned and Mrs. Bouncer, the owner of a small lodging-house in which Mr. Box and Mr. Cox had rooms. One of the male parts was played in London by Keeley and the other by J. B. Buckstone, a rival of Keeley's in broad comedy. The two men belonged to just the same class in life—one was a journeyman hatter and the other a journeyman printer. Each was a prosaic and stupid personage, but the different orders of stupidity were rendered to the very life and even to the imagination by the two performers. Buckstone represented fussy, perky, and restless stupidity, while Keeley was, after his own fashion, the type of the slow-going, ponderous dulness he especially loved to picture. Nothing could be more amusing than the contrast exhibited in every passage of the play by these two actors. It seemed to me that of the two there was more of artistic imagination required for the creation of Keeley's part. The piece is made up of the bewilderment and antagonism of these two men, caused by the peculiar conditions which had made them, without their knowledge or consent, the alternate occupants of the one room under the same roof. Buckstone we understood from the beginning, and could see into the very depths or rather through the shallows of his fussy impatience and fretful temperament. But we never could quite follow at the opening of each passage the slow workings of that property in Keeley's man which he would probably have called his mind. There was always some little surprise awaiting us at the manner in which this personage at last, and after many ponderings, got a glimpse of the actual meaning of some fact or statement which came up for his study and comprehension. Just at the moment when it began to seem impossible that any gleam of the reality could force its way through the thickness of that skull a look came over the face and at last shone into the eyes which told us that the light was breaking in and that in another moment the personage whose inner struggles we were eagerly contemplating would begin to understand what his comrade or his landlady were talking about. Then there came that look of stolid triumph into the face, and we saw that stupidity had begun to exult once more over the success of its unconquerable intellect. If that expression could have been reproduced to the life on canvas or in marble, the world might have had a never-fading embodiment of stupidity working out by sheer patience the meaning of a riddle and exulting at last over the prize of its patient efforts. I saw Keeley in many parts of greater pretension, and requiring no doubt a higher degree of artistic skill, but I never before or since saw anything like so perfect an illustration of self-possessed and self-satisfied stupidity.

Keeley had a wife who was herself one of the best comic actresses of her time, and they had two daughters, both of whom won distinction on the stage. One of them married Albert Smith, who wrote the amusing novel, *The Adventures of Mr. Ledbury and His Friend Jack Johnson,* a book which had an immense popularity, and who also won celebrity and made money by his lecture on the ascent of Mont Blanc. Mrs. Keeley long outlived her husband, and received many marks of public honor from the members of her profession on the occasion of her later birthdays, when she was attaining what might be described as a patriarchal age. Not very many years have passed since I had the pleasure of meeting her at a London garden-party, and she then seemed full of life and animation, and could enter into bright conversation with each and all of the friends who crowded around to testify their respect and admiration. At that time an entirely new generation had arisen with whom the dramatic performances of Keeley and most of his stage contemporaries were but a tradition of the past, to be read about in books or described by veterans who were proud of their superior knowledge.

We have had new schools of comic actors since the days of Keeley's successes. In his time the brilliant and delightful world of topsy-turveydom created by the genius of Gilbert and Sullivan had not come into existence. I have been an observer of the comic drama in most of its phases during these later years, but I must say that my recollection of Keeley's dramatic skill in the kind of performance he chose as adapted to his own powers remains clear and undimmed, and in such parts he has had no rival in my estimation. There were and there are some comic actors who succeed in parts requiring higher artistic gifts and exhibiting far greater variety of artistic expression than any of those in which

ROBERT KEELEY

[*See page* 278

FREDERICK ROBSON

[*See page* 283

Keeley made his mark. I do not set him forth as one of the great creative artists in comedy who adorned the age of Queen Victoria, but I am quite certain that in the peculiar kind of part he made his own he has not had an equal. I am glad to have an opportunity of paying this tribute to his memory and to his success. That success, such as it was, was achieved in genuine comedy, and in comedy which derived none of its effect from any unwholesome element. The most scrupulous daughter might have safely taken her mother to enjoy any of Keeley's performances, and the good lady might have laughed her fill over his looks and his utterances without any dread of a censorious world.

The first appearance of Frederick Robson at the Olympic Theatre was an event in the history of the London stage. Robson was born in humble life, was brought up as an apprentice to a copper-plate engraver, but he soon developed a love for the stage, whither his genius led him, and devoted himself entirely to the dramatic profession. He played for many years in provincial theatres and for a long time in Dublin, but I have no reason to believe that he was appreciated during all this early part of his career. He worked merely as a stock actor, never playing any part which gave him a chance for the development of his splendid gifts. I can remember the whole of his career as an actor in London, for his life came to a premature close about mid-way in the sixties, at a time when the London world had come to regard him as one of the most successful and original performers of the generation, and of many preceding generations. His genius was first displayed in the performance of mere burlesque, or at least what would have been mere burlesque in the hands of any other actor. His burlesque, however, was of an order which proved that he had not alone the gift of genuine comedy but also of genuine tragedy. Even when he most broadly caricatured a Shakespearian part he was able to show that the spirit of Shakespeare's tragedy as well as of his higher comedy had thoroughly taken possession of his soul. When he had ranted some passage of the burlesque in the broadest style of dramatic caricature, there suddenly flashed out from him some words of the most true and touching pathos or of impassioned tragedy.

I have heard many great critics say that if Robson had given himself up to purely tragic parts he might have become the equal of Edmund Kean. At one period of his career there was a common conviction among the lovers of the drama that his ultimate destiny would be to abandon burlesque altogether, and to win fame as a tragedian of the highest order. But Robson's own genius guided him, and compelled him to keep to the style of acting for which nature had intended him, and he created a series of impersonations thoroughly original and entirely his own. I do not suppose that Robson was guided in his dramatic course by careful thought and deliberate resolve, but the style he was to adopt came in his way and he found it. That style consisted of the sudden blending of the broadly comic and the intensely pathetic and tragic, and I have never seen an actor who could play such parts as Robson played them. I have been told by many who knew him that he was not an intellectual man, or one who profoundly studied the principles and the masterpieces of the drama. He went whither his genius directed him or drove him, and it is certain that he could not have done better by any artistic process of thinking out the dramatic forms he adopted, and in which, as far as I know, he has never been rivalled. He could embody the very passion of terror, of anger, or of pity in such a shape that it became a living reality, and that the spectators saw before them not an actor but a human illustration of humanity's various moods. When he passed away from acting burlesques he took to parts the success of which depended on this extraordinary blending of the strongest emotions belonging to man's life. There was a play in which he had to act the part of a miser, and while in one sentence he showed you the miser in his meanest, most ignoble, and most ridiculous moods, in the next sentence he filled the spectator with the deepest pity for the poor, degraded creature, and then in another moment the actor seemed literally shaken with furious, ungovernable anger, which sent a thrill of something like terror through the whole house. One never knew where to have him or what to expect, and yet even the most rapid transmission of moods and expression belonged to the very life of the part, and the moods grew out of each other by a perfectly natural evolution. Owing to his marvellous skill his most amazing contrasts did not seem as if brought out with the purpose of contrast, but as human emotions expressing themselves in the tones and gestures of a mortal like one of ourselves. The feelings which any one endowed with a faculty for self-study or with imagination might have found in his own heart, but would in the ordinary course of life keep locked up there, were made to live upon the stage when Robson appeared in one of his favorite parts. The audience broke out in irrepressible laughter at one moment, found tears spring unbidden to their eyes at another, and yet again were made to tremble with the very passion of terror as the actor abandoned himself to another of his moods. It was not like acting, and even if you knew Robson personally, and knew that in his ordinary life he was but a commonplace sort of man, you could not help feeling that the creature before you was expressing his own natural emotions with no effort to convince or conquer. The parts he played belonged to some pieces in which he was the principal and all-absorbing character, and the whole success of each play depended altogether on his acting. Yet even in his most sudden and surprising changes he seemed a more real and living being than any of his comrades who had to speak some unimportant lines such as any one might speak in every-day life. Probably Robson's genius was naturally adapted to the realization of these electrical contrasts of mood, and it may be that if he had followed the advice of many admirers and given himself up wholly to tragedy, he might not have been equal to the prolonged sustainment of the part at its highest possible level. The world has, however, no reason to regret that Robson kept to that style of dramatic performance which he had created for himself, and did not attempt to become the rival of Edmund Kean or even of Macready. We have had, and still have, great actors of the higher tragedy and the higher comedy, but we have only had one Robson.

I have often heard during the zenith of Robson's career that his dazzling success led to the waste of his physical powers and to his early death. Success was too much for him, it was said, and gave him the means of indulging habits which were fatal to his health. I do not care to dwell upon this darker side of his brief history, but I believe there were many evidences at the time which proved that, in certain instances at least, nothing fails like success. I think that in any case the mere wear and tear wrought upon his muscles and nerves by his style of acting must have been of itself enough to sap the powers of one who could not boast of liberal resources of physical strength. He was a small man, so much below the average height as to appear sometimes almost dwarfish, and the parts he especially loved to play were such as seemed naturally to suit his appearance and for dramatic purposes to set it off. His neck was bent, his shoulders were stooped, and when one saw that unrobust frame shaken and even convulsed by the fits of fury, of grief, or of shuddering terror which he was able to present as no one but he could have done, it was not difficult to foretell that such a man must soon wear himself out by his too life-like representations of conquerable and unconquerable emotions. Robson's appearance would not have lent itself to any parts associated with the higher creations of the drama. One cannot imagine a Macbeth or a Shylock with such a form and face, although Robson was so well able to illumine his burlesques of these parts by occasional flashes of genuine and overmastering tragic passion. There was a time when Robson had made himself one of the most popular actors in London by displays of what might well be called buffoonery. One comic song of his, "Villikens and his Dinah," was the rage of London for a while, and was as well known to, and as often imitated by, the midnight crowds in the East End streets as the once famous music-hall song "Champagne Charlie." Probably he might have gone on playing such parts or even repeating that one part during the rest of his life, and have always retained his full power over the audiences crowding his theatre, who would have been quite satisfied if his genius had never sent out any flame of thrilling emotion; but the highest of his faculties was the peculiar dramatic gift enabling him to bring out that extraordinary combination of the comic and the tragic, which contained the secret of his crowning success and his abiding fame. I have often wondered why since his days we have never found any man whose star lighted him on to such artistic performances. I know one English actor of our day who, if he got the chance of a suitable part, might, I believe, work up the elements of comedy, pathos, and passion into some such representation as that which Robson made his own in the old days of the Olympic Theatre. But I suppose when audiences get fond of one particular style of comic acting they always want to keep the performer to the kind of part in which they especially admire him, and the managers support them by discouraging any desire of his to make an experiment in a new direction. Robson was, however, a man who knew his own capacity and would have his own way. The managers and the public alike came to understand that whatever he believed he could do he was certain to accomplish with success. His name remains forever linked in my mind with those early days, and I cannot recall the living London of that period without a mental picture of him as one of the most characteristic figures of an epoch which accomplished many wonderful successes on the British stage. A stranger could not then visit London even for a few days without being asked by the friends whom he met there, or whom he talked with on his return home, whether he had been fortunate enough to get a seat in the Olympic Theatre and see and listen to Robson. To have seen him might be described, in the famous phrase which was applied in a different sense, as a liberal education—at least in the capabilities of the drama.

Benjamin Webster, who undertook the management of the Olympic Theatre in 1866, was for more than forty years identified with a high order of comedy and melodrama on the London boards. He had been brought up for the navy, but when he was only fifteen years of age the peace of 1815 brought to a close the long struggle between England and France, and seemed to offer to the boy Webster but little chance of active service in the navy. He had always had a taste and apparently some natural endowments for music. He studied for the musical profession during some years, but he soon discovered that his real gifts and aptitudes were for the career of an actor. He played with success in the provinces and soon came to London, where he was not long in establishing himself first as a successful actor and then as actor and manager alike. His style was decidedly original, and there were many parts which he played so well that one remembered them afterwards only in connection with his own name and his own peculiar style. When we had seen Webster in one of his successful parts we got into the way of thinking only of that part and not of the play. It seems a strange link in the past, for those who remember him well in his greatest days, as I do, to remember also that he might have continued to be a sailor but for the fall of Napoleon. Webster was for a long time associated in the drama with Madame Celeste, who seemed to be regarded even in the sixties as belonging to the prehistoric days of the English stage, but who continued still to act, and even occasionally to dance, with all the vivacity of youth, and only took her farewell of the British stage in 1870. She began as a dancer after the fashion of those great dancers whose fame was still living and whose traditions she endeavored to maintain, the Taglionis, the Fanny Elsslers, and the Carlotta Grisis, and she soon settled into the acting of parts in which on occasions belonging to the piece itself she introduced an illustration of her earlier art. She delighted generations by her acting in a piece then universally popular, and made especially popular by her, called "Green

Bushes." I remember reading in one of the comic papers of the time, a paper started in futile rivalry to *Punch,* an article professing to be the story of a man whose earliest theatrical memories enshrined that performance, who afterwards travelled far and wide, returned to London after many years to be delighted by the same actress in the same part. Returning to London again after another prolonged absence when he was becoming an old man, he found Madame Celeste in the freshness of eternal youth drawing new crowds of the passing generation to applaud her in "Green Bushes." It makes one feel very old, indeed, to remember that one saw Madame Celeste in "Green Bushes," and that she and the piece have long since become mere traditions of the stage. Madame Celeste was as well known and as successful in the United States as in England, although it was not then the habit of every one who made a triumph on the English stage to seek out new audiences in the theatres of the American republic.

Webster could not, perhaps, be regarded as one of the really great actors adorning our London boards, for it could not be said of him that he had created a style of acting absolutely original and entirely his own. But he never assumed any part which he was not able to work out to its very best, and he thus became thoroughly identified with the characters he assumed and played in such lifelike fashion. His principal characteristic was the moderation and realism of his acting. He often appeared in parts which had little or no dramatic or literary merit, but he always made the spectators believe that they were looking at and listening to the very man whom the author endeavored to set forth as his leading figure. I remember seeing him more than once in the familiar part of the melodramatic villain. Now we are all prepared to make great allowances for that melodramatic villain, and we do not expect that he shall move and speak and generally behave himself in the manner of an ordinary mortal. But however absurd or melodramatic might be the author's typical villain, Webster always compelled us, for the time, to believe in the reality of that extraordinary creature, and to feel that what we saw and heard was exactly what might have been seen and heard if any human being had been ordained by nature to perform his villanous part in our presence. Webster never indulged in the theatrical strides and halts, the startling gestures and bewildering tones which gallery audiences were then led to regard as inherent constituents or accompaniments of melodramatic villany. Webster conducted himself from first to last after the manner in which humanity is wont to express even its most censurable emotions and projects. His thrilling passages were spoken in the tone and with the gestures of a fellow-mortal in real life, and yet he impressed us with a much deeper sense of obnoxious and dangerous malevolence than we could have got from a performance modelled after the traditional style. I dwell upon this remarkable gift of his because it distinguished him from all other actors of the same time who were compelled by stage exigency to endeavor to realize that now almost forgotten character, the melodramatic villain.

Webster could play with equal success many parts which had nothing to do with melodrama, and he always left us with the same impression that we had been looking on the very man whom the author of the play desired to set before our eyes. I never saw him attempt any character to which he was not thoroughly adapted, and which he had not recognized as coming fully within the range of his capacity. Some of our greatest actors have at all periods attempted parts not suitable to them, and have had to give them up and to acknowledge the failure. But I can say with confidence that I never saw Webster in any part which he did not succeed in making entirely his own. Whatever he attempted to do appeared to be done with perfect ease and complete success. Each part I saw him play remains to this hour absolutely identified in my mind with the acting of Benjamin Webster. I do not know that I should be justified in calling him a versatile actor, but I admit that in estimating the variety of his powers we have to take into account his own instinctive reluctance to venture upon a part which did not seem to him suitable for his best work. I do not mean that Webster limited his performances to characters of the same or a similar order. I have seen him play parts utterly unlike each other in every quality, and play each with an equal success. I have seen him play parts which were for the most part steeped in a quiet pathos, and I have seen him play other parts whose chief qualities were overflowing animal spirits and good-humored, roistering self-assertion, and the one style of performance remains in my memory as characteristic as the other, of the actor who made them live on the stage. I do not know that we have any English actor just now who could be compared with Webster. I do not say this in any disparagement of our present time or as a mere panegyrist of the past, for I know well that we have some living actors who have accomplished greater triumphs in their art than were ever achieved by Webster. What I desire to say is that we have few actors now who can attain the same high level of success in so many different parts and yet without displaying a marked individuality in any of them. We generally see the actor himself in each of the plays, no matter how we may be carried away by the dramatic power of the performance. But Webster had no marked style of his own, and the spectator thought all the time rather of the character in the play than of the man on the stage. The capacity for creating this effect on the minds of his audience seems to me to have been Webster's highest quality. It will not of itself make a Garrick or a Kean, but it can create within its limitations a consummate artist, and such I believe Webster to have been.

CHAPTER XXII

THE BANCROFTS

MARIE EFFIE WILTON, now Lady Bancroft, began her career in the management of a London theatre as partner of the late H. J. Byron in the conduct of the Prince of Wales Theatre, London, at the Easter of 1865. She had been an actress from her very childhood and had played in several English theatres, especially in the Bristol Theatre Royal. Her first appearance in London was made in 1856 at the Lyceum Theatre, when she played the part of a boy in "Belphegor," and she afterwards had several engagements in London before she entered on the responsibility of management. My first recollections of her belong to the time when she was the central figure in the burlesques at the Strand Theatre which made the fame and fortune of that house and filled it every night with enthusiastic audiences. It was out of the question that any one could then visit London without making his way to the Strand, and it was said at the time that the rush of provincial and foreign visitors to that house was so great and so incessant that the ordinary Londoner had to make his arrangements far in advance if he hoped to have a chance of seeing Marie Wilton. The Bancrofts have since published their memoirs, which make most delightful reading and render it superfluous for me to attempt any description of the successful careers of her and her gifted husband, now

Sir Squire Bancroft. The Bancrofts were married in December, 1867. They carried on their joint management of the Prince of Wales Theatre until the opening of 1880, when they became lessees of the famous and historical Haymarket Theatre.

The name of H. J. Byron was for a long time inseparably associated with a form of burlesque much of the humor of which consisted in the device and the delivery of bewilderingly ingenious puns. Is not the story told of Dr. Johnson that when somebody in his presence set down punning as the lowest form of wit, the authoritative doctor declared that the definition was just, inasmuch as punning was the foundation of wit? At the period with which I am now dealing the Strand Theatre became the recognized fountain-head of that species of humor, and the attempt to rival or at least to imitate the punning of the Strand burlesques grew to be a favorite amusement in every circle which counted play-goers among its members. It was told at the time that H. J. Byron said that his one great artistic ambition was to produce a burlesque in which there shall be a pun on every word. He never quite realized this peculiar desire, but he went as near to its accomplishment as human ingenuity could go. We have lost our passion for puns during these later periods of the drama, and it would be impossible now to invoke the power of that curious spell which for many years held such a mastery over English audiences.

Marie Wilton soon took to better work than the production of comedies having puns for their foundation; she gave up mere burlesque acting altogether and devoted herself alike as manageress and actress to the revival of genuine English comedy. I speak of this as a revival in the strictest sense, because for a long time there had been little or nothing of real comedy seen upon the English stage. The theatres which did not give themselves up to tragedy, to the romantic drama, or to burlesque, made their only attempts at comedy by reproductions from the successful pieces of the French stage. It had come to be the opinion of many London managers and actors that there was no chance of success for English comedy. The great demand was for translations from the French. I remember some of us arguing the point with a friend, the late Leicester Buckingham, who had written and produced many successful comedies avowedly adapted from the French. We in our ignorance were expressing our wonder that he did not give us an English comedy, and he answered us by declaring that no London manager would run the risk of producing any comedy which had not already passed successfully through the ordeal of performance on a Paris stage. Some of the most brilliant achievements of Charles Mathews, one of the greatest light comedians who ever lived, were in plays which proclaimed themselves as adaptations from the works of French dramatists. Charles Mathews had his retort upon the Paris drama when he translated one of his own comedies into French and performed its principal character with complete success on the boards of a great Parisian theatre. On that occasion one of the most famous among French dramatic critics devoted a long article to the play and the performance and had only one fault to find with the acting of Charles Mathews. This was in itself but an ingenious compliment, and was intended as such by the critic. Mathews had to play the part of "Un Anglais Timide," as the play was called in Mathews's version, and the fault found by the critic was that Mathews spoke French with a Parisian accent, which it would have been utterly impossible for any ordinary Briton to acquire.

Marie Wilton succeeded in reviving English comedy on the English stage. She brought out the comedies of the late T. W. Robertson, and no reader needs to be told that these were thoroughly English, the scenes and events belonging to English social life and made up of English figures. With Robertson's comedies and Marie Wilton's acting the spell of the French stage was broken for British audiences, and the public of these islands became convinced that English life and English manners might once again be as full and as fresh a source of comedy as they had been in the days of Congreve and of Sheridan and Goldsmith. Since that time English comedy has never lost its hold on the English and the American public, and Lady Bancroft may claim to have borne a leading part in this momentous artistic revival. During each of her theatrical epochs Lady Bancroft was equally successful, although, of course, the field of genuine comedy was a much nobler scene of triumph than any found by her during her earlier career as a leading actress in burlesque. It is only fair to say that even during those younger days, when she had as yet shown no higher ambition than that which found its opportunity in burlesque, she played her parts with a vivacity and an artistic skill which I at least have never seen surpassed. I have the most vivid recollection of her acting in many of these pieces, although I have forgotten everything else belonging to them. The story, the other characters, the incidents, the very name have passed completely from my memory, but I still see Marie Wilton distinct and clear in each part, the Marie Wilton of one piece not to be confounded for a moment with the Marie Wilton of another, but each a separate and individual creation, as real and as much alive now in my thoughts as it was in the delightful old days of the Strand Theatre.

But these were not the parts which won for Marie Wilton her highest artistic reputation and enabled her to accomplish the restoration of true English comedy. Robertson's plays gave her the happiest chance of showing what she could accomplish in dramatic art. While her whole temperament as an actress was exuberant with the very life of comedy, she never indulged in exaggeration. One might have supposed that an actress who had begun her career in burlesque and had accomplished a great success there would when she entered a higher dramatic sphere have carried with her, voluntarily or involuntarily, some of the extravagances which are the charm of the Christmas holiday art. But when Marie Wilton set herself to make a success in that higher comedy which seemed as if it had been written in order to give her a chance of developing her powers, she left entirely behind her all the theatrical peculiarities which naturally belonged to burlesque, and became a perfect living illustration of those lifelike English characters she had to represent. Such parts as that of Polly Eccles in "Caste" must always be identified in the memory of this living generation with the acting of Marie Wilton. There was, to begin with, a complete realization of the part as the author intended it to be, and under the impress of all the conditions with which the author had surrounded it. Like all true comedians, she was able to blend the pathetic with the comic, and there were passages in which the poor girl whose trials and humors all belonged to every-day English life, could touch the hearts of the listeners with an emotion of tearful sympathy not always to be called forth by even the accomplished queen of tragedy declaiming her sorrows in the well-measured intonations appropriate to her more exalted lot.

Marie Wilton was realistic in the higher and better sense of the word—she could express human emotion exactly as it might express itself in the life of an English home, but at the same time she had that true dramatic instinct which enabled her to divine the deeper feelings belonging to every part, feelings that might never reveal themselves to the ordinary observer, in the passing movements of commonplace and prosaic existence. She was able, where she had the opportunity, to show gleams of the poetic in and through the utterly prosaic; she could give that touch of nature which makes the whole world kin and brings Polly Eccles into companionship and sisterhood with the heroine of romance. I must, therefore, always regard Marie Wilton as having created a new epoch in the development of modern English drama, and we can see the effect of her work on the English stage of to-day as distinctly as we could have seen it when she was still moving enthusiastic audiences in her London theatre. Her success was complete and unbroken; she never touched any part without adorning it, and there was one universal feeling of regret when she made up her mind—all too early as many of us thought — that she had played her parts long enough, and was fairly entitled to quit the field of work before the evening shadows had yet begun to fall. Most other actors and actresses who have made a great success are anxious to keep to the realm of their triumphs up to the last, and will not yield to the reminders from outside, growing more and more frequent and audible, that they have done enough for fame, and had better not mar what they can no longer make. Marie Wilton erred, if she erred at all, on the other side. She withdrew into private life before she had given any sign whatever that she was ceasing to hold the homage of the public. She had won celebrity and wealth and most other constituents of happiness, and she made up her mind that she had done her fair share of work, and was free to seek for quiet and repose before time had given her any hint that the season of her triumph must draw to a close.

Marie Wilton, or Lady Bancroft, as she ought now to be called, was as fortunate in the artistic companionship which her marriage created for her as in the other conditions of her life. In Sir Squire Bancroft she found a master of his own dramatic art, and a man peculiarly gifted with the qualities which make a successful theatrical manager. Sir Squire Bancroft was a consummate actor in the parts which he believed suited to him, and he never allowed himself to be tempted into the feverish effort after success in entirely new and uncongenial fields, which has disturbed and marred for a time so many a great dramatic career. In such comedies as those of Robertson, Bancroft's successes came upon a level with the successes won by his brilliant wife, and thus made their dramatic partnership memorable. Bancroft's acting was always natural, always in the true sense dramatic, but it was never melodramatic, and he never sought to produce any effects which might not be associated with the incidents of ordinary human life in the every-day world with which we are all familiar. I do not mean to convey the idea that Bancroft limited his art to such plays as those of Robertson, or to the representation of English life as it then appeared, for he made a great success as Joseph Surface in "The School for Scandal" and as Triplet in "Masks and Faces." During the earlier part of his dramatic career, when he was still a provincial actor, he had won a reputation for the manner in which he played some Shakespearian parts.

It seems somewhat strange to us who now associate Bancroft altogether with modern comedy to be reminded that at one period his name was in the playbill with the names of tragedians like Charles Kean, Phelps, and G. V. Brooke. But even during Bancroft's latest performances at the Haymarket any intelligent spectator could see that he had a capacity for acting which was not limited to the faithful reproduction of modern manners. Every now and then would come from his lips some sentence delivered with perfect colloquial ease, and in the tone of London society, but showing that the actor had an amount of dramatic intensity and a depth of expression which might have found their full effect in scenes of more passionate emotion. It has always seemed to me that Bancroft at an early period of his career made up his mind as to the kind of part which best suited his tastes and his capacity, and held to that line by deliberate choice. My impression is that he is by nature capable of great versatility in acting, but that he soon found out where his best success must lie, and of his free will confined himself to that realm of the drama.

The portrait of Lady Bancroft which appears at the opening of the book, written in collaboration by the husband and wife and entitled *Mr. and Mrs. Bancroft on and off the Stage,* Lady Bancroft regards as, on the whole, the best and most characteristic reproduction of her face and figure at the time, and I need hardly say that there were many reproductions of that face and figure during those early years of her career as an actress and the opening of her enterprise as the joint manager of a theatre. Sir Squire and Lady Bancroft were as familiar figures in London society after they had both retired from the stage as they were when their nightly performances were still crowding the stalls and boxes and galleries of the Haymarket. The Bancrofts had always distinguished themselves by the zeal and generosity with which they took part in every project for the advancement of some benevolent purpose, and their charitable help was freely given to beneficent organizations which had nothing to do with the theatrical profession. They could be counted on to give the help of their talents and their money to every deserving cause, whether public or private, and I have heard of many instances in which the generous and timely help of the Bancrofts never sought or received any manner of notice in the newspapers. Since their retirement from management and from the boards of the theatre they have both appeared in dramatic entertainments, got up for the benefit of some charitable institution or for some theatrical comrade of former days who had fallen upon evil times and was in need of a helping hand. Sir Squire and Lady Bancroft have always been social favorites, and there was an absolute and cordial approval given by all classes to the graceful act of recognition by which Queen Victoria expressed her sense of the services Bancroft had rendered to the drama. Lady Bancroft is in private life alike delightful as hostess and as guest. She is one of the most brilliant talkers whom I have the good fortune to know; she can tell the most amusing stories and say the brightest things without the slightest appearance of one who is talking for effect and who desires to produce an impression on the listening company. Her humorous sallies, her droll stories, her sparkling phrases, come from her with all the simple and unaffected ease of one who is merely joining in ordinary conversation and has no purpose of making a display. I have been so

MARIE EFFIE WILTON

(*Lady Bancroft*)

TERESA TITIENS

[*See page* 304

fortunate of late years, during my retirement from life and work in London, as to be a near neighbor of Sir Squire and Lady Bancroft in a very picturesque part of Westgate-on-Sea. I shall not endeavor to express in words the inestimable advantage of such a companionship.

It may be safely predicted that the career of the Bancrofts will always have a chapter to itself in the history of the British stage. The pair were as successful in their management as in their individual art, and every theatre of which they took charge was sure to become a model institution. The husband and the wife were very different in their styles of art, and each had a marked and distinct individuality. But they were very much alike in one valuable quality—they could both accomplish the greatest successes in comedy without calling in the spurious aid of farcical exaggeration. In this happy gift they are both entitled to rank with the best actors of the Parisian school, who can keep an audience in constant delight and give the fullest effect to the most amusing and humorous passages in a comic scene without going outside the limits of nature and of art. Neither one nor the other seemed to be acting even where it was certain that the very realism of the performance must have been the result of careful thought and study. Each could thus make even a poor and unreal part seem lifelike and credible, and each with a really good part to play could accomplish the author's highest purpose and convert his imaginings into a living and human shape.

CHAPTER XXIII

THREE QUEENS OF SONG

JUST before the opening of the sixties the opera, so far as we knew it in England, seemed to have fallen upon one of those periods of reaction which come every now and then in the history of the drama, of literature, and of painting and sculpture. The great moving influences appeared for the time to have passed away and we had settled down, as is the wont of ordinary mortals, to the gloomy conviction that we had heard the last of the world's famous singers. Grisi and Mario, Persiani, Jenny Lind, and Lablache were heard no more upon our stage, and we were making up our minds that we at least were not to hear their like again. Such is our way with regard to all the arts; we are ever ready to believe that the young people coming up are not likely to be familiar with such a period of artistic success as that which we enjoyed in our earlier days. This was especially the belief we held about the opera just then, and, as often happens during such a season of dearth, a new influence was suddenly borne in upon us which cast for a time our brightest recollections into a shadow and a memory. This happened in the April of 1858, when Teresa Titiens made her first appearance in the theatre then called Her Majesty's in London. The triumph of the singer was instant and complete. A great musical critic declared that "a voice so rich in quality, so extensive and so flexible, combined with a temperament so passionate and a dramatic perception so exact, carries us back to the highest standard of lyric excellence." The critic went on to say that the great line which commenced with Pasta and was sustained by Malibran and Grisi found its new vindication in the genius of Mademoiselle Titiens.

When the sixties had begun Titiens was the ruling star of opera. The portrait set forth in this chapter represents her in the part of Marguerite in "Faust," one of her most successful lyrical performances. She was a great actress as well as a great singer, and for several seasons following she was the reigning queen of opera in Her Majesty's Theatre. There was not a tone of pathos, of grief, of love strong as death, of the gentler tragic emotion, which did not find its full and exquisite expression in Titiens' rendering of Marguerite. Yet even that part did not show her most characteristic qualities at their highest reach. Her genius showed itself at its best and truest in the illustration of characters embodying the most passionate moods of human nature. Such a part as that of Media in Cherubini's thrilling opera, or that of Norma, more familiar to English audiences, by the once popular Bellini, gave her a more complete opportunity for the display of her marvellous dramatic as well as lyrical powers. It may be questioned whether any great singer ever became more thoroughly identified with a part in the admiration of English audiences than Titiens did in that opera of "Norma," which is now so seldom presented on an English stage. Titiens was Hungarian by extraction; she was born in Hamburg and made her first great success in Germany during 1849. She was still a young woman when she achieved her splendid triumph in the London opera-house. Many years later she visited the United States, and there, too, accomplished a complete success. Titiens was as great in oratorio as in the lyrical drama, and no one who ever heard her sing sacred music is ever likely to forget the impression it wrought upon him. She was not exactly beautiful in feature, but her face and her eyes had such expression that the listening gazer had little thought of criticism so far as mere personal appearance was concerned, and found all his faculties absorbed in admiration for her voice and her acting. Every note which she sang received new meaning from her eyes and her looks, her gestures and her movements. She was, indeed, a queen of her art. In her own line she had not in my recollection any rival, and when I recall in memory all the great operatic singers whom I have heard, I still find that in the parts she made her own she stands unrivalled.

The public does not now hold in much esteem the operatic works of Bellini, but so long as Titiens reigned upon the lyric stage the world became a willing captive to her impassioned rendering of poor Norma's love and troubles. Even the younger generation, which has all but forgotten Norma and her story, and to whom Titiens herself is becoming something like a tradition, is still impressed by the profound conviction that the fame of the great singer is one of the events which make an epoch in the history of the opera. She had a dramatic power which in its more tragic forms Jenny Lind never could command and only Grisi could rival. She made one of the familiar topics of conversation during her time, and to hear Titiens was in itself an ample reason for making a visit to London from the most distant parts of the British Islands. I have always had a feeling I could hardly define in critical terms, a feeling which associates her with the great American actress Charlotte Cushman. It often

ADELINA PATTI

LYDIA THOMPSON

[*See page* 318

came into my mind that Titiens was another Charlotte Cushman, with a voice which made her supreme in opera. As Charlotte Cushman was one of the greatest English-speaking actresses of the more modern stage, the most devoted admirer of Titiens will see that I am not uttering any disparagement of her gifts when I say that she was another Charlotte Cushman endowed with a divine voice and a musical genius. The artistic career of Titiens was not very long; she passed away at an early age from opera and oratorio in England. She had not gone far beyond her prime when death slit the thin-spun life, but not the praise. She will be remembered forever in the history of the world's great singers.

The early sixties brought a new diva to the operatic world in London. Adelina Patti made her first appearance at the Italian Opera-House, Covent Garden, in the May of 1861. That first appearance was in the part of Amina in "La Somnambula," and was a brilliant and complete triumph. The new singer was then a little more than eighteen years of age, and she had already accomplished a great success in the United States. She ought to have had music in her soul, for she was of Italian extraction and was born in Spain. If the atmosphere of Italy and Spain are not conducive to music, one is at a loss to know under what skies its birth could find more favorable auspices. No one who lived in London during 1861 can ever forget the effect created by Patti's singing and acting. She had in her the genius of the singer and of the actress. Her voice was exquisite in all the unending variety of its tone, and it had a range and a compass which the comparatively fragile appearance of the young singer would not have led one to expect. She appeared in a great many parts and in all with something like equal success. She was most popular, perhaps, in parts combining delicate pathos with bright and graceful humor, but she accomplished more than one triumph in characters which demanded tragic force and the deepest tones of passionate grief. She was not a queen of exalted lyric tragedy like Titiens, but when rendering into music and into dramatic expression all the gentler emotions of the human heart, the maidenly love, the intense womanly sorrow, the bright and delicate playfulness of happy girlhood soon to be crossed by suffering, she has never within my recollection had a superior on the operatic stage. Her personal charms and the grace of her movements seemed to be the natural accompaniments of her voice and her lyric power. She had all London at her feet, and although other great singers came up from time to time, she was for many seasons the star of a London opera-house, and always maintained the same place in public admiration, I might even say in public affection, which she won on the night of her first appearance in London. I remember having heard with much interest during Patti's first season in London about her love for the open air and her anxiety to escape as soon as possible every evening from the streets of London's West End—inclinations not often to be found among the celebrities of the opera and the stage. During a great part of her early London career she occupied a house in the unfashionable region of Clapham Common — I wonder whether any other queen of song has ever lived there at the height of her fame—and it used to be a delight to her to drive every night from Covent Garden into the roads of South London and to enjoy the atmosphere of the breezy common with its rare trees and its little lake. In later years, as we all know, she made her home for the most part in the Welsh castle of which she became the owner, and where she created an exquisite private theatre for the delight of her friends and herself. Madame Patti was always great in concerts as well as in opera, and was ever ready to give her help, the help of her voice, her genius, and her fame, to the cause of any deserving public charity. The English people came in the end to regard her as one of themselves, and although she still accomplished great operatic tours to distant countries, it was always taken for granted that she would return in due course to her home on British soil. One of her greatest successes was achieved in Russia, where she received from the reigning emperor the honorable and honorary appointment of first singer at the imperial court. She did not, however, restrict her appearances to the countries where emperors and kings could be among her listeners, for she won splendid success and received large sums of money during two seasons in that very much outlying country the Argentine Republic. I do not remember any great operatic singer of our time who won a more unqualified popularity among her audiences of whatever country than that achieved by Madame Patti. Her real gifts were at once discerned and recognized, she had a place to herself, and was hardly ever made a subject of disparaging comparison with other great singers. She was not, as I have said, set up as a rival to the great singers of more impassioned tragedy; she was taken for exactly what she was, for a singer who had created her own style of sweet, playful, gentle, and pathetic emotion.

Even at the height of Grisi's fame there were some critics who made a sort of school of their own by endeavoring to find fault with the style of that thrilling queen of opera, and who seemed to think it a proof of their own superior culture that they could find fault with her rendering of this or that passage in an opera, or even with her whole conception of some one part. But everybody took Patti exactly as she was, and cordially recognized that she accomplished to absolute perfection every part she undertook. I may also say that I do not think any foreign singer ever became so fully at home in English life as Patti did almost immediately after her first great success in London. One heard of her everywhere in English social life. She was the ornament of London receptions and evening parties; she was always taking a part in this or that enterprise for the benefit of a public charity; she became a leading member of all manner of societies having no direct association with the stage. I have not heard her or seen her for many years, but it seems an impossibility even to think of Adelina Patti as growing old. It is my ill fortune to have heard Jenny Lind only in her later days, when she sang at a concert given in London for some charitable purpose, and then, indeed, it seemed hard to realize that this was the singer who, within my own recollection, had bewitched the world by her voice. My memory of Patti must be ever the same, and with her there must remain in my mind the charm of eternal youth. If years have changed her in any way I at least have not known it.

The first appearance of Christine Nilsson in London may well be described as one of the events of the sixties. This great singer suddenly arose like a new star in the sky of the lyric drama. She had made a splendid success in Paris during 1864; but Londoners in the days of the sixties did not follow the course of operatic meteors arising above other horizons with the close attention which is easy in these days of rapid telegraphic intercourse between the British metropolis and foreign capitals. The men and women in London society who made a study of music and took a deep interest in every new musical career had come to know long before 1867 that another Swedish Nightingale was following in the path of Jenny Lind. But the British public in general took only a languid interest in the foreign stage, and especially in foreign opera, so the announcement of Christine Nilsson's first appearance was not awaited with intense expectation by the ordinary visitors to the two rival opera-houses. We had made up our minds to the belief that there could be only one Swedish Nightingale, that Jenny Lind was that bird of song, and Jenny Lind had had her full triumph, her unsurpassed success, and was then living upon her fame. Therefore, while all students of music and accomplished musical critics had learned already that there was an event to be looked for when the new singer should challenge the judgment of a London audience, the usual opera-goer was quite content to know that an interesting novelty might be looked for, and that it would be a good thing for him to have a seat in the opera-house on the occasion of that first appearance.

I had the pleasure of being present on that memorable night, and I have some personal as well as other reasons for remembering the event. I was then concerned in the editorial conduct of a London daily newspaper which has long since ceased to exist, and I was lucky enough to have a box for Christine Nilsson's first night in London. It was part of my ordinary work to go down to the editorial rooms in the city after an evening spent in the theatre or in private society and throw my soul, as well as I could, into my newspaper business. Therefore, I naturally assumed that when the curtain fell on the last scene of the opera I should have to turn my attention to my editorial work and to occupy my mind with home and foreign politics, with the doings of Parliament and the threatenings of continental war. But while seated in my box, before the new singer had made her appearance, I received a startling message from my newspaper office which for the moment cast for me a bewildering cloud over the operatic stage. This message was to the effect that our regular musical critic, a lady of great accomplishment in that art, who has since died, had been suddenly taken ill and was unable to attend that night, and that I, as the only member of the newspaper staff then in the theatre, would have to give an account of the event and pass judgment on the new singer for the benefit of our readers next morning. Not often, I think, has a mere literary man been placed in so perplexing and so responsible a position. I knew nothing of music in the cultured and scientific way; I was fond of the opera and of music in general, as I suppose rational persons usually are; I might have ventured confidently enough on dashing off a criticism concerning a new play or a new actor, but to attempt to express critical judgment on the merits of a new singer was beyond any power I had ever claimed or ever had the right to claim. But there I was—seated in that opera-box, the sole representative there of the newspaper which owned my services; there was no time to lose in the quest, probably the hopeless quest, for a more fitting substitute, and my only choice seemed to be either to sit out the opera and write the criticism myself or to leave my newspaper to come out next morning without any account of the great event.

I have always regarded the success of that evening as one which shed some of its good fortune upon me. My stroke of good luck consisted in the fact that before the first act was over I became filled with the conviction that a complete and splendid success had been accomplished by Christine Nilsson. There could be no question as

CHRISTINE NILSSON

to the judgment passed by the astonished and delighted audience. Even those best qualified to form an opinion from their knowledge of the singer's recent career must have found their highest expectations realized alike in the success of Christine Nilsson and in the unanimous recognition which it received from that crowded house. I had no difficulty in making up my mind that a new queen of opera had come to London, and that I was entitled to proclaim with the utmost confidence to my readers that she had actually come into her own. But let me do myself justice, although I never made any pretension to play the part of a qualified musical critic. I did recognize from the first the genius of Christine Nilsson and the exquisite beauty, the marvellous range, and the ever-varying intonations of her voice. I think I may say that even though the house in general had failed to rise to the occasion, and had listened without emotion, were such a thing possible, to that voice, I should have felt able to declare on the strength of my own convictions that a new singer of the very highest order had come to delight us in London. I should have known, too, that in Christine Nilsson we had not merely a great singer, but an actress who in her own field could find no superior. However, I was not put to the risk of any heroic enterprise on that occasion. I called to mind the story told of Edmund Kean, when he returned from his first great performance in a London theatre to his anxious wife who was awaiting him at home. She asked him in breathless eagerness what a certain noble lord, who was a patron of Kean, had said of his performance. "Never mind his lordship"—I believe he used a stronger expression—the great actor replied; "all I know is that the house rose at me." This much I knew of Christine Nilsson—that the house rose at her—and I knew that I need have no hesitation about the full outpouring of my own praises in print.

Christine Nilsson's position was secured in London by this great opening success. She had won for herself a place in English opinion among the greatest singers of modern times. She had a distinct style of her own, both in singing and in acting. Her sphere was not that more exalted region of thrilling lyric tragedy in which Grisi reigned so long supreme, nor had her style the almost infinite variety of Patti's, nor did it display the occasional bursts of tempestuous grief and passion with which Pauline Lucca could electrify her audiences. Christine Nilsson's style was all tenderness, sweetness, exquisite pathos, intense womanly love, these moods of human life which seem to come in with the evening shadows, and where passion itself puts some restraining measure on the vehemence of its expression. She belonged, according to my judgment, to the romantic order of the lyric drama, and she went through this mood of the lyre with full and exquisite mastery. At one time there used to be an actual controversy, not about her performance of "La Traviata," but about the story of that opera, which was made the subject of public discussion. "Was it right," one set of disputants asked, "that the story which the opera embodied should be put on the lyric stage with the attractions of a great singer and actress to allure the young and the innocent into the contemplation of La Traviata's career? Are we not coming upon evil days when English mothers will bring their daughters to look upon and listen to such a character set forth in living presentation, and to find their hearts stirred into sympathy with such a heroine by the voice and the acting of the lyric artist who plays the part?" The arguments on the other side of the question amounted merely to the contention that no human creature was likely to suffer moral harm by the natural sympathy felt for the heroine of so pathetic a story, even though that heroine had yielded to the overpowering temptation of her life. The discussion would hardly awaken very profound interest in our times, for we are not much given of late to troubling ourselves about the direct ethical lesson to be taught by every dramatic performance which attracts our attention, but at that time there was a very keen debate as to the moral effect of "La Traviata." There can be no doubt that a good deal of maudlin and morbid sentimentality was awakened by the story of La Traviata in minds of a certain order, as there had been by the novel "La Dame aux Camélias," on which it was founded; but assuredly the prevailing tone of "La Traviata" as we heard it, under the inspiration of Adelina Patti and of Christine Nilsson, was one of pure and generous sympathy with all that was noble even in a frail and erring human being. The success of the great Swedish singer in London lasted just as long as she gave London a chance of testifying its appreciation. Whenever she returned to one of our opera-houses she found her popularity and her fame still on the increase. She visited the United States, where she made a success not less complete than that which she had won in France and in England, and where she is said to have made a considerable fortune in money. Again in 1872 she appeared at a London theatre, and she might have gone on appearing and reappearing there as long as it suited her to appeal to a London audience. After that time she performed at St. Petersburg and put in an occasional appearance at the theatres of other continental cities. She did not, however, linger on the operatic stage, and the musical world knew of her only while she was still in the full possession of all the charms of her voice and her lyric genius. The zenith of her fame belongs to the sixties, and especially to her appearance in the London opera-houses. She passed, in music, out of sight. Hers was one of the most remarkable instances of genius asserting itself in spite of all early difficulties. She was born to poverty and to hard struggle, the daughter of a poor Swedish laborer, and she first displayed that gift of music which was in her by performing on the violin at fairs and markets. At this early period of her life, when she was yet only fourteen years old, her skill with the violin and the flute attracted the attention of a man of fortune and position who saw that she was made for a great musical career, and undertook the cost of having her educated by the best instructors to be had at Stockholm and afterwards in Paris. Then followed her first appearance in the Paris opera-house, and from that time forth there was nothing but success first and honored retirement afterwards. Her face was of a beauty which seemed made for the expression of the music she sang with such exquisite effect, and of those dramatic passages suited to her genius. I have not often been present at any event on the stage which marked itself so distinctly in dramatic and musical interest as the first appearance of Christine Nilsson in London. I can look upon the whole scene now as I saw it then, and can hear once more that voice of marvellous power and harmony, those tones of indescribable pathos and sweetness. I offer the portrait in this chapter and the pages I have written to accompany it as if they were the flowered wreaths which we throw at the feet of a conquering queen of song.

CHAPTER XXIV

THREE STAGE GRACES

Lydia Thompson was unquestionably one of the theatrical lights of the sixties. Her light did not ascend very high or float very far, but it was distinct and clear in its time, and it won for her a full popularity. She was singer, actress, and dancer, all in one. She was not a great singer, she was not a dancer belonging to that order in which Fanny Elssler and Cerito won their fame, and she made no pretensions to be a great actress. She played in farcical light comedy which had occasional episodes of song and dance, and whatever she tried to do she did well. She had a pretty and expressive face and a beautiful figure. The charms of her form were humorously described in a saying which became popular in her time—the assertion that Lydia Thompson was the only woman then living who could support a whole theatre upon her legs. She would at a later day have made a most graceful and welcome figure in our modern musical comedy, and she would have danced and sung and acted quite well enough to bear a conspicuous part in it. When one looked at her graceful form, heard her sweet, soft voice, and saw how her expressive eyes and charming features lent new meaning to every sentence she spoke, one was not inclined to make any invidious comparisons, but yielded himself up unresistingly to the attractiveness of the performer. It was quite certain that the manager who had secured the services of Lydia Thompson could count upon full houses and applauding audiences. When I first settled in London, Lydia Thompson was a star, not of the first magnitude, but of a brightness which made itself distinctly seen in the theatrical firmament. After many seasons of London success and of provincial tours, where she was always welcome, she, like most rising actors and actresses in our days, went to the United States, where she won popular applause and secured remunerative engagements. I saw her during the early seventies in New York and Philadelphia and other American cities, and was much pleased to find that she still carried with her all the youthful grace of form and of movement which had made her so attractive a figure in London at the opening of the sixties. She did not keep to the stage for very long, but retired into private life before time had done anything to impair the charms which had captivated so many cities and towns. Her great artistic merit was that she never attempted any part, never tried song or dance, which was not suited to her style and within the range of her powers. She appeared to have an instinctive knowledge as to the compass of her voice, her capacity for acting, and the limitations of her skill as a dancer. The praise might be accorded to her that whatever she attempted on the stage she did as well as any other actress, singer, or dancer could have done it, and that she had attractions of face and figure which the greatest singers and actresses do not always possess. She could not be described as belonging to that order of mediocrity to which, according to a great authority, gods and men have alike forbidden the poet to belong. Hers would have been mediocrity if one compared her with really great actresses, singers, and dancers, but she never invited the comparison, and she won for herself a place which was altogether her own. I have the most agreeable recollections of my many visits to some of the theatres where she made her first triumphs, and I feel certain that nothing but real artistic capacity could have enabled her to win so complete a success within the limitations beyond which she apparently had no ambition to pass. Her portrait is well entitled to a place in this volume.

In one of the burlesques which were the rage during the sixties a song was introduced describing satirically the dramatic events of the time. The song declared that "the last sensation out is Miss Adah Isaacs Menken"—the last word being pronounced for the imperative purpose of rhyme as "Menkeen"—"whose classical style of dress does not much trouble the sewing-machine." Miss Menken, who was a poetess as well as an actress, was born in one of the Southern States of America, and made her first London appearance in 1864. She played in "Mazeppa," a sort of drama adapted to the purposes and effects of the circus, and taken, of course, from Byron's poem. She created an immense sensation and became the subject of a keen controversy, but the sensation and the controvesy were not caused so much by her dramatic powers as by the peculiarity of her stage costume, to which the lines just quoted made sarcastic allusion. Miss Menken, when strapped to the fiery Cossack horse, exhibited herself in the costume of the ordinary athlete when displaying, or, at all events, when practising, his professional occupation. Of course she was carefully made up from neck to ankles in close-fitting tights, but her ostensible and acknowledged covering was of the scantiest dimensions. I do not know that there was anything in her make-up which ought to have astonished or scandalized spectators who were accustomed to the ballet, but the preliminary announcements of her appearance seemed designed to attract attention to something of audacity in her manner of presenting herself, and the effect was an indignant protest on the part of a large section of the public, a pleading for consideration and artistic independence on the part of her admirers, and, therefore, a controversy and a sort of scandal. Given the peculiarity of costume, there was nothing whatever in Miss Menken's style of acting which suggested indecorum of any kind, and she played her part as becomingly as any one could. She had no claims, so far as I could judge, to be considered a great actress, but it was in one sense her misfortune that the public controversy put out of consideration altogether her merits as a dramatic performer, and that she was discussed and criticised almost entirely with reference to the extent of her clothing.

There was at one time during the early sixties an exhibition in one of the London theatrical halls which was described as "The Walhalla," and was introduced, if I remember rightly, by a manageress called Madam Warton. The exhibition consisted of the presentation of living statues — that is to say, of men and women who represented famous groups of statuary and who in some instances, while covered completely by silk tights, exhibited otherwise no more drapery than each sculptor had given to his marble figures. The London music-halls have much more lately made us familiar with this sort of display through what were called living pictures. Miss Menken was somewhat unfairly regarded by many as merely another illustration of these living statues, and the immediate result was, as I have said, that her dramatic merits, whatever they may have been, were wholly forgotten in the discussion as to her costume. For a time at least she was more talked about and argued about than almost any other actress of the day, and there were family circles in which to acknowledge that one had seen Miss Menken's Mazeppa was to confess one's self indifferent to the recognized standards of social propriety. Miss Menken, I believe, wrote several volumes of poetry, and whatever may have been the qualities of her poems, they certainly did not, so far as I know, contain anything which could have created a public scandal. One volume of her poems was dedicated to Charles Dickens, who had been very kind to her, and she was among the first to recognize the poetic genius of Algernon Charles Swinburne, who was just then making his earliest appeals for that fame which he was destined so surely to win.

Adah Menken was a widow when she first made her appearance in London, and she afterwards married Heenan, the "Benicia Boy," whose famous pugilistic encounter with Sayers, the English champion of prize-fighting, created one of the greatest sensations known to the early sixties. I believe Adah Menken entered the marriage state more than once afterwards, but I am not recounting her personal history and am only concerned in describing the peculiar effect which she produced on the London public by her performance or exhibition as Mazeppa. I think she died young. I have always heard her well spoken of by those who knew her privately, and I am aware that she had the friendship of some distinguished Englishmen who were not likely to bestow it on undeserving objects. She was unfortunate in the manner by which those who managed her performances had purposely or unconsciously introduced her to the British public and thus created a scandal about a piece of dramatic impersonation which would otherwise have been judged merely by the standard of dramatic merit. The sensation which she created and the fact that she proved herself by her poetic efforts to be a woman possessed of some really high artistic qualities entitle her portrait to a place in this chapter. From what I have been told, by some who knew her well, about her sincere aspirations after dramatic success and after the higher purposes and moods of life, and from the melancholy tone of many of her poems, I have always thought that there was something tragic in the fate which doomed her to be remembered almost altogether as the heroine of a controversy about the proprieties or improprieties of theatric or amphitheatric costume.

The opening of Nellie Farren's life as an actress made one of the theatric events of the sixties. Her first appearance was at the Victoria Theatre, a theatre known as the Coburg in earlier days when it had a dramatic history of its own, commemorated in some famous novels of the time. She appeared there in March, 1864, and a few months after went up a step in her profession by her engagement at the Olympic. There she made a distinct success, but it was not until she became one of the company at the Gaiety Theatre, under the management of my old friend Mr. John Hollingshead, towards the close of 1868, that she attained to her true position as one of the foremost living actresses in her own style. She was then recognized as an unsurpassed actress in burlesque, and she maintained that position so long as her health allowed her to keep up the severe physical exertion demanded by the performances in which she took the leading part, and was almost always on the stage. Burlesque of this order was then somewhat of a novelty in London. It was not sheer burlesque—that is to say, broad caricature of the higher drama—but had in it much of poetic feeling and of artistic illustration, combined with light comedy and extravagant humor. It never degenerated into buffoonery, and Nellie Farren, at least, was always able, even in her broadest comedy, to suggest that she herself could thoroughly appreciate the higher sentiments and purposes of the characters and the performances which she satirized. It might, in fact, be described as a sort of overture to that order of high-class comic opera which was made immortal by Sir Arthur Sullivan and W. S. Gilbert. Nellie Farren had all the qualities needed to achieve a complete success in the style of performance then new to the London stage. She was a genuine actress, and, therefore, a genuine artist; she had grace of form and movement; she could put meaning into every side glance and into every half-suppressed tone; she was always comic, but in her uttermost comedy she could now and then touch the hearts of the spectators by a note of tenderness or even of deep emotion, which showed that in her, as in all true comedians, the faculty of arousing laughter is in close association with the qualities appealing to the higher emotions. She had especially the gift of fascination, and she made her audiences her willing captives.

I remember an amusing little poem which appeared in one of the comic papers during her earlier Gaiety triumphs, a poem professing to be the work of a devoted admirer who for obvious reasons could never hope to be her suitor. It is necessary, perhaps, that I should explain to my readers at the present day that there was a pun concealed in this word "suitor" which gave it a personal significance. The lady whose stage name was Nellie Farren was in reality Mrs. Soutar, and the somewhat obvious pun explained the regret of her poetic admirer that he could not be hers in that sense. The poet got over all difficulties as to the nomenclature of his heroine by describing her as " Little What's-Her-Name." He declared in one of his closing verses, so far as I can recollect, that he could seek no higher honor and could ask no higher fame than a corner in the memory of " Little What's-Her-Name." I feel no doubt that there was an immense number of admiring young men in London and throughout the provinces at the time who sympathized to the full with the expressions of admiration and of tender regret poured forth in this lyrical tribute. The best days of her success belonged to a period later than the close of the sixties, but the opening of her brilliant theatrical career must always be associated with the decade to which this volume is devoted. Most of my readers will remember her best in the later days of her stage career, when she was the especial attraction of the crowds who filled the Gaiety Theatre for season after season, and delighted her public as the leading actress in many famous burlesques, from " The Forty Thieves " to " Ruy Blas."

In those days one could never get quite outside the range of Nellie Farren, even if it were possible to imagine anybody desirous to do so, because her praise was on everybody's lips, she was the subject of talk in every household, her portraits appeared in every shop window where portraits could be exhibited, the music of her songs echoed in every street and square, and ladies who had but little qualification for such a task were constantly trying to imitate her rendering of this or that popular ballad. Nellie Farren had the immense advantage that she appealed to every sort of audience. Even those who most firmly asserted their claims to the possession of the highest culture were not afraid or unwilling to acknowledge the enjoyment they derived from her delightful and really artistic burlesque performances. One might see some of the most eminent figures in literary, political, and scientific life in the stalls and boxes when Nellie Farren was playing one of her most successful parts. We all know that there have been clever comic performers and singers, men and women, who could only command unqualified success with what might be described as music-hall audiences and who win a fame which never ascends above the level of such audiences. But Nellie Farren, even in her most popular burlesques, was always able to attract the attention and compel the admiration of a cultivated and intellectual order of play-goers, and no suggestion of vulgarity or of extravagant burlesque ever marred the artistic charm of her acting and singing and her graceful movements as a dancer. Nellie Farren was compelled to withdraw prematurely from the stage by a severe illness which made quietude a necessary condition to the prolongation of her life. Only a few years ago her theatrical friends and admirers, who comprised, indeed, the whole dramatic and lyric profession, organized a benefit performance on her behalf which proved one of the most splendid exhibitions of combined theatrical art ever set before a London public, and realized an amount of money enough to secure the popular and brilliant actress against any chances of poverty during ill health and the descent of life into old age. It seems almost impossible to associate the idea of old age with a figure like that of Nellie Farren, which showed as if it were meant to illustrate the living possibility of perpetual youth. Still it was only too certain that although the fascinating actress and singer might be able to appear now and again at intervals before an admiring public, her career of continuous acting had run its course, and nothing could have been more to the honor of the English public and of the dramatic profession than the practical recognition which these in combination contrived to make of the claim which Nellie Farren had established upon their sympathy and support. Such a recognition did honor alike to those who gave and to her who received it. I am now passing beyond the natural limits of my subject, but I am sure my readers will readily accept my excuse for having thus followed the career of Nellie Farren down to a period which leaves the sixties far behind. My own recollections of her are naturally associated most with that period of her early triumphs when she came upon London as an astonishing and fascinating novelty, even in those days of varied and original dramatic successes.

CHAPTER XXV

SOME QUEENS OF SOCIETY

THE collection of photographs to which this book is dedicated contains some which remind me that I ought to give a chapter to three at least of the queens of society who reigned and held their courts during the sixties. I am now concerned especially with the women who made their reception-rooms a rallying-place for politicians, risen and rising, who belonged to one or other of the great political parties or had as yet not quite decided under which flag they were to rally. At all times in the social history of every civilized country there have been queens of society who were thus able to render direct and substantial service to the political cause they had at heart, by making their houses a meeting-ground for the leaders of their own party and for men whom a mere admission to the sacred social circle might prevail upon to lend a willing ear to the claims of that party. In England the sixties were especially favorable to the purposes of ladies who desired to win by their courtesy and hospitality new adherents to the government or the opposition as the case might be. That was a time when men saw a remarkable breaking-up and remoulding of the old traditional political groups. Great reforms in the franchise, in the construction of constituencies, and in the qualifications for a seat in Parliament were expected, or had actually taken place, and a new political world was forming itself throughout the British Islands. The old divisions of parties were becoming less and less recognizable; the old names and catch-words were falling into disuse, and nothing in the past could make it certain whether the new men coming up into activity might attach themselves to the government or to the opposition. Under these conditions the influence of a leading woman in society might be of much importance in winning new adherents to either side of some great, new, political controversy. A writer in an influential American magazine described this period of England's public life as marked by a sudden and wide increase of that influence which he described in the title of his article as "The Petticoat in English Politics." I do not venture to say whether that petticoat influence was really much greater during the sixties than at earlier or later periods in the history of English public life, but for the reasons I have just given that influence had in those days especial chances of exercising its power and of making itself conspicuous. The most influential and distinguished among these queens of society in the sixties was Lady Palmerston, the wife of the statesman who held for so many years the most commanding administrative position in England's political affairs. It is needless to say that Lady Palmerston's reign as a queen of society came to a close with the earlier sixties, for her husband died in the October of 1865. Lady Palmerston undoubtedly gave invaluable assistance to her husband during the most important passages of his career as a statesman.

Palmerston was a man of the most attractive manners, who could make himself agreeable to everybody by his courteous ways, his facility for always saying the most suitable thing at the most convenient time to the person whom he especially wished to influence. He had also a great kindliness of disposition and a gift of sympathy which enabled him to bring himself into genial relations with all who came under his notice, and on whom a winning word or two would not be thrown away. Lady Palmerston played her part as his companion and helpmate with consummate tact and with happy effect. Her receptions were always thronged with eminent men and women from all countries, and she took care to be on terms of friendliness with foreign ambassadors and envoys and with the ladies of their families. She had an especial gift of putting foreigners and strangers of every kind at their ease, and she opened her rooms freely to all who had any claims upon her hospitality. She did not confine her welcome merely to the eminent and influential visitors who might naturally be supposed to have some right to the attention of the prime-minister's wife, but she had a quick eye for distinguishing young men of capacity and promise in their own spheres who might not in the usual course of things come within the range of her courteous dominion. Some newly elected member of the House of Commons might come to London a complete stranger to the great world of society, and a word or two of recommendation from one of her friends would be enough to secure a ready invitation to her home for this yet unrecognized stranger. It is needless to say that this newly elected member of Parliament found himself touched and delighted by the honor thus unexpectedly conferred on him, and Lady Palmerston had always the wit to discern the best manner of gaining his confidence and gratitude.

In the political conditions then prevailing it is easy to see that many a supporter could thus be gained for Lord Palmerston and his policy who otherwise might have wandered into some different camp. Palmerston was not what we should now call an advanced Liberal, though there were some questions on which he wholly agreed with Liberals in general. On the other hand, there were many subjects on which he showed a distinct leaning towards the views of the moderate Conservatives. At a former day the distinction between Whig and Tory had been too marked to allow of much opportunity for neutrality, and the changes had not taken place in the construction of constituencies which gave to any but a decided partisan of one side or the other a chance of obtaining a seat in the House of Commons. The later years of Palmerston's political life were therefore exactly the time when a capable and ready-witted wife could render immense service to her husband by her readiness to form new acquaintances and to win the friendly allegiance of those for whom public life had not yet determined their sphere of action. She never fell into the mistake which a less clever woman might have made of allowing her invitations to be indiscriminate, and seeking for mere popularity by welcoming everybody who happened to bring himself or to be brought under her notice. It was always a distinction to be invited to Lady Palmerston's house, and to be seen there was enough to secure for a rising man the consideration of those around him. She thoroughly understood that if you want to conciliate a man you must pay attention to his wife and daughters, and also the importance of securing the gratitude of women as well as of men. Many anecdotes were told at the time of how Lady Palmerston had thus been successful in securing the allegiance of some previously unknown politician to the cause which her husband had most immediately in view. Such a man would naturally feel a thrill of delight when he saw it recorded in the newspapers of his locality that he and his wife had been present at one of Lady Palmerston's receptions and that the wife of the great prime-minister had treated them with marked attention. The next division in the House of Commons on some question of temporary interest might prove, in the most practical manner, the immediate effect of her hospitality and her kindness.

The enduring success of an administration does not depend altogether on the votes called forth by some great national question in which a man's course of action must be decided by mere party principles. There are many occasions in the House of Commons when the success of a government may greatly depend on votes in the division lobby which are not decided by the accepted creed of Liberal or Conservative, and on all such occasions the influence of Lady Palmerston showed its practical effect in securing for her husband a commanding majority. I am very far from wishing to describe Lady Palmerston's receptions as given up altogether to the welcome of politicians and the promotion of political objects. Lady Palmerston's interests and tastes were of wide and varied range, and she was always glad to receive in her rooms any distinguished representative of letters, art, or science, any successful explorer, or any philanthropist who had done honor to his name by some charitable work. But it is quite certain that Lady Palmerston as a queen of society made it her object to rule over a political world. The queens of society may generally be divided for the purposes of description into three orders. There are those who direct their influence especially, as Lady Palmerston did, to the promotion of political interests through personal and private influence. There are others who go in mainly for the picturesque, the attractive, and the brilliant, and who desire to gather within their sphere witty, fashionable, celebrated, and clever men and graceful and beautiful women, and to make their coterie a living illustration, after modern fashion, of the House Beautiful. Then there is a third set of fair rulers who only care for notoriety, and with whom the mere fact that a man or woman has been much talked about in the newspapers is a passport of admission. Lady Palmerston belonged unquestionably to the first of these orders, and although she loved to receive celebrities of every kind, she did not care about mere notorieties, and unless the notoriety gave some promise that he might under proper guidance become useful in the political sense he would not have had much chance of an invitation to one of her receptions.

Another queen of society in the sixties was Frances Countess Waldegrave, the wife of Chichester Fortescue, who was Under Secretary of State for the Colonies in two of Lord Palmerston's administrations. He was appointed Chief Secretary to the Lord Lieutenant of Ireland in 1865, and held the same office under Mr. Gladstone three years later, being then made a member of the cabinet, a position which is not always occupied by the Chief Secretary for Ireland. Chichester Fortescue, who held other administrative offices at a later date, was a man of considerable ability, and was regarded with much respect by the House of Commons. He was an aristocrat by birth, and represented an Irish county in the liberal interest for many years. At that time there was something remarkable in the very fact that an English Liberal should be chosen to represent an Irish county when the influence of the landlord class in Irish county constituencies was generally all-powerful and was not likely to be given to the support of a candidate who advocated liberal opinions. To a large section of Londoners — that section with which an admission into society is the darling object of life—

Chichester Fortescue was better known as the husband of Lady Waldegrave than for his own personal or political recommendations. Lady Waldegrave made her receptions an institution of the West End. An invitation to one of them was held to be in itself a recognition of social distinction. Lady Waldegrave, however, did not go in especially for playing the game of politics, but loved to see herself surrounded by men and women who had acquired celebrity in any field. I have again and again heard some one recommended to favorable notice by the mere assurance that "I meet him often at Lady Waldegrave's parties." I remember being greatly amused by the reasons which the editor of an English provincial journal gave me for the satisfaction he felt on being invited to Lady Waldegrave's house. My friend was a man of great ability and many accomplishments, who afterwards obtained a seat in the House of Commons and won distinction there during his short parliamentary career. At the time of this conversation he had not yet stood for Parliament, and seemed to me not in the least likely to be ambitious of a place in society; I was, therefore, a little surprised when I saw his name mentioned as one of Lady Waldegrave's guests. I expressed my surprise frankly, and he gave me as frankly the reason why he had felt gratified by the invitation and delighted to accept it. Now what does the reader suppose was his one motive in allowing himself to be drawn from his professional retirement into the glittering world of West End society? It was not because it pleased himself or pleased his wife, but simply and solely because he thought it would annoy the editor of the rival journal in the provincial city where he lived. I had had enough journalistic experience to understand how an editor's interest in the newspaper he conducted might induce him to welcome an invitation which would show the rival editor that he was the representative of a journal entitled to this recognition of superior political influence.

At Lady Waldegrave's parties it could be taken for granted that nobody was to be met who had not some claim to distinction, if not to actual celebrity, and a modest man who was only beginning to make his way might well have felt almost bewildered by the number of real celebrities by whom he was surrounded at one of these delightful receptions. Lady Waldegrave was a charming hostess, and made all her guests feel happy by her genial manner and the unaffected sincerity of her welcome. There was a larger infusion of the literary, scientific, and artistic elements at her house than was usually to be found at Lady Palmerston's, and there was no suggestion, so far as I have ever heard, that one was invited there merely because it was hoped that he might be able to acknowledge his invitation by any service to be rendered to this or that side in a parliamentary division. Every one who was fortunate enough to obtain admission to those social gatherings had the same opinion as to their delightful character, as to the interest which the hostess took in the happiness of her guests, and as to the opportunities which these receptions gave of mingling freely with men and women whom it was a pleasure to meet.

The next portrait I have to introduce is that of Mrs. George Cavendish Bentinck, whose rule as a queen of society began during the course of the sixties, but extended to a period well within the recollection of readers whose memories do not go so far back as the years to which this volume is dedicated. She was the wife of a man who held at one time a considerable position in parliamentary and public life, but she did not go in merely for political society in the home to which

MRS. GEORGE CAVENDISH BENTINCK

so many guests were made welcome each London season. She kept open house for society in general, but she was anxious to bring under her roof all who were celebrities in letters and arts, in science and politics, in fashion and in sporting life as well. Her luncheon-parties used to be one of the institutions of the London season. George Cavendish Bentinck, her husband, held office, if I remember rightly, in more than one administration. He is not to be confounded with the other Bentinck who was familiarly known to the House of Commons as "Big Ben," and with whom I was often brought into association during the earlier days of my parliamentary life. Cavendish Bentinck did not make quite so remarkable and so peculiar a figure in the House of Commons as "Big Ben," who in those days might well have been regarded as one of the curiosities of parliamentary life. "Big Ben" was a stout Tory in politics, but he went in now and then for independence of action, and occasionally displayed his independence with an aggressive ostentation. At one period of his career he seemed to make himself a foreshadowing of the Fourth party, although when he did thus assert his right to freedom of action his party consisted of himself alone. During the sixties he once made a vehement attack on the policy and the action of his titular leader, Disraeli, and the jest went round at the time that his intention was to set himself up as a rival candidate for the leadership of the tory party. A satirical poem on the subject appeared in one of the London daily papers and created a good deal of amusement, rather perhaps because of the prompt timeliness of its satire than because of its claim to poetic humor. It was called "The Panther and the Hippopotamus," and it professed to describe a quarrel among the animals in the Zoological Gardens, whose leadership by the brilliant panther was disputed by the ponderous hippopotamus. I need hardly tell my readers which of these two animals was supposed to represent Disraeli and which "Big Ben."

George Cavendish Bentinck, the husband of the lady whose portrait appears here, was a less self-assertive and eccentric personage, and he followed his parliamentary career without occupying, to any extent, the attention of the outer world. Mrs. Cavendish Bentinck made her fame as a leader of society, and I believe that those who were frequent guests in her hospitable house were sure to meet there almost every one who had won distinction or seemed likely to win distinction in any field of success, including the field of fashion. There is always in London some queen of society endowed with the same natural and pardonable ambition to make her home the meeting-place of celebrities. I think Mrs. Cavendish Bentinck was the first who within my own recollections of London life began to win such a position. She accomplished her task with unquestionable success, and is entitled to a place among these portraits from the sixties. I have met with many distinguished foreigners whose first introduction to the social life of the West End was made in the house of Mrs. Cavendish Bentinck. Her name will be long and gratefully remembered by many men and women from all parts of Europe and the United States.

CHAPTER XXVI

LAST WORDS

I HAVE now gone through the collection of photographs which it was my purpose to introduce to my readers in this book. In my opening chapter I explained that, while these portraits are all taken from the sixties and are characteristic of the epoch to which they belong, they do not profess to be anything like a complete gallery of pictures of the eminent men and women who were conspicuous figures of English life throughout those years. I have described them as one might describe some portrait-gallery of the present day in which it happened that many remarkable portraits were not included, as one might describe the contents of the annual exhibition of the Royal Academy without professing thereby to give a complete illustration of British art for that season. In this volume every portrait is characteristic of the time which the volume surveys, and when I have gone through the collection my work of description is completed. There is not a single picture in the gallery which does not in itself help to bring back to the public mind a distinct recollection of men and women who made the sixties an important and peculiar period in modern English history. In politics, letters, arts, science, and social life the sixties have a history of their own, and none of the figures I have set forth in these pages is without its appropriateness and importance in the revival of those memories. The sixties constitute an epoch of great change in almost every department of England's public and social life, and many of the changes which are still only in process of development owed their beginning to some of the men and women whose portraits I offer to the public, around which I have intertwined recollections of my own. It is no feeling of idle curiosity which prompts us all to take an interest in the accounts given of a past time by one who can say that he has seen and known the men and women whom he is describing, and that he does not derive his impressions merely from the study of contemporary pictures or from the reading of contemporary books. That was the feeling with which I undertook the writing of this volume. I have carried out the work to the best of my ability, with the hope that it might do something to bring my readers into closer association with the life of those memorable years.

The sixties were memorable years in every sense. They saw the opening and they saw the close of many a great career. Two of the greatest English novel-writers of all time, Dickens and Thackeray, died within that period, Thackeray during its earlier part and Dickens just before its close. With these deaths there would appear to have come to an end two great schools of British fiction. There have, indeed, been, and are still, many pupils of either school working in the same field, but no new master has since arisen or seems likely to arise. The influence of Carlyle, of Tennyson, and of some other writers of the highest order, reached its zenith during the sixties, and although these men lived and worked on to a much later day, yet they could not well have added anything to the fame they had already won. The career of Algernon Charles Swinburne, and the career, as a poet, of Dante Gabriel Rossetti, began in the sixties, and will always be associated with that period. Some of the greatest names belonging to the dramatic and lyric stage were made known to the world during the same years. In politics the sixties made a deep and lasting mark. Some of the most important changes in our political constitution were accomplished during those years, and the parliamentary history of these islands may be said to have begun a new era within that momentous period. The sixties also saw the sudden uprising of Prussia to its position among the greatest European powers; saw the first evidences of the approaching fall of Louis Napoleon's empire in France; saw the settlement of the great controversy which had so long divided the Northern and Southern States of America. The work of Darwin and of Huxley took its first recognized form during the earlier part of that richly productive era. I only glance at these facts with the object of reminding the reader that the sixties have a history entirely their own, and may claim to be ranked as a distinctive epoch. I question whether any equal space of time in England's history produced a larger amount of original matter. Every portrait, therefore, which illustrates any phase of that period must have its abiding interest for the readers of succeeding generations. It is with me a delightful memory to have seen so many of the great figures of those days, and to have seen so many other figures which, although not as great, were yet conspicuous in the same epoch, and in their way characteristic of it. Perhaps I could not more fittingly enshrine those closing and opening eras than by mentioning the facts that on the 9th of January, 1860, Lord Macaulay was buried with honor in Westminster Abbey, and that on the 1st of January, 1870, the Emperor Louis Napoleon declared at the annual reception of the diplomatic body in the Tuileries that the year 1870 was destined to consolidate the general agreement between his government and the foreign powers, and thus tend to the increase of concord, peace, and civilization. I need not add that the year 1870 saw one of the greatest continental wars known to modern European history, the fall of Louis Napoleon's empire and the rise of the third French republic. These events may serve as historical landmarks for the opening and the closing of the sixties, and may illustrate the importance of the historical period they enclosed. With this brief retrospect I think my collection of portraits from the sixties may now be thrown open to the public.

THE END